WordPress 4.x Complete

Get your website up and running and beautify it with WordPress

Karol Król

PUBLISHING

BIRMINGHAM - MUMBAI

WordPress 4.x Complete

First published: November 2006
Second edition: January 2011
Third edition: November 2013
Fourth edition: April 2015

Production reference: 1240415

Published by Packt Publishing Ltd.
Livery Place
35 Livery Street
Birmingham B3 2PB, UK.

ISBN 978-1-78439-090-7

www.packtpub.com

Credits

Author

Karol Król

Reviewers

Matt Cohen

Cyril Pierron

Olivier Pons

Ardian Yuli Setyanto

Commissioning Editor

Dipika Gaonkar

Acquisition Editor

Neha Nagwekar

Content Development Editor

Siddhesh Salvi

Technical Editor

Taabish Khan

Project Coordinator

Nidhi Joshi

Copy Editors

Hiral Bhat

Pooja Iyer

Tani Kothari

Sonia Mathur

Khushnum Mistry

Shambhavi Pai

Vikrant Phadke

Kriti Sharma

Sameen Siddiqui

Proofreaders

Safis Editing

Paul Hindle

Indexer

Hemangini Bari

Production Coordinator

Manu Joseph

Cover Work

Manu Joseph

About the Author

Karol Król is a WordPress developer, PHP programming specialist, professional blogger, and writer. He has been building expertise in WordPress ever since his early years at Silesian University of Technology, Poland, where he graduated with a master's degree in computer science. Early in his career, he worked as a freelance website developer for several years. Later, he decided to shift his focus toward popularizing WordPress as the perfect solution for all web-based projects and devoted his time to developing his writing career. His articles have been featured on websites such as NewInternetOrder.com, About.com, MarketingProfs.com, SmashingMagazine.com, ProBlogger.net, Six Revisions, Web Design Ledger, and many more. Currently, Karol's two main projects are providing business advice to normal people online through his website at `http://newinternetorder.com/` (normal people who don't have hours upon hours of time to spend sitting on their computer, watching yet another business training and trying to figure things out in the middle of the night), and offering his writing services through his main hub at `http://karol.cc/`.

I'd like to thank everyone at Packt Publishing for working with me and making this book a reality. Also, many thanks to everyone who has supported me along the way. Last but not least, I'd like to thank the WordPress team for building and constantly improving an incredible tool. If it wasn't for you guys, I'd be out of work.

About the Reviewers

Matt Cohen is the Chief Product Officer at WooThemes, market leaders in premium WordPress products and the creators of WooCommerce. He spends his day managing his engineering team and a growing team of product managers.

With a deep love of web development, Matt began tinkering with HTML4 in high school (before CSS existed) and developed a strong bond with early web development languages and principles. Then, he worked as a senior developer at a handful of agencies before joining WooThemes as a senior web developer in late 2010. A love for product creation, customer experience, and well-architected products led Matt to move into the chief product officer's role, where he now oversees the design and creation of all products developed within WooThemes.

Matt loves WordPress deeply and is an engineer at his core, with a strong interest in creating amazing customer experiences. In his free time, he enjoys nature, punk rock, and forgotten 90s television.

Cyril Pierron is a tech-savvy and life-curious engineer and web addict. He started programming at the age of 8 and has been working in the field of telecommunications for 12 years. He has been a solution architect in the e-commerce sector since 2011. He is married and the father of a lovely girl.

As an e-commerce expert, Cyril has noticed an increasing requirement to blend both the online store and marketing content into one consistent unified experience for consumers.

I would like to thank Packt Publishing for giving me the opportunity to work on this book as a reviewer, after my first experience with *jQuery 1.4 Animation Techniques Beginner's Guide, Dan Wellman, Packt Publishing*, a few years ago. I would also like to thank Karol Król, who did a wonderful job writing it, and my wife, who showed quite a lot of patience and support as I kept working on this book after hours.

Content management systems (CMS) are the key to brands sharing information and reaching out to their communities and fans. WordPress is a reference, one of the best known systems in this market, and this book will definitely give you, the reader, a complete view of its capabilities and usages.

Olivier Pons is a senior developer who's been building websites since 1997. He's a teacher at IngeSup (École Supérieure d'Ingénierie Informatique, http://www.ingesup.com/ and http://www.y-nov.com); the University of Sciences (IUT) in Aix-en-Provence, France; ISEN (Institut Supérieur de l'Électronique et du Numérique); and École d'Ingénieurs des Mines de Gardanne, where he teaches state-of-the-art web techniques: MVC fundamentals, Symfony, WordPress, PHP, HTML, CSS, jQuery / jQuery Mobile, Node.js, AngularJS, Apache, NoSQL, Linux basics, and advanced VIM techniques. He has already done some technical reviews, including *Ext JS 4 First Look, jQuery Hotshot, jQuery Mobile Web Development Essentials, WordPress Complete*, and *jQuery 2.0 for Designers Beginner's Guide*, all by Packt Publishing. In 2011, he left a full-time job as a Delphi and PHP developer to concentrate on his own company, HQF Development (http://hqf.fr). He currently runs a number of websites, including http://krystallopolis.fr, http://artsgaleries.com, http://www.battlesoop.fr, http://www.livrepizzas.fr, http://www.papdevis.fr, and http://olivierpons.fr, which is his own web development blog. He works as a consultant, teacher, project manager, and sometimes helps big companies as a senior and highly skilled developer.

Ardian Yuli Setyanto, S.Kom, has been programming since his high school days. He featured in the national selection for Tim Olimpiade Komputer Indonesia (TOKI, which means Indonesia Computer Olympiad Team) twice, in 2002 and 2003. This persuaded him to study computer science at Gadjah Mada University (UGM). He graduated in 2009, the first among his other friends, with a score of 3.5 out of 4. He also used WordPress for his essay during his bachelor's degree. Ardian developed his own plugin and combined it with a GSM phone to read and send SMS (text messages), instead of the usual e-mail service used to manage WordPress comments, which he discussed in his essay.

After graduating from the university, he started working as a freelancer using WordPress and PrestaShop. These CMSes are widely used in his home country, Indonesia. Ardian was a technical reviewer for *PrestaShop 1.3 Beginners Guide, Packt Publishing*, written by John Horton. He was also selected as a local moderator for the PrestaShop forum in the Indonesia region.

Nowadays, he works as a backend developer, using PHP and Ruby. Some of his favorite frameworks are Symfony2, Rails, and Sinatra. You can read his blog at `http://www.ardianys.com`, which discusses programming and his beloved family — Niela, Dzulqarnain, and Nusaibah. If you have any technical questions about this book, you can contact him via Twitter at `@ardianys`.

Many, many thanks and kudos to Packt Publishing for selecting me again as a technical reviewer, although I could not completely finish my work because my father was not well. Mainly, thanks to Ms. Nidhi Joshi, who patiently accepted my conditions.

www.PacktPub.com

Support files, eBooks, discount offers, and more

For support files and downloads related to your book, please visit www.PacktPub.com.

Did you know that Packt offers eBook versions of every book published, with PDF and ePub files available? You can upgrade to the eBook version at www.PacktPub.com and as a print book customer, you are entitled to a discount on the eBook copy. Get in touch with us at service@packtpub.com for more details.

At www.PacktPub.com, you can also read a collection of free technical articles, sign up for a range of free newsletters and receive exclusive discounts and offers on Packt books and eBooks.

https://www2.packtpub.com/books/subscription/packtlib

Do you need instant solutions to your IT questions? PacktLib is Packt's online digital book library. Here, you can search, access, and read Packt's entire library of books.

Why subscribe?

- Fully searchable across every book published by Packt
- Copy and paste, print, and bookmark content
- On demand and accessible via a web browser

Free access for Packt account holders

If you have an account with Packt at www.PacktPub.com, you can use this to access PacktLib today and view 9 entirely free books. Simply use your login credentials for immediate access.

Table of Contents

Preface   **xi**

Chapter 1: Introducing WordPress   **1**

  Getting into WordPress   **2**

    Using WordPress for a blog or a website   3

      Starting the journey – what is a blog?   3

  Understanding the common terms   **4**

    Post   4

    Categories and tags   4

    Comments   5

    Themes   5

    Plugins   5

    Widget   6

    Menus   6

    RSS   6

    Page   6

    Home page   7

    Users   7

  Why choose WordPress   **7**

    A long time in refining   7

    Active in development   8

    A large community of contributors   8

    Amazingly extendable   8

  Getting to know the WordPress family   **8**

  Digging into WordPress – the features   **9**

  Getting familiar with the new feature list since 3.7   **10**

    Learning more   11

  Learning more with online WordPress resources   **12**

  Staying updated through WordPress news   **12**

Understanding the Codex	**13**
Getting support from other users	**14**
Using theme and plugin directories	**14**
Summary	**15**
Chapter 2: Getting Started with WordPress	**17**
Building your WordPress website – start here	**18**
Using WordPress.com	**20**
Publishing your first content on a WordPress.com blog	22
Installing WordPress manually	**24**
Preparing the environment	24
Downloading WordPress	24
Upgrading from an earlier version of WordPress	25
Uploading the files	25
Installing WordPress	27
Installing WordPress through a hand-built configuration file	30
Learning more	33
Installing WordPress through an auto-installer script	**33**
The wp-admin panel	**37**
Changing general blog information	41
Creating your first post	43
Writing your first comment	44
Retrieving a lost password	47
Getting a Gravatar	**47**
Summary	**48**
Chapter 3: Creating Blog Content	**49**
WordPress admin conventions	**49**
Lists of items	50
Posting on your blog	**52**
Adding a simple post	52
Common post options	54
Categories and tags	55
Images in your posts	57
Videos and other media in your posts	63
Using the Visual editor versus the Text editor	67
Lead and body	68
Drafts, pending articles, and timestamps	69
Advanced post options	71
Excerpt	71
Sending pingbacks and trackbacks	72
Discussion	73
Custom Fields	74
Working with post revisions	75

Changing the author of the post	77
Protecting content	77
Pretty post slug	78
Custom post format settings	79
Additional writing options	**81**
Press This	81
Posting via e-mail	82
External blogging tools	82
Mobile apps for iOS and Android	83
Discussion on your blog – comments	**85**
Adding a comment	**85**
Discussion settings	**86**
Submission, notification, and moderation settings	86
When to moderate or blacklist a comment	88
Avatar display settings	89
Moderating comments	**90**
How to eliminate comment spam	**92**
Getting an Akismet API key	93
Activating Akismet	95
Adding and managing categories	**96**
Summary	**97**
Chapter 4: Pages, Menus, Media Library, and More	**99**
Pages	**99**
Adding a page	100
Parent	102
Order	102
Managing pages	102
Menus	**103**
Adding a Menu	103
Displaying a Menu	106
Header	**107**
Background	**109**
Advanced site customization	**112**
Media library	**113**
Media Manager	115
Adding an image gallery	118
Choosing a post or page	118
Selecting or uploading images	119
Importing/exporting your content	**123**
Importing content	124
Exporting content	125
Summary	**126**

Chapter 5: Plugins and Widgets   **127**

Breaking down plugins – what are they?   **127**

Why use plugins   **128**

Where to get plugins from   **128**

Finding new plugins   **130**

Installing a plugin – the how-to   **131**

Manual plugin installation   131

Auto-installation   134

The must-have pack of plugins   **137**

Backing up   137

Enabling Google Analytics   140

Caching   142

Search engine optimization (SEO)   143

Securing your site   145

Social media integration   148

Jetpack   151

Widgets   **152**

Summary   **155**

Chapter 6: Choosing and Installing Themes   **157**

Finding themes   **158**

WordPress Theme Directory   158

Main types of themes   161

Finding more themes   162

Some not-design-related theme basics   **164**

The structure of a theme   164

Factors to consider when choosing a theme   165

The purpose of the theme   165

Theme licensing   168

Up-to-date themes only   168

Themes that are customizable   169

Themes with responsive structure   169

Support, reviews, and documentation   170

Installing and changing themes   **170**

Adding a theme within the wp-admin   170

Downloading, extracting, and uploading   173

Summary   **176**

Chapter 7: Developing Your Own Theme   **177**

Setting up your design   **178**

Designing your theme to be WordPress-friendly   178

Three paths of theme development   179

Building a theme from the ground up   180

Building a theme with a framework   180

Building a theme with a starter theme	181
Converting your design into code	**182**
Examining the HTML structure	182
Examining the CSS	184
Converting your build into a theme	**190**
Creating the theme folder	190
How to create basic WordPress content	193
The functions.php file	193
The <head> tag	198
The header and footer	199
The sidebar	201
Main column – the loop	202
Creating template files within your theme	**207**
Understanding the WordPress theme	208
Breaking it up	208
The header.php file	208
The footer.php file	209
The sidebar.php file	209
Your four template files	210
Archive template	211
Single template	212
Page template	214
Generated classes for the body and post	216
Other WordPress templates	217
Creating and using a custom page template	218
Making your theme widget-friendly	**225**
Going back to our sidebar	225
Working with the functions.php file	226
Adding some widgets	226
Additional widgetizing options	227
Enabling a menu in your theme	**228**
Creating a child theme	**228**
Creating the new theme folder	229
Creating the style sheet	230
Using your child theme	230
Sharing your theme	**231**
Summary	**233**
Chapter 8: Feeds, Podcasting, and Social Media Integration	**235**
Getting started with feeds	**236**
Working with built-in WordPress feeds	**238**
Adding feed links	**239**
Feeds for the entire website	240

Feeds for comments   241
Podcasting   **242**
  Creating a podcast   243
    Recording yourself   243
    Making a post   244
    Dedicated podcasting   245
  Podcasting plugins   246
  Using a service to host audio files for free   247
Integrating social media   **248**
  Making your blog social media friendly   248
  Setting up social media share buttons   249
  Setting up social media APIs' integration   249
  Setting up automatic content distribution to social media   250
    The Jetpack plugin   251
    The Revive Old Post plugin   251
  Setting up social media metrics tracking   253
Summary   **254**
Chapter 9: Developing Plugins and Widgets   **255**
Plugins   **256**
  Building plugins from scratch   256
  Plugin code requirements   257
  Basic plugin - adding link icons   257
    Naming and organizing the plugin files   258
    Writing the plugin's core functions   260
    Adding hooks to the plugin   261
    Trying out the plugin   264
  Adding an admin page   265
    Adding management page functions   265
    Modifying the doctype_styles_new_regex() function   268
    Adding hooks   268
    Trying out the plugin   269
  Testing your plugins   270
  A plugin with DB access – capturing searched words   271
    Getting the plugin to talk to the database   272
    Adding management page functions   273
    Trying out the plugin   274
  Learning more   276
Widgets   **276**
  Custom tag cloud widget   276
    Naming our widget   277
    The widget structure   278
    The widget initiation function   279
    The widget form function   280
    The widget save function   281

The widget print function	282
Custom widget styles	283
Initiating and hooking up the widget	284
Trying out the widget	284
Learning more	285
Bundling a widget with an existing plugin	286
Shortcodes	**286**
Shortcodes and the way they work	286
Types of shortcodes	286
Creating a simple shortcode	287
Enabling shortcodes in widgets	290
Summary	**291**
Chapter 10: Community Blogging	**293**
Concerns for a multi-author blog	**293**
User roles and abilities	**294**
Administrator	294
Editor	295
Author	296
Contributor	298
Subscriber	298
Managing users	**299**
Enabling users to self-register	301
User management plugins	**303**
Summary	**303**
Chapter 11: Creating a Non-blog Website Part 1 – The Basics	**305**
The must-do tasks	**307**
Static websites	**307**
The process	308
Building your home page	309
Creating easy-to-grasp menus	311
Corporate or business websites	**311**
Picking a clean theme	312
Branding elements	313
Good navigation	314
Custom home page	315
Optional slider	316
Meteor Slides	317
Master Slider	318
One-page websites	**321**
Picking a one-page theme	323
Branding elements	324

High-quality images	324
Summary	**326**
Chapter 12: Creating a Non-blog Website Part 2 – Community Websites and Custom Content Elements	**327**
Membership websites	**327**
Taking the simple approach	328
Using membership plugins	329
Taking the free approach	330
Installing the plugin	331
Using the plugin	333
Video blogs and photo blogs	**334**
Exploring themes for video and photo sites	336
Getting plugins for video and photo sites	336
Social networks	**338**
Installing a social network	339
Designing your social network	341
Extending the functionality	341
Introducing custom post types	**342**
Registering a new post type	342
Adding labels	344
Adding messages	344
Creating book template files	346
Registering and using a custom taxonomy	352
Customizing the admin display	354
Summary	**355**
Chapter 13: Administrating WordPress	**357**
System requirements	**357**
Enabling permalinks	**358**
The importance of backing up	**358**
Easy, quick, and frequent content backups	358
Backing up everything	359
Getting a managed solution	360
Upgrading WordPress	**360**
Steps for upgrading	360
Backing up your database	361
Backing up your WordPress files	361
Running the WordPress upgrade feature	361
Updating permalinks and .htaccess	362
Installing updated plugins and themes	362
Migrating or restoring a WordPress website	**363**
Acting in case of a site crash	**364**
Setting file permissions	**365**

Explaining file permissions	365
Permissions for WordPress	366
How to set permissions	366
Troubleshooting	**366**
Troubleshooting during installation	367
Headers already sent	367
Page comes with only PHP code	367
Cannot connect to the MySQL database	367
Basic troubleshooting	368
Cannot see posts	368
I don't receive the e-mailed passwords	369
Tips for theme development	**369**
Template tags	369
Class styles generated by WordPress	372
Learning more	373
Summary	**373**
Index	**375**

Preface

WordPress 4.x Complete will take you through the complete process of building a fully functional WordPress site from scratch. The journey goes all the way from teaching you how to install WordPress to the most advanced topics, such as creating your own themes, writing plugins, and even building non-blog websites. The best part is that you can do all of this without losing your shirt along the way. Moreover, once you get some practice, you will be able to launch new WordPress sites within minutes (not a metaphor, by the way; this is completely true).

This book guides you along the way in a step-by-step manner to explain everything there is to know about WordPress. We'll start by downloading and installing the core of WordPress, where you will learn how to choose the correct settings in order to guarantee a smooth experience for yourself and your visitors. After that, this book will teach you all about content management functionalities for your site, from posts and pages to categories and tags, all the way to links, media, menus, images, galleries, administration, user profiles, and more. Next, you will find out what plugins and themes are and how to use them effectively. Finally, you'll learn how to create your own themes and plugins to enhance the overall functionality of your website. Once you're done with *WordPress 4.x Complete*, you'll have all the knowledge required to build a professional WordPress site from scratch.

What this book covers

Chapter 1, Introducing WordPress, explains what makes WordPress an excellent software that can run your website (blog or not). WordPress is packed with excellent features and is so flexible that it can really do anything you want. It has a wealth of online resources. Additionally, it's super easy to use, and you need no special skills or prior experience to use it. Last but not least, it is free!

Chapter 2, Getting Started with WordPress, describes how to install WordPress on a remote server, change the basic default settings of your blog, write posts, and comment on those posts. This chapter also shows you how to work with sites hosted on WordPress.com, which is one of the branches of the WordPress world.

Chapter 3, Creating Blog Content, teaches you everything you need to know to add content to your blog and then manage that content, be it posts, categories, and comments, or tags, spam, and excerpts.

Chapter 4, Pages, Menus, Media Library, and More, explores all of the content WordPress can manage that's not directly about blogging. You also get to learn about static pages, menus, headers and backgrounds, the media library, image galleries, and more.

Chapter 5, Plugins and Widgets, discusses everything there is to know about finding the best plugins for WordPress and then using them effectively. Plugins are an integral part of every WordPress site's lifespan, so it's hard to find a successful site that isn't using any of them.

Chapter 6, Choosing and Installing Themes, describes how to manage the basic look of your WordPress website. You also get to learn where to find themes, why they are useful, and how to implement new themes in your WordPress website.

Chapter 7, Developing Your Own Theme, explains how to create your own theme. With just the most basic HTML and CSS abilities, you can create a design and turn it into a fully functional WordPress theme.

Chapter 8, Feeds, Podcasting, and Social Media Integration, explains what an RSS feed is and how to make feeds available for your WordPress blog. This chapter also explores how to syndicate an entire blog or just posts within a certain category, and how to create your own podcast with the help of plugins. Finally, it goes on to discuss social media integration and how it can help you build a popular website.

Chapter 9, Developing Plugins and Widgets, teaches you everything you need to know about creating basic plugins and widgets: how to structure the PHP files, where to put your functions, and how to use hooks. This chapter also teaches you to add management pages and a widget that is related to a plugin.

Chapter 10, Community Blogging, explains how to manage a group of users working with a single blog, which is a community of users. Community blogging can play an important role in a user group or a news website. This chapter also explains how to manage the different levels of privileges for users in the community.

Chapter 11, Creating a Non-blog Website Part 1 – The Basics, explores the endless possibilities of WordPress when it comes to using it to launch various types of websites. This chapter presents the first batch of our non-blog websites and explains in detail how to build them on top of a standard WordPress installation.

Chapter 12, Creating a Non-blog Website Part 2 – Community Websites and Custom Content Elements, goes through some additional types of non-blog websites and also presents some technical aspects of building them (caution—code talk inside!).

Chapter 13, Administrating WordPress, covers many of the common administrative tasks you may face when managing a WordPress website. This includes backing up your database and files, moving your WordPress installation from one server or folder to another, and doing general problem-solving and troubleshooting.

What you need for this book

- A computer
- A web browser
- A plain text editor
- FTP software

You may consider a text editor that highlights code (such as Coda, TextMate, HTMLKit, and so on), but a simple plain text editor is all that's required. You may like to run a local copy of WordPress on your computer, in which case you may need a server such as Apache and MySQL installed (though WAMP and MAMP can take care of all that for you). But even this is not necessary, as you could do the entire thing remotely.

Who this book is for

This book is a guide to WordPress for both beginners and those who have slightly more advanced knowledge of WordPress. If you are new to blogging and want to create your own blog or website in a simple and straightforward manner, then this book is for you. It is also for people who want to learn to customize and expand the capabilities of a WordPress website. You do not require any detailed knowledge of programming or web development, and any IT-confident user will be able to use this book to produce an impressive website.

Conventions

In this book, you will find a number of text styles that distinguish between different kinds of information. Here are some examples of these styles and an explanation of their meaning.

Code words in text, database table names, folder names, filenames, file extensions, pathnames, dummy URLs, user input, and Twitter handles are shown as follows: "The `wp-config.php` file allows us to set this, too."

A block of code is set as follows:

```
<!DOCTYPE html>
<html dir="ltr" lang="en-US">
<head>
<meta charset="UTF-8" />
<title>Blog title</title>
<style type="text/css">@import url("style.css");</style>
```

When we wish to draw your attention to a particular part of a code block, the relevant lines or items are set in bold:

```
function ahs_doctypes_regex($text) {
$types = get_option('ahs_supportedtypes');
$types = ereg_replace(',[ ]*','|',$types);
$text =
```

Any command-line input or output is written as follows:

```
chmod -R wp-admin 744
```

New terms and **important words** are shown in bold. Words that you see on the screen, for example, in menus or dialog boxes, appear in the text like this: "To add a new page, go to your wp-admin and navigate to **Pages | Add New**."

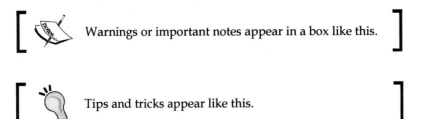

> Warnings or important notes appear in a box like this.

> Tips and tricks appear like this.

Reader feedback

Feedback from our readers is always welcome. Let us know what you think about this book—what you liked or disliked. Reader feedback is important for us as it helps us develop titles that you will really get the most out of.

To send us general feedback, simply e-mail feedback@packtpub.com, and mention the book's title in the subject of your message.

If there is a topic that you have expertise in and you are interested in either writing or contributing to a book, see our author guide at www.packtpub.com/authors.

Customer support

Now that you are the proud owner of a Packt book, we have a number of things to help you to get the most from your purchase.

Downloading the example code

You can download the example code files from your account at http://www.packtpub.com for all the Packt Publishing books you have purchased. If you purchased this book elsewhere, you can visit http://www.packtpub.com/support and register to have the files e-mailed directly to you.

Downloading the color images of this book

We also provide you with a PDF file that has color images of the screenshots/ diagrams used in this book. The color images will help you better understand the changes in the output. You can download this file from: https://www.packtpub.com/sites/default/files/downloads/B04045_ColorImages.pdf.

Errata

Although we have taken every care to ensure the accuracy of our content, mistakes do happen. If you find a mistake in one of our books—maybe a mistake in the text or the code—we would be grateful if you could report this to us. By doing so, you can save other readers from frustration and help us improve subsequent versions of this book. If you find any errata, please report them by visiting http://www.packtpub.com/submit-errata, selecting your book, clicking on the **Errata Submission Form** link, and entering the details of your errata. Once your errata are verified, your submission will be accepted and the errata will be uploaded to our website or added to any list of existing errata under the Errata section of that title.

To view the previously submitted errata, go to `https://www.packtpub.com/books/content/support` and enter the name of the book in the search field. The required information will appear under the **Errata** section.

Piracy

Piracy of copyrighted material on the Internet is an ongoing problem across all media. At Packt, we take the protection of our copyright and licenses very seriously. If you come across any illegal copies of our works in any form on the Internet, please provide us with the location address or website name immediately so that we can pursue a remedy.

Please contact us at `copyright@packtpub.com` with a link to the suspected pirated material.

We appreciate your help in protecting our authors and our ability to bring you valuable content.

Questions

If you have a problem with any aspect of this book, you can contact us at `questions@packtpub.com`, and we will do our best to address the problem.

1
Introducing WordPress

Have you ever wanted to get yourself a shiny new website at a low cost, without the need to hire a team of developers and designers, without learning advanced PHP, and with almost unlimited extension possibilities? Or maybe you want to get into the world of website creation and becoming the next expert. If that's a yes to any of these questions, then WordPress is likely to be the platform you should look into.

These days, everyone has a good reason to have a website. It's not just large companies anymore. Individuals, families, freelancers, and small or independent businesses can all benefit from having one. Many individuals and small businesses may not have the financial resources to hire a website development company or a freelance web developer to create a website for them. This is where WordPress comes into play.

In short, WordPress is an open source web software application that you can use to create and maintain a modern website, even if you don't have any technical expertise. Since WordPress is a web application, it doesn't need to be installed on your home computer, or any other machine under your control. It can live on a server (a kind of computer) that belongs to your website hosting company. WordPress is free, easy to use, and packed with excellent features.

Originally, WordPress was an application meant to run a blog website. However, it has now evolved into a fully-featured **Content Management System (CMS)**. Actually, at the time of writing, WordPress powers over 23 percent of the entire Internet. If that's not enough, the newest version of the platform has been downloaded over 25 million times (you can see the live numbers at `https://wordpress.org/download/counter/`). It seems that joining the craze is, indeed, a wise thing to do.

In this chapter, we'll explore:

- The reasons that will make you choose WordPress to run your website
- The greatest advantages of WordPress
- Online resources for WordPress
- The complete list of features in the newest versions of WordPress

Getting into WordPress

WordPress is an open-source content management system. **Open source** means that the source code of the system is made available with a license, whereby the copyright holder provides the rights to study, change, and distribute the software to anyone and for any purpose (as Wikipedia defines it). **Content management system** means a software application that can run a website (for example, a blog) and allows you to publish, edit, and modify the content. It's a piece of software that lives on the web server and makes it easy for you to add and edit posts, themes, comments, and all of your other content.

Even though WordPress was originally a blog engine—used primarily to run blogs—it's now being used by a number of big (by today's standards) online agencies to run their sites. Outlets such as The New York Times, The Wall Street Journal, Forbes, and Reuters use WordPress as the base of their web publishing platforms.

Undoubtedly, the platform has evolved a lot over the years, and even though a large number of new functionalities have been introduced, WordPress still remains one of the easiest to use web publishing platforms out there.

 Originally, WordPress was a fork of an older piece of software named **b2/cafelog**. WordPress was developed by Matt Mullenweg and Mike Little, but is now maintained and developed by a team of developers that includes Mullenweg.

Using WordPress for a blog or a website

There are generally two popular types of websites for which WordPress is meant to be used:

- A normal website with relatively static content—pages, subpages, and so on.
- A blog website—chronologically organized and frequently updated, categorized, tagged, and archived.

However, as experience shows, these days WordPress is successfully used to run a wide variety of other sites as well, such as:

- Corporate business sites
- E-commerce stores
- One-page profile sites
- Membership sites
- Video blogs
- Photo blogs
- Product sites
- Education sites (e-courses) and more

For those of you unfamiliar with blog websites and blogging terminology, let's take a look at the basics.

Starting the journey – what is a blog?

Originally, **blog** was short for **weblog**. According to Wikipedia, the term weblog was first used in 1997, and people started using blogs globally in 1999. The terms *weblog*, *weblogging*, and *weblogger* were added to the Oxford Dictionary in 2003, though these days most people leave off the "we" part.

Just to give you a more plain-English explanation, a blog is a website that usually contains regular entries made by an author. These entries can be of various types, such as commentary, descriptions of events, photos, videos, personal remarks, tutorials, case studies, long opinion pieces, political ideas, or whatever else you can imagine. They are usually displayed in a reverse chronological order, with the most recent additions at the top. Those entries can be organized in a variety of ways—by date, topic, subject, and so on.

One of the main characteristics of a blog is that it's meant to be updated regularly. Unlike a site where the content is static, a blog behaves more like an online diary, wherein the blogger posts regular updates. Hence, blogs are dynamic with ever-changing content. A blog can be updated with new content and the old content can be changed or deleted at any time (although deleting content is not a common practice).

Most blogs focus their content on a particular subject—for example, current events, hobbies, niche topics, and technical expertise. This doesn't mean that blogs are meant to be published only by individuals sharing their personal opinions on given matters. On the contrary, these days, blogs have become a major part of the online presence for many businesses and corporations. The modern practice of "content marketing" is now one of the most widely accepted web marketing methods, and its core is based on publishing quality content, often in blog form.

Understanding the common terms

If you are new to the world of blogging (sometimes called "blogosphere", which is a fairly popular expression these days), you may want to familiarize yourself with the following common terms.

Post

Each entry in the blog is called a **post**. Every post usually has a number of different parts. Of course, the two most obvious parts are title and content. The **content** is text, images, links, and so on. Posts can even contain multimedia (for example, videos and audio files). Every post also has a publication timestamp, and most have one or more categories and tags assigned to them. It is these posts, or entries, that are displayed in a reverse chronological order on the main page of the blog. By default, the latest post is displayed first, in order to give the viewer the latest news on the subject.

Categories and tags

Categories and **tags** are ways to organize and find posts within a blog and even across blogs. Categories are like topics, while tags are more like keywords. For example, for a blog about food and cooking, there might be a category called **Recipes**, but every post in that category might have different tags (for example, soup, baked, vegetarian, and dairy free).

The purpose and correct usage of tags and categories is one of the widely discussed topics among bloggers. Although there are basic guidelines such as the ones presented here, every blogger develops their own approach after a while, and there are no rules "written in stone".

Comments

Most blogs allow visitors to post comments about the posts. This gives readers the opportunity to interact with the author of the blog, thus making the whole experience interactive. Often, the author of the blog will respond to comments by posting additional comments with the single click of the reply button, which enables a continuous public online conversation or dialog.

Comments are said to be one of the most important assets for a blog. The presence of a large number of comments shows how popular and authoritative the blog is.

Themes

The **theme** for a blog is the design and layout that you choose for your blog. In most blogs, the content (for example, posts) is separate from the visual layout. This means you can change the visual layout of your blog at any time without having to worry about the content being affected. One of the best things about themes is that it takes only minutes to install and start using a new one. Moreover, there are a number of very good free or low-cost themes available online.

That being said, you need to be careful when working with free themes from unknown developers. Often, they contain encrypted parts and code that can hurt your site and its presence on Google. Always look for user reviews before choosing a theme. Most importantly, the safest bet is getting your free themes only from the official WordPress directory at https://wordpress.org/themes/. The themes there have been tested and checked for any suspicious code.

 You can learn more about this whole issue at http://newinternetorder.com/free-wordpress-themes-are-evil/.

Plugins

WordPress **plugins** are relatively small pieces of web software that can be installed on a WordPress site. They extend the native functionality to do almost anything that the technology of today allows. Just like WordPress itself, the code within plugins is open source, which means that anyone can build a new plugin if they have the required skill set. Every WordPress website or blog can work with an unlimited number of plugins (although it is not a recommended approach). The most popular functionalities introduced through plugins include: spam protection, search engine optimization, caching, social media integration, interactive contact forms, and backups.

Widget

In short, **widgets** are a simplified version of plugins. Furthermore, they display a direct, visible result on your blog by using small content boxes (depending on the exact widget you're using, this content can be very diverse). The most common usage of widgets is to have them showcased within the sidebars on your site. Typically, your current theme will provide you with a number of widget areas where you can display widgets (as mentioned, many of these are located in the sidebar). Some of the common usages for widgets are to display content such as categories and tags, recent posts, popular posts, recent comments, links to archived posts, pages, links, search fields, or standard non-formatted text.

Menus

We need to talk some history to explain the meaning of menus in WordPress. Back in the day, WordPress didn't allow much customization in terms of tweaking navigation menus and hand-picking the links we wanted to display. This changed in version 3.0, whereby the new **Custom Menus** feature was introduced. In plain English, it allows us to create completely custom menus (featuring any links of our choice) and then display them in specific areas on our sites. To be honest, this feature, even though it sounds basic, is one of the main ones that has turned WordPress from a simple blogging tool into a fully-fledged web publishing platform. I promise this will sound much clearer in the following chapters.

RSS

RSS is an acronym for **Really Simple Syndication**, and *Chapter 8, Feeds, Podcasting, and Social Media Integration*, addresses the topic of feeds in detail. For now, let's say that RSS and feeds are a way to syndicate the content of your blog so that people can subscribe to it. This means people do not actually have to visit your blog regularly to see what you've added. Instead, they can subscribe and have new content delivered to them via e-mail, or through a feed reader such as **Feedly**.

Page

It's important to understand the difference between a page and a post. Unlike posts, pages do not depend on timestamps and are not displayed in a chronological order. Also, they do not have categories or tags. A **page** is a piece of content with only a title and content (an example would be **About Me** or **Contact Us**—the two most popular pages on almost any blog). It is likely that the number of pages on your blog remains relatively static, while new posts can be added every day or so.

Home page

A home page is simply the main page that visitors see when they visit your website by typing in your domain name or URL address. In the early days of WordPress' existence, a home page wasn't something we talked about as a separate kind of page. Originally, a home page was generated automatically from the newest posts—it was a listing of those posts in a reverse chronological order. Right now, however, WordPress allows us to build a completely customized home page and display whatever content we wish on it.

Users

As mentioned earlier, WordPress is now a complete web publishing platform. One of its characteristics is that it is capable of working with multiple user accounts, not just a single account belonging to the owner (main author) of the site. There are different types of user accounts available, and they have different credentials and access rights. WordPress is clearly trying to resemble a traditional publishing house where there are authors, editors, and other contributors all working together. Even though the possibility of creating an unlimited number of user accounts won't be that impressive for anyone planning to manage a site on their own, it can certainly be a more than essential feature for big, magazine-like websites.

Why choose WordPress

WordPress is not the only publishing platform out there, but it has an awful lot to offer. In the following sections, I've called attention to WordPress's most outstanding features.

A long time in refining

In web years, WordPress has been around for quite a while and was in development the whole time, and so constantly getting better. WordPress very first release, Version 0.70, was launched in May 2003. Since then, it has had 24 major releases, with a number of minor ones in between. Each release came with more features and better security.

Each major release comes with a codename honoring a great Jazz musician, and this has become a tradition in the WordPress world. For instance, the latest version, 4.1, is codenamed Dinah (in honor of jazz singer Dinah Washington).

Active in development

WordPress is a continually evolving application. It's never left alone to stagnate. Developers are working on WordPress constantly to keep it ahead of spammers and hackers, and to evolve the application on the basis of the evolving needs of its users.

A large community of contributors

WordPress is not being developed by a lonely programmer in a dark basement room. On the contrary, there is a large community of people working on it collaboratively by developing, troubleshooting, making suggestions, and testing the application. With such a large group of people involved, the application is likely to continue to evolve and improve without pause.

Amazingly extendable

In addition to having an extremely strong core, WordPress is also quite extendable. This means that once you get started with it, the possibilities are nearly limitless. Any additional functionality that you can dream of can be added by means of a plugin that you or your programmer friends can write.

Getting to know the WordPress family

WordPress as a platform and as a community of users has evolved in two main areas. The first one is gathered around WordPress.org—the native, main website of the WordPress project. The other is WordPress.com—a platform providing free blogs for every user who wants one:

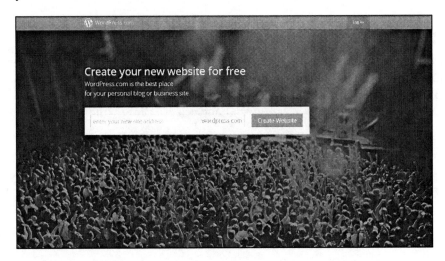

Essentially, WordPress.org is about developing the platform itself, sharing new plugins, discussing the technical aspects of WordPress, and being all "techie" in general. WordPress.com (the preceding screenshot) is a purely community-driven site where bloggers can meet with each other, and publish their content on free blogs under the `wordpress.com` subdomain (for example, something like `http://my-blog-name.wordpress.com/` is a subdomain). That being said, there are paid plans available at WordPress.com as well.

In *Chapter 2, Getting Started with WordPress*, we will discuss all of the differences between having your blog on WordPress.com and downloading the software from WordPress.org and hosting it yourself, but the basic difference is the level of control. If your blog is on WordPress.com, you have less control over plugins, themes, and other details of the blog because everything is managed and made worry-free by the WordPress.com service, which obviously has its pros and cons.

Digging into WordPress – the features

Here is a list of some of the features that WordPress has to offer:

- Compliance with the **World Wide Web Consortium (W3C)** standards, although this does depend on the theme you're using
- Unlimited categories and subcategories
- Unlimited tags
- Automatic syndication (RSS and Atom)
- Use of the XML RPC interface for trackbacks and remote posting
- Ability to post via e-mail and mobile devices (there are apps available for all major mobile platforms, including iOS and Android)
- Support for plugins and themes
- Import of data from other blogs (Moveable Type, Textpattern, Greymatter, b2evolution, and Blogger)
- Easy to administer and blog without any previous experience
- Convenient, fully functional, built-in search
- Instant and fast publishing of content—no re-building of pages required
- Multilanguage capability
- Ability to password protect content
- Comments manager and spam protection

- Built-in workflow (write, draft, review, and publish)
- Intelligent text formatting via a **What You See Is What You Get (WYSIWYG)** editor
- Multi-user and multi-author support for user accounts
- Feature-rich **Media Library** for managing photos and other non-text content through a visual and highly usable interface
- Social media integration capabilities
- Dynamic and scalable revision functionality with post (edit) locking
- Built-in embed functionality through shortcodes (compatible with services such as YouTube, Vimeo, Flickr, and SoundCloud)
- An admin panel that's accessible via all modern devices, operating systems, and web browsers
- Pre-made color schemes for the admin panel
- User-friendly image editing, plus a drag-and-drop image importing feature
- Advanced **Search Engine Optimization (SEO)** features through plugins and themes

Getting familiar with the new feature list since 3.7

Since the last edition of this book was published, quite a staggering number of new features have been added to the WordPress software. If you're new to WordPress, this list may not mean a whole lot to you, but if you're familiar with WordPress and have been using it for a long time, you'll find this list quite enlightening:

- Introduction of a new, modern admin panel design (uncluttered, with clean typography, improved contrast, responsive structure, and better theme management)
- Inclusion of eight new admin color schemes
- Introduction of Open Sans as the new font for the WordPress admin panel
- New default theme—**Twenty Fifteen**
- Update of the external libraries used in WordPress
- Improved **right-to-left (RTL)** support

- New click-to-add interface for adding widgets to sidebars
- Introduction of a smoother media editing experience (better visual editing, quicker access to scaling, and crop and rotation tools)
- Drag-and-drop file importing into the editor itself
- Image gallery previews right in the editor
- Live widget previews inside the **Customizer**
- Introduction of a new theme browser
- Enabling of HTML5 markup to be used for captions and galleries
- Improved database layer
- Media Library listing now appearing on a grid layout
- Improved visual editor that expands to fit the content being worked on
- New fixed toolbar in the editor
- Embeddable content previews right in the visual editor
- Inclusion of a new grid view of the plugins page for finding and installing new plugins
- Introduction of the Customizer API
- Improved WordPress installation in languages other than English
- Improved media experience on small screen sizes

Learning more

If you'd like to see detailed lists of all the new features added since WordPress version 3.7, take a look at the articles on these links:

- `http://codex.wordpress.org/Version_3.8`
- `http://codex.wordpress.org/Version_3.9`
- `http://codex.wordpress.org/Version_4.0`
- `http://codex.wordpress.org/Version_4.1`

Also, you can read a fully explained feature list at `https://wordpress.org/about/features/`.

Learning more with online WordPress resources

One very useful characteristic of WordPress is that it has a large, active online community. Everything you will ever need for your WordPress website can likely be found online, and probably for free. In addition to this, these days we can also find many paid resources and training programs that offer expert advice and training, revolving around many different possible usages of a WordPress site.

Staying updated through WordPress news

As WordPress is constantly being developed, it's important to keep yourself up-to-date with the software community's latest activities.

If you visit the dashboard of your own WordPress site regularly, you'll be able to stay up-to-date with WordPress news and software releases. There are widgets on the dashboard that display the latest news and announcements, and an alert always appears when there is a new version of WordPress available for download and installation.

If you prefer to visit the website, then the most important spot to visit or subscribe to is WordPress Releases. Whenever there is a new release, be it a major release, or an interim bug fix, or an upgrade, it will be at `https://wordpress.org/news/category/releases/`.

Also, be sure to stay tuned to the main WordPress blog at `https://wordpress.org/news/`.

Some additional resources worth mentioning are as follows:

- `https://wordpress.org/`: The absolute main hub for WordPress
- `https://wordpress.com/`: The main platform for free WordPress blogging
- `http://jobs.wordpress.net/`: Job listings for anyone searching for employment in various areas related to WordPress (or anyone searching for WordPress help)

- `http://wordpress.tv/`: A great source of top-notch WordPress tutorials, how-to advice, case studies, product demonstrations, and WordPress-related conference presentation recordings
- `http://central.wordcamp.org/`: WordCamp is a conference that focuses on everything WordPress, it takes place a number of times during the year in different locations around the world, and this site is the central point for the conference

Understanding the Codex

The WordPress **Codex** is the central repository of all the information that the official WordPress team has published to help people work with WordPress.

The Codex has some basic tutorials for getting started with WordPress, such as a detailed step-by-step discussion of the installation, and lists of every template tag and hook. Throughout this book, I'll be providing links to specific pages within the Codex, which will provide more or advanced information on the topics in this book.

The Codex can be found at `http://codex.wordpress.org/Main_Page` (the following screenshot):

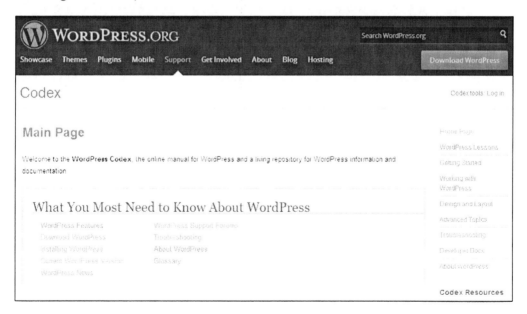

What's also worth pointing out is that, recently, the WordPress team released one more resource that will come in handy for new and experienced developers alike. It's called the WordPress Code Reference and it can be found at `https://developer.wordpress.org/reference/`. It delivers a lot of education on WordPress's functions, classes, methods, and hooks.

Getting support from other users

The online WordPress community asks questions and responds with solutions on the WordPress forum at `https://wordpress.org/support/`. It's an excellent place to go if you can't find the answer to a problem in the Codex. If you have a given question, then probably someone else has had it as well, and WordPress experts spend time in the forum answering them and giving solutions.

Using theme and plugin directories

There are official directories for themes and plugins on WordPress.org. Though not every theme and plugin is available here, the ones that are have been vetted by the community to some extent. Anything you download from these directories is likely to be relatively bug-free. Plugins and themes that you get from other sources can have malicious code, so be careful. You can also see what the community thinks of these downloads by looking at ratings, comments, and popularity.

Additionally, plugins in the Plugin Directory are automatically upgradable from within your WordPress administration panel (wp-admin), while other plugins have to be upgraded manually. We'll cover this in detail in a later chapter. You can find the **Theme Directory** at `https://wordpress.org/themes/` (the following screenshot) and the **Plugin Directory** at `https://wordpress.org/plugins/`.

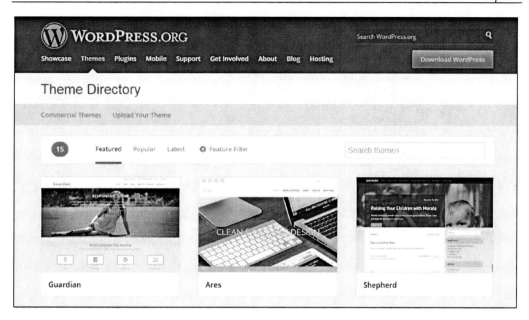

Summary

Having a website of your own is essential these days, whether you are an individual, a small business, or some other group, or you are blogging regularly or want some accurate static content up on the Internet. In this chapter, we reviewed basic information about blogging and common blog terms for those of you who are new to the concept.

WordPress is an excellent software application that can run your website (blog or not). It's packed with excellent features and is so flexible that it really can do anything you want, and it has a wealth of online resources. Additionally, it's super easy to use, and you don't need any special skills or prior experience to use it. Last but not least, it is free!

In the next chapter, we will explore the choices and steps involved in installing WordPress and getting started.

2
Getting Started with WordPress

This chapter will guide you through the process of setting up WordPress and customizing its basic features. You can choose between a couple of options regarding where your WordPress installation will live. Keep in mind that WordPress is relatively small (less than 10 MB) as well as easy to install and administer.

WordPress is available in easily downloadable formats at `https://wordpress.org/download/`. WordPress is a free, open-source application and is released under GNU **General Public License (GPL)**. This means that anyone who produces a modified version of the software released under the GPL is required to maintain the same freedoms, and that people buying or using the software can also modify and redistribute it. Thus, WordPress and other software released under the GPL are maintained as open source. In this chapter, you will learn how to:

- Create a free blog on WordPress.com
- Install WordPress manually on your web host
- Perform basic setup tasks in the WordPress admin panel (the wp-admin)
- Publish your first content

Building your WordPress website – start here

The first decision you have to make is where your blog is going to live. You have two basic options when creating your site:

- Do it at `https://wordpress.com`
- Install on a third-party web server (hosted or your own)

Let's look at some of the advantages and disadvantages of each of these two options.

The advantage of using WordPress.com is that they take care of all the technical details for you. The software has already been installed, and it will be upgraded for you whenever there's an upgrade. You're not responsible for anything else but the management of your content. A major disadvantage is that you lose almost all of the theme and plugin control you'd have otherwise. WordPress.com will not let you upload or edit your own theme, though it will let you (for a fee) edit the CSS of any theme you use. WordPress.com will not let you upload or manage plugins at all. Some plugins are installed by default (most notably Akismet, for spam blocking, and also plugins supporting Google Sitemaps, caching, Carousel slideshows, polls, site stats, and some social media buttons), but you can neither uninstall them nor install others. Additional features are available for a fee. Furthermore, you can sign up with WordPress.com Enterprise and get access to a range of optional plugins. The current list features nearly 100 plugins (WordPress.com Enterprise is available at `http://en.wordpress.com/enterprise/`). This chapter will guide you through the creation of a blog on WordPress.com, and the next chapter will acquaint you with navigation around the wp-admin. However, much of what this book covers will be impossible on WordPress.com.

A major advantage of installing WordPress on another server (which means either a server that belongs to the web host with which you signed up, or a server you set up on your own computer) is that you have control over everything. You can add and edit themes, add and remove plugins, and even edit the WordPress application files yourself if you wish to (however, don't do this unless you're confident about your WordPress skills). You'll have to keep your own WordPress software up-to-date, but that's relatively simple, and we'll cover it in this chapter. The only disadvantage is that you have to perform the installation and maintenance tasks on your own, which, as you'll see, shouldn't be too intimidating. Moreover, some web hosts provide a one-click or easy-to-use installer, which lets you skip over some of the nitty-gritty steps involved in manual installation.

In this chapter, we'll discuss how to create a new blog on WordPress.com and how to start working with it on a daily basis. However, if you want to accomplish any of the more advanced tasks with reference to the topics in this book, you will have to install WordPress on your own server as opposed to using WordPress.com.

The following table is a brief overview of the essential differences between using WordPress.com and downloading an installation package from WordPress.org and then installing it on your own server:

	WordPress.com	**WordPress.org (installation on your own server)**
Installation	No need to install anything, just sign up.	Install WordPress yourself, either manually or via your host's control panel (if offered).
Themes	Use any theme made available by WordPress.com.	Use any theme available anywhere, written by anyone (including yourself).
Plugins	No ability to choose or add plugins (unless you sign up to the premium paid WordPress.com Enterprise).	Use any plugin available anywhere, written by anyone (including yourself).
Upgrades	WordPress.com provides automatic upgrades.	You have to upgrade it yourself when upgrades are available.
Widgets	Widget availability depends on available themes.	You can widgetize any theme yourself.
Maintenance	You don't have to do any maintenance.	You're responsible for the maintenance of your site.
Advertising	No advertising of your own allowed. However, WordPress.com itself sometimes runs ads on your site.	You can advertise anything and in any amount you like.
Ownership	Even though the content belongs to you, WordPress.com can take down your blog at any moment if they consider it being inappropriate.	You have complete control over your site, and no one can force you to take it down.

	WordPress.com	WordPress.org (installation on your own server)
Domain	Your site is available as a subdomain under .wordpress.com by default, but you can also upgrade to the Premium package (for a fee) and use your own, manually registered domain.	You can use any manually registered Internet domain.

Using WordPress.com

WordPress.com (https://wordpress.com) is a free service provided by the WordPress developers, where you can register a blog or non-blog website easily and quickly with no hassle. However, because it is a hosted service, your control over some things will be more restricted than it would be if you hosted your own WordPress website. As mentioned earlier, WordPress.com will not let you edit or upload your own themes or plugins. Apart from this, WordPress.com is a great place to maintain your personal site if you don't need to do anything fancy with your theme or the source code of your site in general. To get started, go to https://wordpress.com and enter your new site address—the address of the site that you'd like to have created. Then, click on the loud blue-and-white **Create Website** button. You will be taken to the sign-up page:

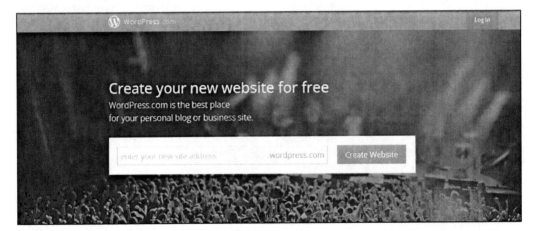

The following screenshot shows an example sign-up page where you need to enter your e-mail address (please triple-check when entering yours; it's where the confirmation e-mail will be sent), username (this is what you will sign in with in the future), password (note that the password measurement tool will notify you whether your password is strong or weak; there's also a **Generate strong password** link available next to the field), and finally blog address (WordPress.com also allows you to register a custom domain in place of the standard .wordpress.com subdomain):

After providing this information, you need to click on the **Create Blog** button at the bottom of the screen (shown in the following screenshot). Now, at this point, WordPress will try to sell you one of their premium packages (WordPress.com Premium and WordPress.com Business). Some of the additional functionalities inside the premium packages include a free .com, .net, .org, or .me domain, advanced customization capabilities, access to a range of premium themes, the possibility to store videos directly on your WordPress.com account, additional disk space (the free account offers 3 GB), and direct e-mail support or live chat support.

For now, we're going to stick with the basic, free account.

You'll be redirected to the final settings page, where you will be able to set some additional details about your new blog, such as the blog title, tagline, and default language. After that, you will have the chance to do the one thing that's usually the most exciting part about building a new blog—picking a new theme. There are some free and paid themes available. Additionally, after clicking on a specific theme, you'll have some limited possibilities to customize it. This is not too fancy. For more in-depth tuning, one of the WordPress.com premium packages is required.

Clicking on the **Next Step** button a couple more times will finally get you to the end of the process, where you will have the chance to publish your first piece of content (more on that shortly). At this stage, you will also be prompted to visit your inbox and search for the activation e-mail that has just been sent to you. The e-mail itself is very clear and only requires you to click the big **Activate Blog** button. If you can't see the images, then you might need to check your e-mail software's settings.

Right now, your new WordPress.com site is fully installed and visible to the world, and you can begin to publish and promote content, and build your audience.

Publishing your first content on a WordPress.com blog

All you have to do in order to publish some content on your WordPress.com blog is click on the New Post link in the top menu:

When you do so, you're presented with a handy online text editor window, where you can type in the contents of your post. Every post needs a title, the actual content, and some optional parameters such as tags and categories. You can add a photo for your publication.

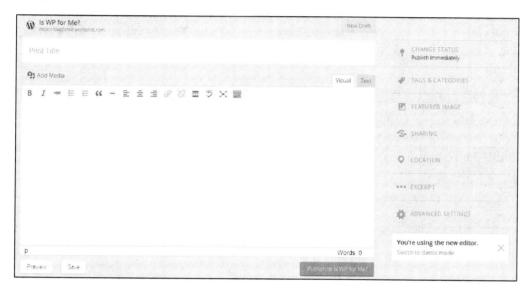

Once you have finished editing, you can either save the write up as a draft (for further modifications), preview what it's going to look like on the blog, or publish it straight away with the **Publish to [YOUR SITE]** button.

Essentially, a WordPress.com blog can be managed just like any other WordPress site (content wise), so you do get access to the Dashboard (explained later in this chapter), where you can edit and publish your content, too. The interface described here is a specially designed panel that can't be found on any other type of blog. In other words, you won't get it with a regular WordPress site (a standalone site on your own domain and hosting). Therefore, if WordPress.com is your preferred way of launching a blog, then you should skip the next section of this chapter, which is all about installing WordPress manually as a standalone site.

Installing WordPress manually

The WordPress application files can be downloaded for free if you want to perform a manual installation. If you've got a website host, this process is extremely easy and requires no previous programming skills or advanced blogging experience.

Some web hosts offer automatic installation through the host's online control panel. One of these automatic installation methods is described later in this chapter.

Preparing the environment

A good first step is to make sure you have an environment setup that is ready for WordPress. This means you need to ensure that the server meets the minimum requirements and that your database is ready.

For WordPress to work, your web host must provide you with a server that fulfills the following requirements:

- Support for PHP version 5.2.4 or greater (recommended is PHP 5.4 or greater)
- Provision of a MySQL database (full access) of version 5.0 or greater (recommended is MySQL 5.5 or greater)

Additionally, these minimum requirements tend to change occasionally. The most current requirements can always be found at `https://wordpress.org/about/requirements/`.

You can determine whether your host meets these two requirements by contacting the support team at your web host. If it does, you're ready to move on to the next step.

Downloading WordPress

Once you have checked your environment, you need to download WordPress from `https://wordpress.org/download/`. On that page, the `.zip` file is shown as a big blue button because this will be the most useful format for people to identify what to download. If you are using Windows, Mac, or Linux operating systems, your computer will be able to unzip that downloaded file automatically. (The `.tar.gz` file is provided because it is preferred by some Unix users.)

A further note on location

We're going to cover remote installation of WordPress. However, if you plan to develop themes or plugins, it is recommended that you install WordPress locally on your own computer's web server. Testing and deploying themes and plugins directly to the remote server will be much more time-consuming than working locally. If you look at the screenshots depicting WordPress installation throughout the book, you'll notice that all these are examples of working locally.

After you download the WordPress `.zip` file and extract the files, you'll get a folder called `wordpress`.

Upgrading from an earlier version of WordPress

If you are upgrading an existing installation of WordPress, you should probably leave this chapter and instead read the section *Upgrading WordPress* in *Chapter 13, Administrating WordPress*, of this book.

Uploading the files

Now, we need to upload all these files to our web server using any **FTP** client (or simply put them in our local server directory on our local computer). FTP stands for **File Transfer Protocol**. There are several FTP clients available on the Internet that are either freeware (no cost) or require a small fee. If you don't already have an FTP client, try one of the following:

- **Filezilla**: `https://filezilla-project.org/download.php?type=client` (for Mac or Windows)
- **Fetch**: `http://fetchsoftworks.com/` (for Mac only)
- **SmartFTP**: `http://www.smartftp.com/` (for Windows only)

You can also download the popular web-based FTP application net2ftp from `http://www.net2ftp.com`. These services are useful if you don't want to install a desktop application on your computer. You can also check whether your host provides browser-based FTP software.

A note about security

Whenever possible, you should use **Secure FTP (sFTP)** rather than regular FTP. If you're using sFTP, all of the data sent and received is encrypted. With FTP, data is sent in plain text and can easily be nabbed by hackers. Check both your FTP software and your hosting options and select sFTP if it's available.

Using your FTP client or service, connect to the FTP server using the server address, username, and password provided to you by your host. Next, open the folder where you want WordPress to live. You may want to install WordPress in your root folder, which will mean that visitors will see your WordPress website's home page when they go to your main URL—for example, `http://yoursite.com`. Alternatively, you may want to install WordPress in a subfolder—for example: `http://yoursite.com/blog/`.

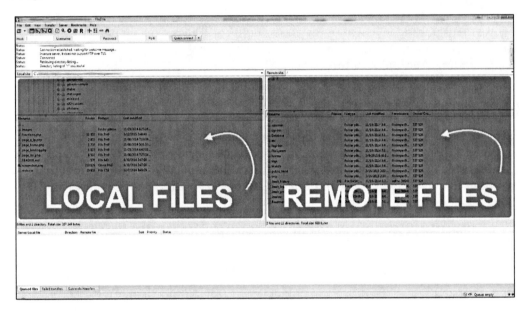

On the left side, you will see the files from your local folder, and on the right side, you will see your remote folder. (Note that the FTP client you are using may have a slightly different layout, but this is the general idea.)

Now select all of the WordPress files on your local machine from the left pane, and drag them onto the right pane. You can watch as your FTP client uploads the files one at a time and they appear on the right panel. This may take a few minutes, so be patient.

If you're installing WordPress on your local server, just be sure to place the WordPress files in the correct `webroot` directory on your computer.

Once all of the files have been uploaded, you're ready to proceed with the installation.

Installing WordPress

Now it's time to proceed with the famous 5-minute installation of WordPress (the fact that WordPress can be installed in 5 minutes or less is widely advertised on the official WordPress website). If you access your WordPress URL via your browser, you will see a short introduction message instructing you to choose the language that you want to perform the installation in:

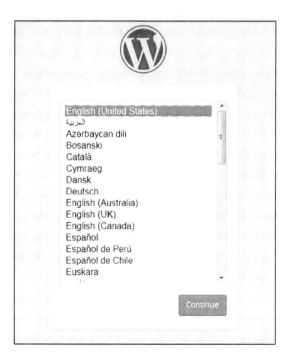

After this, you will be presented with another screen, informing you of all the required details that you'll need in order to complete the installation successfully. Currently, the following are the required details:

- **Database name**: For example, this can be `wptestblog`.
- **Database username**: For example, this can be `localdbuser`.
- **Database password**: For example, `62dcx%^_0hnm`—the more complex the password, the better.
- **Database host**: For example, this can be `1.1.1.1`—most of the time, you will be required to provide an IP address of your database host (if needed, you can take a look at this handy cheat sheet for an in-depth explanation of all the possibilities: `http://codex.wordpress.org/Editing_wp-config.php#Possible_DB_HOST_values`). In the case of servers running locally on your own machine, the database host is most likely localhost.

The big question, therefore, is where to get all this information from. The answer is your web host. Most of the large web hosts offer you a way to create your own databases via an online control panel, with usernames and passwords of your choice. If you're not sure how to do this, just e-mail or call your hosting provider for assistance. Professional support teams will be glad to help you with this.

Once you have those four parameters, you can press the **Let's go!** button and proceed to the next step of the installation. The following is a screenshot of the main setup form:

As you can see, the details are the same as those shown in an earlier screenshot. Of course, your details will be different. Also, another important point to note is that there's an additional field labeled as **Table Prefix**. This is the default prefix that every table in your database will have before its name. The default value in that field is wp_. It is recommended that you change this to any two- or three-letter word of your choice and end it with an underscore (_), just as a safety precaution against standard database attacks on known WordPress tables. The one used here is wtb_.

After pressing the **Submit** button, you will be redirected to the final confirmation page. All you have to do here is click the **Run the install** button.

At this point, things can either go well, or not that well. In the latter case, proceed to the next section, *Installing WordPress through a hand-built configuration file*. Fortunately, such problems are rare. The best indication that the online installation is going well is the presence of the following screen:

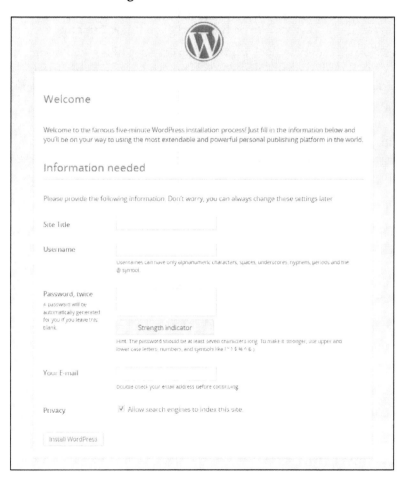

This is the final setup page. Here, you set up the core details of your new site. (If you've ever installed an earlier version of WordPress, you'll notice some differences, such as the ability to choose your first username and password.) Now, fill out the installation form (you will be able to change all of these later, so don't be too worried about getting locked into your choices):

- **Site Title**: Fill in the name of your blog (it can be something simple, such as "Daily Cooking").

- **Username**: It's in your best interest to choose a username that's not obvious. For instance, if you go with "Admin", it will be very easy to guess for anyone who might want to hack into your blog. Also worth pointing out is the fact that this account is the administrator account, which has the most privileges and access rights in all areas of the site. Opt for something difficult to guess, such as "Site-Master-45" and don't worry, silly is good.

- **Password, twice**: Choose a secure password, one that has both upper and lowercase letters, a number or two, and even a few punctuation marks.

- **Your E-mail**: Double-check that this is correct. This is the e-mail address WordPress will use to contact you about the blog, comments, and so on. If you do not get an e-mail from your WordPress site shortly after installing it, check your spam folder.

- **Privacy**: This is the final checkbox, yet possibly one of the most important settings on this list. If you leave it checked (recommended), your site is going to be accessible through Google and other search engines. Unchecking it means banning your site from the search engines.

Now, click on **Install WordPress**. You're done with the installation!

You can click on **Log In** to get to the login page. Alternatively, you can always enter your WordPress Admin panel (also known as the wp-admin) by pointing your browser to `http://yoursite.com/wp-admin`. If you're not already logged in, this URL will redirect you to the login page.

Installing WordPress through a hand-built configuration file

Now, in some cases, your web hosting account will prevent WordPress from creating a valid configuration file. This issue may be caused by access rights limitations. However, it's not a big obstacle because you can always create a configuration file manually. To do this, just open the `wordpress` folder and find the file named `wp-config-sample.php`. Make a copy of this file and name it `wp-config.php`. We'll modify this file together.

You need not be a PHP programmer to do this. Just open this file with a simple editor such as Notepad. The following is the copied text from the original `wp-config.php` file. Note that most of the comments have been removed, so that we can focus on the items we need to change. One thing to know about PHP is that any text that comes after a double slash (//), or between a slash-star and star-slash (/* and */), is a comment. It's not actual PHP code. Its purpose is to inform you what that line or that section is about:

```php
<?php
/** The name of the database for WordPress */
define('DB_NAME', 'database_name_here');

/** MySQL database username */
define('DB_USER', 'username_here');

/** MySQL database password */
define('DB_PASSWORD', 'password_here');

/** MySQL hostname */
define('DB_HOST', 'localhost');

/** Database Charset to use in creating database tables. */
define('DB_CHARSET', 'utf8');

/** The Database Collate type. Don't change this if in doubt. */
define('DB_COLLATE', '');

define('AUTH_KEY',         'put your unique phrase here');
define('SECURE_AUTH_KEY',  'put your unique phrase here');
define('LOGGED_IN_KEY',    'put your unique phrase here');
define('NONCE_KEY',        'put your unique phrase here');
define('AUTH_SALT',        'put your unique phrase here');
define('SECURE_AUTH_SALT', 'put your unique phrase here');
define('LOGGED_IN_SALT',   'put your unique phrase here');
define('NONCE_SALT',       'put your unique phrase here');

$table_prefix  = 'wp_';
```

As you can see from the code, you can insert a number of settings here, but they do resemble the ones we were filling out in the online installer just a minute ago. Let's walk through the most important ones.

Just as in the online installation, we fetched the database information, but this time we put it in the `wp-config.php` file:

```
// ** MySQL settings ** //
define('DB_NAME', 'wptestblog');
define('DB_USER', 'localdbuser');
define('DB_PASSWORD', '62dcx%^_0hnm');
define('DB_HOST', 'localhost');
```

Next, for security purposes, you need to put some unique phrases into the keys. The secret keys are used by WordPress to add random elements to your passwords and in some other situations. This will help to keep your WordPress installation uniquely protected. No one else is likely to choose the same unique keys that you chose, and therefore, breaking or hacking into your site will be more difficult. You can get some secret keys generated from `https://api.wordpress.org/secret-key/1.1/salt/` (the sample config file itself will remind you of this through the in-code PHP comments). Once you have finished, you will get the following code snippet, which you can paste directly onto the default code in `wp-config.php`:

```
define('AUTH_KEY', 'uu|6#00Pc/3h?Pg5:Zc#:S=;<3mdw-ai');
define('SECURE_AUTH_KEY', 'vy1.@Nr@Zb^G|0Vfz-|TH5&W');
define('LOGGED_IN_KEY', 'sryMVd'jVpiMWWQqx~!v XE5@fJMTt2[Z');
define('NONCE_KEY', 'i,+UPpMR>Mj3o}(B**^<T:/md,YFF76d]Kf');
define('AUTH_SALT', 'n.8Li=9OjV+_p|}e5yN2k<s{!KJs|[S&Zh');
define('SECURE_AUTH_SALT', 'I#2vPT^u[5vLX|'MzPg/J*y]RTfr');
define('LOGGED_IN_SALT', 'gR%QP^c*jfFUy,iQ}-0g_%;%H)pN0B5');
define('NONCE_SALT', '&L);.IH'v{]zYLO2:h_t#J0D-p)cvyc');
```

 Important! Don't ever get the salt keys from anywhere other than `https://api.wordpress.org/secret-key/1.1/salt/`. This is an important security mechanism that protects your browser's session from being hijacked and then used for unauthorized access to your WordPress site.

Finally, we have the aforementioned table prefix. The `wp-config.php` file allows us to set this, too. Again, here's the prefix of our choice:

```
$table_prefix = 'wtb_';
```

The WordPress Codex has a long and detailed page that describes everything about editing your wp-config.php file: http://codex.wordpress.org/Editing_wp-config.php. Once you save the wp-config.php file and either upload it onto your web host or place it on your local server, you can visit your site through your domain name (like http://yoursite.com/). You should be presented with the final setup page—the one visible in the earlier screenshot. All you have to do now is proceed according to the instructions described earlier in this chapter.

Learning more

If you'd like to see an even more detailed step-by-step guide for manual installation, take a look at this page in the WordPress Codex at http://codex.wordpress.org/Installing_WordPress.

Also, you can find more detailed installation instructions as well as specifics on changing file permissions, using FTP and languages, importing from other blogging engines, and so on in the WordPress Codex at http://codex.wordpress.org/Getting_Started_with_WordPress#Installation.

Installing WordPress through an auto-installer script

Some web hosts provide their customers with access to a range of auto-installer scripts for various web platforms, including WordPress. Most of these auto-installers have quite similar functionalities, and the actual process of installing a new WordPress site is similar as well. Here, we're going to focus on one of these scripts, **Softaculous**.

> Note that this is yet another way of installing a WordPress site, and we're covering it here to make this book as complete as it can be. However, if you've already managed to install your site by the methods described earlier, then this section won't be of any use to you at this point.

Softaculous is the preferred method of WordPress installation for many professional developers and bloggers. In some cases, it's the fastest method when dealing with a completely new hosting account maintained by a new web host. Softaculous is provided on hosting accounts running on many management platforms, such as cPanel, Plesk, DirectAdmin, InterWorx, and H-Sphere. Most likely, your hosting account (a commercial hosting account you've bought from a respected provider) is certain to be using one of these platforms. The following screenshot shows cPanel, which is one of the platforms:

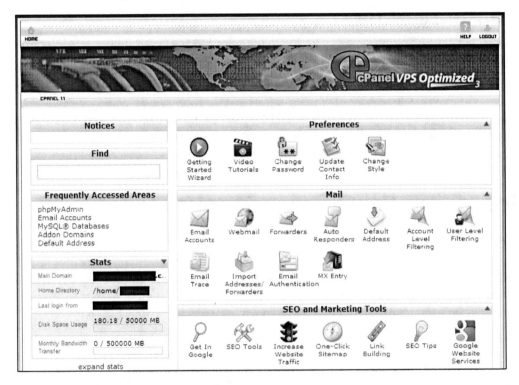

Although such platforms have different user interfaces, the core functionalities from a user's point of view remain mostly the same. To access Softaculous, just scroll down until you see the main icon labeled **Softaculous**. When you click on it, you will be redirected to the control panel of Softaculous, where you can see the WordPress icon in the center, along with an **Install** button that becomes visible when you hover your mouse over the icon.

The whole idea of using this script is to make things quicker and more hassle-free, so that you don't have to take care of creating databases manually, or setting configuration files. Softaculous will handle all of this for you. The following is the site creation form:

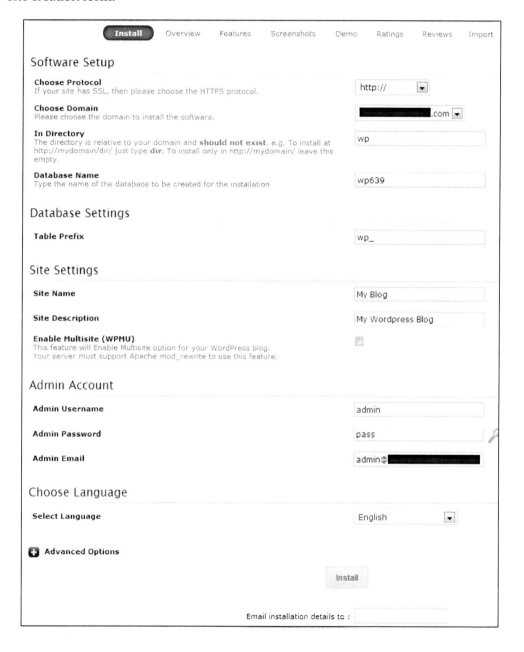

Here's a breakdown of all the fields and what details to fill them out with:

- **Choose Protocol**: You can stick with the default value of `http://`.

- **Choose Domain**: If you have more than one domain assigned with your hosting account, then you get to choose which one you want to use here. For single-domain accounts (most likely the case), this drop-down field has only one option.

- **In Directory**: If you want to install your WordPress site under a subdirectory, then input its name here (just the name). If you want to install the site in the main directory (`http://yoursite.com/`), then make sure the field is blank.

- **Database Name**: You can confidently go with the default value.

- **Table Prefix**: As discussed earlier in this chapter, change this to something unique (in my case, it's `wp_`).

- **Site Name**: This is the name of your site (in the present case, "My Blog").

- **Site Description**: This is the tagline (in the present case, "Exploring cooking every day of the week").

- **Enable Multisite (WPMU)**: Leave this unchecked unless you're an advanced user planning to launch a multisite installation.

- **Admin Username**, **Admin Password**, and **Admin Email**: These are the details of your admin account, similar to the ones we had to provide during the manual WordPress installation.

- **Select Language**: WordPress has many localized versions of the platform, not only English, and you can choose one here.

Clicking on the **Install** button starts the installation process. The process itself requires no supervision, and you will be able to access your site as soon as it finishes after roughly one or two minutes. You can check whether the installation has been successful through the standard `http://yoursite.com/` and `http://yoursite.com/wp-admin/` URLs. In other words, this is the end of the installation process through Softaculous. As you can see, it's much simpler and quicker than manual installation. Furthermore, Softaculous always installs the most recent version of WordPress, so you don't have to worry about getting something out of date.

 You can also encounter other auto-installer scripts, which are similar to Softaculous, such as Fantastico, Installatron, and SimpleScripts.

The wp-admin panel

WordPress installs a powerful and flexible administration area where you can manage all of your website content and do much more. Throughout the book, this will be referred to in shorthand as the **wp-admin** or **WP Admin**.

Now that you've successfully installed WordPress, it's time for our first look at the wp-admin. There are some immediate basic changes that are recommended to make sure your installation is set up properly.

You can always get to the wp-admin by visiting `http://yoursite.com/wp-admin/` (this URL is also the reason why we're calling it the wp-admin, by the way). If it's your first time there, you'll be re-directed to the login page. In the future, WordPress will check whether you're already logged in, and if so, you'll skip the login page.

To log in, just enter the username and password you chose during the installation. Then, click on **Log In**.

Whenever you log in, you'll be taken directly to the **Dashboard** section of the wp-admin. Following is a screenshot of the wp-admin that you will see immediately after you log in to the blog you just installed:

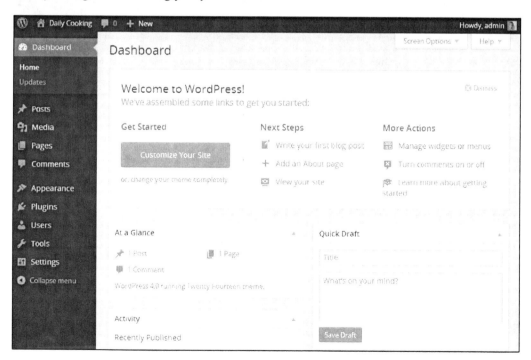

You'll see a lot of information and options here, which we will explore throughout this book. For now, we will focus on the items that we need to consider right after a successful installation. First, let's take a brief look at the top of the wp-admin and the **Dashboard** section.

The very top bar, referred to as **top bar** or **admin bar**, is mostly dark grey and contains the following:

- A rollover drop-down menu featuring a set of links to **About WordPress** (some details about the current installation of WordPress), **WordPress.org**, **Documentation**, **Support Forums**, and **Feedback**

- A link to the front page of your WordPress website (in this example, the title of the whole site is **Daily Cooking**)

- An updates and activity section containing either links to the newest comments or to pending updates

- A rollover drop-down menu with handy links to **New Post**, **New Media**, **New Page**, and **New User**

- Your username linked to your profile, which is yet another drop-down menu containing a link labeled as **Edit My Profile** and another one, namely the **Log Out** link

You'll also notice the **Screen Options** tab, which appears on many screens within the wp-admin. If you click on it, it will slide down a checklist of items on the page to show or hide. It will be different on each page. I encourage you to play around with that by checking and unchecking the items, as you find whether you need them or not:

Right next to the **Screen Options** tab, you find the **Help** tab. Just like the **Screen Options** tab, this one also appears on many screens within the wp-admin. Whenever you're in doubt regarding a specific screen, you can always check the **Help** tab for instructions. Accessing the **Help** tab is always quicker and, in most cases, more effective than searching for solutions online.

On the left side of the screen is the main menu:

You can click on any word on the main menu to be taken to the main page for that section, or you can hover your cursor over a given link to see all of the possible subsections you can visit. For example, if you hover your cursor over **Settings**, you'll see the subpages for the **Settings** section, and at that point, you can click on either of the subpages or the main **Settings** link itself:

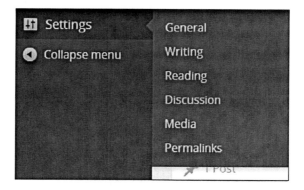

In this book, instructions regarding which page within the wp-admin to navigate to are indicated by phrases such as "navigate to **Settings | General**" or "navigate to **Posts | Add New**". This always describes the path you should take to get there via the main menu.

The top menu and the main menu exist on every page within the wp-admin. The main section on the right contains information for the current page you're on. In this case, we're on the **Dashboard** section. It contains boxes that have information about your blog, and about WordPress in general.

In the new versions of WordPress, when you log in for the first time, you're presented with a welcome message, similar to the one that follows:

In short, it's the welcome panel that allows you to access some of the crucial sections of the wp-admin with just one click. Once you click on the **Dismiss** link, the panel will no longer be displayed after login. In its current version, the panel allows you to do the following:

- Customize the current theme, but only if the theme provides some customization features (not all themes do)
- Change the current theme to a new one
- Write your first blog post
- Add an About page, which is usually the most visited page on most WordPress sites
- View your site
- Manage menus and widgets
- Turn comments on or off—by default they are on
- Learn more about how to get started with WordPress, which is an external link pointing to `http://codex.wordpress.org/First_Steps_With_WordPress`

For now, we're not going to focus on this welcome panel because first we need to understand what its content means, in order to use it effectively. In this chapter and the following chapters, we will get to know all of the crucial methods of managing a WordPress site, and once we gain some experience, with time, this welcome panel can make our everyday work much quicker. Therefore, let's jump right into the general site settings section.

Changing general blog information

You may need to change and add some general blog information (such as blog title or one-sentence description) after a successful installation to get your website set up with the correct information. To get started with this, navigate to **Settings** in the main menu.

There are many options you can set here, most of which are self-explanatory. We'll look at the most important ones, and you can explore the rest on your own. Obviously, you can change your blog's title. Mine is called "Daily Cooking", for example. You can also change the blog description, which is used in most themes as a subtitle for the blog, like the subtitle of a book. The default description is "Just another WordPress site". You'll probably want to change that. Let's change ours to "Exploring cooking every day of the week."

One of the things you probably want to take a look at on this page is the **Timezone** option. Whether you have a blog (with timestamps on every post) or not, it's important that WordPress knows what time zone you're in, if you want to schedule a page or post for the future, show users accurate timestamps, or even just make sure that e-mail notifications are correctly time-stamped. Additionally, if you're planning to publish content internationally, meaning that your target audience is located in an entirely different location, it's good to set the time zone to represent your target audience and not yourself.

The pull-down menu will show you different UTC settings, along with the biggest cities around the world. Just choose a city in your time zone. After you save the changes, the time that appears further down the page (next to **Time Format**) will change to the time you chose, so that you can check and make sure it's correct.

Another feature worth considering on this page is whether or not you want to allow user registration on your site. For most sites, this is not particularly useful, but if you're planning to make the site community-driven or utilize some form of crowdsourcing, then this might be worth considering. In that case, it's not advisable to give new users a user role higher than `Subscriber` (the default value).

When you're done making changes to this page, be sure to click on the **Save Changes** button at the bottom of the page.

Finally, there's only one more component you should adjust in your new site's settings before publishing any content: the permalinks. As WordPress defines them, permalinks are the permanent URLs to your individual pages, blog posts, categories, and tags. By default, WordPress links to your new posts using a highly unoptimized URL structure. For instance, if you create a post titled "How to Cook the Best Meal Ever", WordPress will link it as `http://yoursite.com/?p=123` (or something similar). The main problem with this structure is that it doesn't indicate what the page is about. Neither your visitors nor Google will be able to make a guess. In the case of Google, such a structure can also significantly impact on your future search engine rankings. Therefore, to set a more optimized structure, you can go to **Settings | Permalinks**. Here are the available settings:

Common Settings	
● Default	http://localhost/wp-dev-temp/?p=123
○ Day and name	http://localhost/wp-dev-temp/2014/10/11/sample-post/
○ Month and name	http://localhost/wp-dev-temp/2014/10/sample-post/
○ Numeric	http://localhost/wp-dev-temp/archives/123
○ Post name	http://localhost/wp-dev-temp/sample-post/
○ Custom Structure	http://localhost/wp-dev-temp

The best setting from a visitor's point of view, as well as from Google's, is the one labeled **Post name**. Going back to the example with the "How to Cook the Best Meal Ever" post, if you set the permalinks to **Post name**, the URL of this post will be `http://yoursite.com/how-to-cook-the-best-meal/`, which is a lot clearer and predictable.

You can always review the official information on permalinks anytime at `http://codex.wordpress.org/Using_Permalinks`. Further down the page, there are also optional settings for **Category base** and **Tag base**. By default, **Category base** is set to `category`. For example, if you have a category called "recipes", then you can view all posts under this category at `http://yoursite.com/category/recipes`. Some site owners prefer to change this to something more user-friendly, for example, "topics".

Even though it conveys the exact same message, it can be much easier to grasp for visitors who are not that familiar with the standards of web content publishing. In the end, the construction of your category base is solely down to your discretion. The tag base, on the other hand, rarely needs any adjustments.

Creating your first post

For this chapter, and the next few chapters, we'll be focusing on the use of WordPress to run a blog website. In a later chapter, we'll talk more specifically about using WordPress for a non-blog website.

Therefore, with that in mind, let's add the first piece of content to your new blog—a blog post. (This won't be the very first post on the blog itself, because WordPress created a post, a comment, and a page for you when it installed. Nevertheless, it will be "your" first post.) To create a post, just click on **New Post** on the top menu. You'll be taken to the following page:

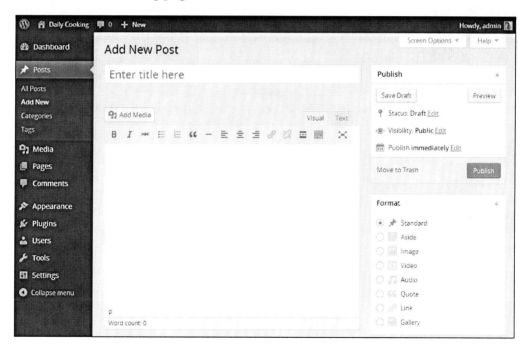

As you can see, there are a lot of options for your post (which we'll explore in more detail in *Chapter 3, Creating Blog Content*). For now, let's just worry about the basics. Every post should have, at a minimum, a title and some content. Therefore, go ahead and type in some text in those two fields (the title field and the big content field). When you are happy with it, click on the **Publish** button.

You'll get a green label note informing you that the post has been published. Take a look at the front page of your site by clicking on the name of your site in the top bar. You'll see the following:

Notice that we are using the default **Twenty Fourteen** theme. If you're using a different one, then the design and the layout of your first post will be different.

Writing your first comment

Now, let's see what it's like to post a comment. One of the great things about blogs is that they give you—the writer—an opportunity to spark a conversation with your readers. WordPress comes with a fantastic commenting system that allows visitors to add comments to your blog. To add your own comment to your first post, just visit the post's permalink URL and scroll down until you see the comment form.

As you're already logged in, all you have to do is write something in the text area and click on **Post Comment**. The comment form you'll see is basic and doesn't leave much room for error:

However, those who are not logged in to the wp-admin will see a slightly different one (the following image):

LEAVE A REPLY

Your email address will not be published. Required fields are marked *

Name *

Email *

Website

Comment

You may use these HTML tags and attributes: `<a href="" title=""> <abbr title=""> <acronym title=""> <b> <blockquote cite=""> <cite> <code> <del datetime=""> <em> <i> <q cite=""> <strike> <strong>`

POST COMMENT

Later, we'll explore how we can control which comments show up right away and which comments have to wait for you to verify them as valid, as well as which fields are required for visitors.

Retrieving a lost password

If you have lost your password and can't get into your wp-admin panel, you can easily retrieve it by clicking on the **Lost your password?** link on the login page. A newly generated password will be e-mailed to you at the e-mail address you provided during the installation process. This is why you need to be sure that you enter a valid e-mail address. Otherwise, you will not be able to retrieve your password.

Getting a Gravatar

One final point that's worth discussing in this chapter is the matter of WordPress avatars. Although WordPress provides a number of possibilities in this area, the most popular one revolves around an external service—**Gravatar**. Gravatar started as a tool meant to provide people with the capability of using the same profile picture (avatar) across the entire web. The name Gravatar actually stands for **Globally Recognized Avatar**.

What this means in plain English is that whenever you sign up with a web service, and if the service is Gravatar-compatible, so to speak, then it will pick your profile picture from Gravatar automatically, instead of forcing you to upload it manually from your computer. Apart from the profile picture, Gravatar also gives you a personal online profile that anyone can see whenever they click on your (Gravatar) profile picture or something called Hovercard. Now, what does all this have to do with WordPress, right? Well, WordPress is one of those services and tools that widely support Gravatar in all possible areas of the platform. For example, if you create a new blog and use an admin e-mail address that's hooked to Gravatar, your profile picture in WordPress will immediately be replaced with the one provided by Gravatar. Moreover, if you ever comment on any WordPress blog with a Gravatar e-mail address, your profile picture will be set as the avatar for the comment itself.

To set your own Gravatar, just go to `http://gravatar.com/` and click on the **Sign In** button in the right corner of the screen. You'll be presented with a login form and a small sign-up link labeled **Need an account?**. If you already have a WordPress.com account, then you can safely log in with it. If not, click on the **Need an account?** link, which will redirect you to the sign-up page. The fields are quite standard, with you being prompted to enter your e-mail address and your preferred username and password. Once you've completed the sign-up process, you can finally set your Gravatar. On the main **Manage Gravatars** page, there's a link labeled **Add one by clicking here!**—this is where you can upload a Gravatar.

The good thing about Gravatar is that you can choose where you want to get the picture from. You can either upload it from your computer, get it from some other place on the web (for example, from a direct link to your Facebook profile image), or use an image that you've uploaded as your Gravatar previously. In the next step, Gravatar allows you to crop and adjust your image. When you're finally happy with the result, you can click the big button and proceed to the rating settings of your image. Every Gravatar can be classified as **G rated**, **PG rated**, **R rated**, or **X rated**. The fact is that if you select anything other than **G rated**, your Gravatar won't be displayed on all sites. Thus, it's a good practice to upload only appropriate images.

When you're done with this step, from now on, your Gravatar is set up and ready to use. Gravatar also enables you to hook up more than one e-mail address to a single account, as well as use more than one image. This is actually a great feature because you can manage each of your e-mail addresses and every form of your online presence with just one Gravatar account, a true timesaver. Now you can go back to your WordPress blog and check whether your new Gravatar has appeared in the profile section within the wp-admin (provided that you've used the same e-mail address for the account).

Summary

You have learned a lot of things from this chapter. Now, you can install WordPress on a remote server, change the basic default settings of your blog, write posts, and comment on those posts.

You also have a basic understanding of how WordPress.com works, and how to handle your online image or brand by using Gravatar.

In the next chapter, we will learn about all the other aspects of a blog post that you can control, and additional ways to add posts, as well as the intricacies of managing and controlling comments and discussions on your blog.

3
Creating Blog Content

Now that your WordPress installation is up and running, you are ready to start creating content. In this chapter, you will first become familiar with the WordPress admin dashboard display (also commonly referred to as wp-admin), editing features and conventions. Then, you'll learn how to control all of the information associated with a post, not just the title and content, but also images and media. You will also learn about comments – what they are for, and how to manage them. Additionally, we will explore how to keep your content organized and searchable using tags and categories.

WordPress admin conventions

In the wp-admin, you have the ability to manage a number of different types of content and content sorting types, including posts, categories, pages, links, media uploads, and more. WordPress uses a similar format for various screens. Let us explore them here.

Lists of items

For every object in WordPress you might want to manage, there will be a screen listing them. For example, let's have a look at what a list of posts might look like:

As you can see, the name of the post type is at the top, and the list of items has columns. Let's take a look at the important elements:

- Each item in the list shows its **Title**. You can always click on an item title to edit it.

- If you hover your mouse over a specific row, as I hovered over **Hello world!** in the preceding screenshot, you will see four additional links. The first three are always the same (**Edit**, **Quick Edit**, **Trash**), while the fourth varies between **View** and **Preview**, depending on whether we're dealing with an already published post or one that's pending. The **Edit**, **Trash** and **View/ Preview** links are pretty self-explanatory, but the **Quick Edit** link deserves an additional word. When you click on it, you will see a panel allowing you to perform some simplified editing (just the basic details and parameters, with no actual content editing):

- You can make changes and then click on **Update**, or click on **Cancel** if you've changed your mind.

- The area above the list of posts lets you choose whether to view **All** (posts), **Published** (posts), **Drafts**, **Pending** (posts), or **Trash**. At the moment, I have only **All** posts and **Published** posts on my list. But with time, the list is bound to get populated some more, as we're going to continue writing new posts (and the same goes for your own site).

- Just below those links is the **Bulk Actions** menu, and its corresponding **Apply** button. Choose one or more posts by clicking on their checkboxes (or check the top checkbox to select every item). Then choose **Edit** or **Move to Trash** from the **Bulk Actions** menu, and after clicking on **Apply**, you'll be able to bulk delete or bulk edit those posts. Additionally, further down the road, so to speak, when you install some third-party plugins, you'll notice that this **Bulk Actions** menu might contain more options on top of the standard two – editing and deleting.

- The **filter menu** lets you choose options from the dates and categories pull-down lists, and then click on the **Filter** button to only show items that meet those qualifications.

- The search field along with the **Search Posts** button provides yet another way of filtering through your posts, to find the specific one you're looking for. This might not seem like a particularly useful feature at first, but once you have more than, say, 200 posts published on the site, finding individual entries becomes quite a challenge.

- At the very top is the **Screen Options** drop-down. This tab, which appears on every screen, will allow you to hide or show particular columns, and choose the number of items to show per page.

Posting on your blog

The central activity you'll be doing with your blog is adding posts. A **post** is like an article in a magazine; it needs a title, content, and an author (in this case, you, though WordPress allows multiple authors to contribute to a blog). A blog post also has a lot of other information attached to it, such as a date, excerpt, tags, and categories. In this section, you will learn how to create a new post, and what kind of information to attach to it.

Adding a simple post

Let's review the process of adding a simple post to your blog, which we carried out in the previous chapter. Whenever you want to add content or carry out a maintenance process on your WordPress website, you have to start by logging in to the **wp-admin** (**WordPress Administration panel**) of your site. To get to the admin panel, just point your web browser to `http://yoursite.com/wp-admin`.

 Remember that if you have installed WordPress in a subfolder (for example, `blog`), then your URL has to include that subfolder (for example, `http://yoursite.com/blog/wp-admin`).

When you first log in to the wp-admin, you'll be at the **Dashboard**. The **Dashboard** has a lot of information on it so don't worry about that right now.

The quickest way to get to the **Add New Post** page at any time is to click on **New,** and then **Post** link at the top of the page in the top bar. This is the **Add New Post** page:

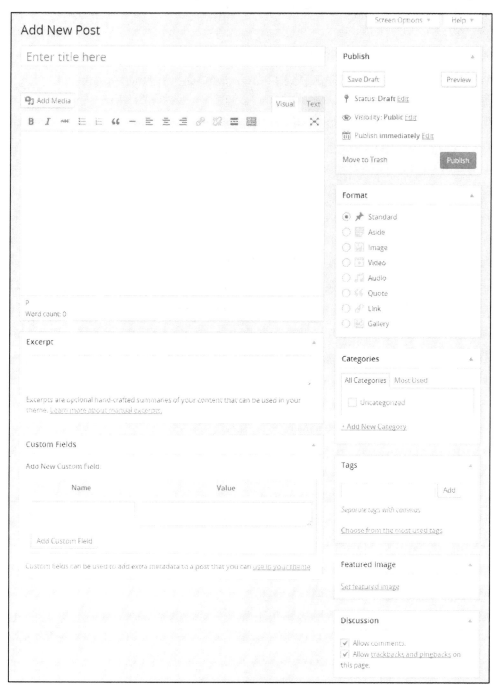

Note that depending on the setup of your computer and your web browser, some of the blocks shown in the preceding screenshot might not be visible by default. However, everything that's crucial for content publication will definitely be on the screen.

To add a new post to your site quickly, all you need to do is the following:

1. Type in a title into the text field under **Add New Post** (for example, `My Top 3 Favorite Dishes`).

2. Type the text of your post in the content box. Note that the default view is **Visual**, but you have a choice of the **Text** view as well:

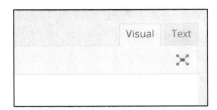

3. Click on the **Publish** button, which is at the far right. Note that you can choose to save a draft or preview your post as well.

Once you click on the **Publish** button, you have to wait while WordPress performs its magic. You'll see yourself still on the **Edit Post** screen, but now the following message would have appeared telling you that your post was published, and giving you a **View post** link:

If you view the front page of your site, you'll see that your new post has been added at the top (newest posts are always at the top).

Common post options

Now that we've reviewed the basics of adding a post, let's investigate some of the other options on the **Add New Post** and **Edit Post** screens. In this section, we'll look at the most commonly used options, and in the next section we'll look at the more advanced ones.

Categories and tags

Categories and tags are two types of information that you can add to a blog post. We use them to organize the information in your blog by topic and content (rather than just by date), and to help visitors find what they are looking for on your blog.

Categories are primarily used for structural organizing. They can be hierarchical, meaning a category can be a parent of another category. A relatively busy blog will probably have at least ten categories, but probably no more than 15 or 20. Each post in such a blog is likely to between one and possibly four categories assigned to it. For example, a blog about food and cooking might have these categories: Recipes, Food Talk, In The Media, Ingredients, and Restaurants. Of course, the numbers mentioned are just suggestions; you can create and assign as many categories as you like. The way you structure your categories is entirely up to you as well. There are no true rules regarding this in the WordPress world, just guidelines like these.

Tags are primarily used as shorthand for describing the topics covered in a particular blog post. A relatively busy blog will have anywhere from 15 to even 100 tags in use. Each post in this blog is likely to have three to ten tags assigned to it. For example, a post on the food blog about a recipe for butternut squash soup may have these tags: soup, vegetarian, autumn, hot, and easy. Again, you can create and assign as many tags as you like.

Let's add a new post to the blog. After you give it a title and content, let's add tags and categories. When adding tags, just type your list of tags into the **Tags** box on the right, separated by commas:

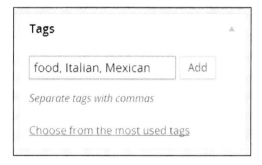

Then click on the **Add** button. The tags you just typed in will appear below the text field with little **x** buttons next to them. You can click on an **x** button to delete a tag. Once you've used some tags in your blog, you'll be able to click on the **Choose from the most used tags** link in this box, so that you can easily re-use tags.

Categories work a bit differently than tags. Once you get your blog going, you'll usually just check the boxes next to existing categories in the **Categories** box. In this case, as we don't have any existing categories, we'll have to add one or two.

In the **Categories** box on the right, click on the **Add New Category** link. Type your category into the text field, and click on the **Add New Category** button. Your new category will show up in the list, already checked. Look at the following screenshot:

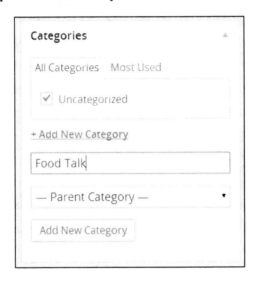

If in the future you want to add a category that needs a parent category, select **Parent category** from the pull-down menu, before clicking on the **Add New Category** button. If you want to manage more details about your categories, move them around, rename them, assign parent categories, and assign descriptive text, you can do so on the **Categories** page, which we'll see in detail later in this chapter.

Click on the **Publish** button, and you're done (you can instead choose to schedule a post; we'll explore that in detail in a few pages). When you look at the front page of your site, you'll see your new post on the top, your new category in the sidebar, and the tags and category (that you chose for your post) listed under the post itself.

Images in your posts

Almost every good blog post needs an image! An image will give the reader an instant idea of what the post is about, and the image will draw people's attention in as well. WordPress makes it easy to add an image to your post, control default image sizes, make minor edits to that image, and designate a featured image for your post.

Adding an image to a post

Luckily, WordPress makes adding images to your content very easy. Let's add an image to the post we've just created a minute ago. You can click on **Edit** underneath your post on the front page of your site to get there quickly. Alternatively, go back to the wp-admin, open **Posts** in the main menu, and then click on the post's title.

To add an image to a post, first you'll need to have that image on your computer, or know the exact URL pointing to the image if it's already online. Before you get ready to upload an image, make sure that your image is optimized for the web; for instance, you can use a service like Kraken (`https://kraken.io/`). Huge files will be uploaded slowly and slow down the process of viewing your site. Just to give you a good example here, I'm using a photo of my own so I don't have to worry about any copyright issues (always make sure to use only the images that you have the right to use, copyright infringement online is a serious problem, to say the least). I know it's on the desktop of my computer. Once you have a picture on your computer and know where it is, carry out the following steps to add the photo to your blog post:

1. Click on the **Add Media** button, which is right above the content box and below the title box:

2. The box that appears, allows you to do a number of different things regarding the media you want to include in your post. The most user-friendly feature here, however, is the drag-and-drop support. Just grab the image from your desktop, and drop it in the center area of the page labeled **Drop files anywhere to upload**:

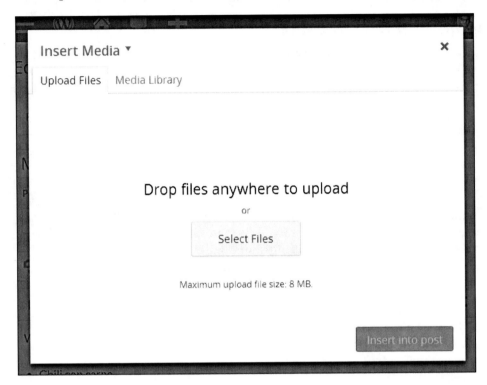

3. Immediately after dropping the image, the uploader bar will show the progress of the operation, and when it's done, you'll be able to do some final fine-tuning:

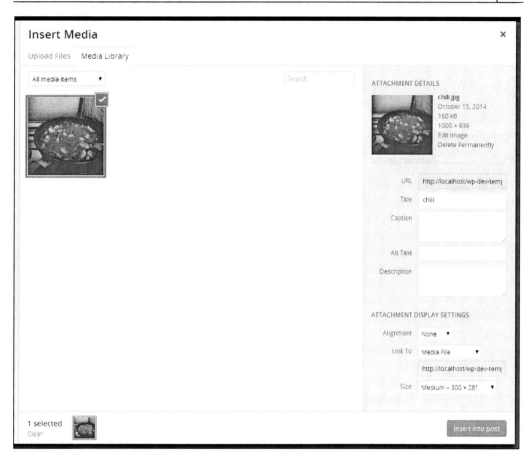

4. The fields that are important right now are **Title**, **Alt Text**, **Alignment**, **Link To**, and **Size**. **Title** is a description for the image, **Alt Text** is a phrase that's going to appear instead of the image in case the file goes missing or any other problems present themselves; **Alignment** will tell the image whether to have text wrap around it and whether it should be right, left, or center; **Link To** instructs WordPress whether or not to link the image to anything (a common solution is to select **None**); and **Size** is the size of the image.

5. Once you have all of these fields filled out, click on **Insert into post**. This box will disappear, and your image will show up in the post – right where your cursor was prior to clicking the **Add Media** button – on the edit page itself (in the Visual editor, that is. If you're using the Text editor, then the HTML code of the image will be displayed instead).

6. Now, click on the **Update** button, and go look at the front page of your site again. There's your image!

Controlling default image sizes

You may be wondering about those image sizes. What if you want bigger or smaller thumbnails? Whenever you upload an image, WordPress creates three versions of that image for you. You can set the pixel dimensions of those three versions by opening **Settings** in the main menu, and then clicking on **Media**. This takes you to the **Media Settings** page:

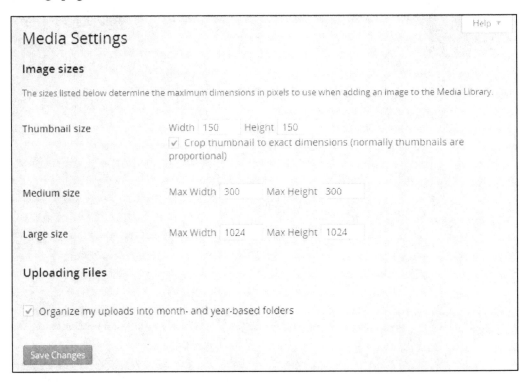

Here you can specify the size of the uploaded images for the following:

- **Thumbnail size**
- **Medium size**
- **Large size**

If you change the dimensions on this page, and click on the **Save Changes** button, only the images you upload in the future will be affected. Images you've already uploaded to the site will have had their thumbnail; medium, and large versions created, already using the old settings. It's a good idea to decide what you want your three media sizes to be early on in your site's lifespan, so you can set them and have them applied to all images, right from the start.

Another thing about uploading images is the craze for HiDPI displays, also called Retina displays. Currently, WordPress is in a kind of a transitional phase when it comes to images and being in tune with modern display technology; Retina-ready functionality was introduced quite recently in WordPress 3.5. In short, if you want to make your images Retina-compatible (meaning that they look good on iPads, modern Android phones and other devices with HiDPI screens), you should upload the images at twice the dimensions. For example, if you want your image to be presented as 800 pixel wide and 600 pixel high then upload it as 1600 pixel wide and 1200 pixel high. WordPress will manage to display it properly anyway, and whoever visits your site from a modern device will see a high-definition version of the image. In future versions, WordPress will provide a more managed way of handling Retina-compatible images.

Editing an uploaded image

Every image that has been previously uploaded to WordPress can be edited. In order to do this, go to the Media Library by clicking the **Media** button in the main sidebar. What you'll see is a new kind of listing, introduced in one of the latest versions of WordPress. Instead of a traditional list, what you get to work with now is a grid-based archive that gives each piece of media much better visibility. Right now, we only have one image in the library, but as you continue working with your site, the list will become much more impressive:

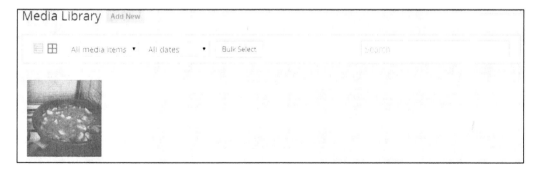

When you click on the image and then on the **Edit Image** button at the bottom of the pop-up window that's going to appear, you'll enter the **Attachment Details** section. Here, you can perform a number of operations to make your image just perfect. As it turns out, WordPress does a well enough job with simple image tuning so that you don't really need an expensive software like Photoshop for this. Among the possibilities, you'll find the option of cropping, rotating, scaling, and flipping vertically and horizontally:

For example, you can use your mouse to draw a box, as I have done in the preceding screenshot. On the right, in the box marked **Image Crop**, you'll see the pixel dimensions of your selection. Click the crop icon (top left), then the **Thumbnail** radio button (on the right), and then **Save** (just below your photo). You now have a new thumbnail! Of course, you can adjust any other version of your image just by making a different selection prior to hitting the **Save** button. Play around a little until you become familiar with the details.

Designating a featured image

As of WordPress 2.9, you can designate a single image that represents your post. This is referred to as the featured image. Some themes will make use of this, and some will not. The default theme, the one we've been using, is named **Twenty Fifteen**, and it uses the featured image to create a great looking background for the post on the front page. Depending on the theme you're using, its behavior with featured images can vary, but in general, every modern theme supports them in one way or the other.

In order to set a featured image, go to the **Edit Post** screen. In the sidebar, you'll see a box labeled **Featured Image**. Just click on the **Set featured image** link. After doing so, you'll see a pop-up window, very similar to the one we used when uploading images. Here, you can either upload a completely new image, or select an existing image by clicking on it. All you have to do now is click on the **Set featured image** button in the bottom right corner. After completing the operation, you can finally see what your new image looks like on the front page. Also, keep in mind that WordPress uses featured images in multiple places, and not only the front page. And as mentioned before, much of this behavior depends on your current theme.

Videos and other media in your posts

These days, the newest versions of WordPress are capable of not only including images into our blog posts, but other types of media too, such as audio files and videos.

Adding videos to blog posts

Luckily for us, the process of adding a video to a standard blog post or page has been made as easy as possible. Let's discuss this step by step.

We're going to start by creating a whole new post. The title we can use is, *Great Baby Back Ribs Recipe*. Creating the post itself is pretty basic. All you need to do is go to **Posts** | **Add New**. You'll see a screen that we've already covered earlier in this chapter. Let's put some example content in place, and try including a video right away. All we have to do in order to achieve this is copy and paste the URL of the video that we'd like to have included in our content. Just a standard copy-and-paste, and nothing else.

 When copying the URL of the video, it's important to make sure that the link is copied as-is in raw-text form (not hyperlinked anywhere: that is, not clickable).

The example I'm going to use here is the video at `http://www.youtube.com/watch?v=hDyHbTxTL-A`.

It's a nice video recipe for some baby back ribs. So in order to include this video in a blog post, all I have to do is take its URL address and just paste it in. This is the raw-text content of the new post that I'm working on now:

```
There's a great video recipe I've found on YouTube. It teaches us how
to prepare killer baby back ribs!

http://www.youtube.com/watch?v=hDyHbTxTL-A

(by Laura Vitale)
```

However, when I save such a post, on the front page of my site, the video URL will be turned into a live video automatically. This is visible in the next screenshot:

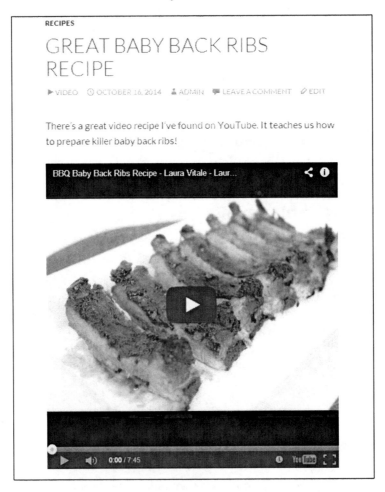

To give the post some more unique presence, I also added a new category – **RECIPES** (which you can see in the preceding screenshot), and I assigned the post to a new content type – **Video**. This is done through the sidebar on the post editing screen. We will talk more about different content types later in this chapter:

The process described here explains how to embed YouTube videos and make them a part of your blog posts, but the same goes for other popular platforms like Vimeo, TED, Hulu, WordPress.tv, and others. To get the full list of supported platforms, please visit `https://codex.wordpress.org/Embeds`.

One more method of adding videos to blog posts, which we left out initially, is uploading the raw video files manually (instead of using a third-party platform like YouTube). Although this is possible in WordPress – you can drag and drop a video file just like you'd do with an image – it's not a recommended solution. Video files are always quite large in size, and having them hosted on your standard web server can become very expensive (bandwidth costs), should the video become popular and end up being viewed by thousands of people. It's a lot more effective and user-friendly to just upload the video to YouTube or a similar platform, and then have it embedded on your site, like we've explained a minute ago.

Adding audio to blog posts

Not surprisingly at this point, it turns out that WordPress makes adding audio to your blog posts, just as easy as adding a video. To demonstrate this, I'm going to create an entirely new post and call it, *Some Paleo Wisdom with Robb Wolf*. In it, I'm going to share a podcast episode of Robb's. To do that, just like with videos, I have to get a direct URL of the audio file that I want to share on the blog.

Going to Robb's site, I quickly find the episode I'm after available at `http://traffic.libsyn.com/robbwolf/PaleoSolution-240.mp3`. So, I take this URL, and just like with video, I paste it right into my new blog post's content box as follows:

```
Check out this great podcast episode by Robb Wolf:
http://traffic.libsyn.com/robbwolf/PaleoSolution-240.mp3
```

WordPress will pick that URL immediately and turn it into a live audio streaming. When I publish my new post, this becomes visible right away. The next screenshot presents what my new post looks like on the front page:

Now, in this example, I used a direct URL address of an audio file (the MP3 podcast), but I can also use a direct URL of an audio recording at SoundCloud, Spotify, or Rdio, plus a bunch of other services. Again, to get the full list of supported platforms, feel free to visit `https://codex.wordpress.org/Embeds`.

Adding raw audio files is possible too. However, this presents the same problems as we mentioned when talking about video files. Even though audio files are always smaller in size than videos, they can still cost you a lot of money if you're attempting to host them on your standard web server. It's therefore always a better solution to upload your audio somewhere else (like, SoundCloud, for example), and then just embed the audio inside of a blog post like we're describing here.

Limited editing possibilities

Unlike with images, WordPress doesn't really give us any editing possibilities when it comes to media like audio or video. It's understandable that images can be manipulated in a lot of ways, for example, they can be rotated, cropped, scaled, and so on. However, there's no such possibility with videos. Once a video file or audio file is produced, we can't alter it in any way. We can only take it and display it on our sites as-is.

Using the Visual editor versus the Text editor

WordPress comes with a Visual editor, otherwise known as a WYSIWYG editor (pronounced "wissy-wig", and stands for What You See Is What You Get). This is the default editor for typing and editing your posts. If you're comfortable with HTML, you may prefer to write and edit your posts using the Text editor – particularly useful if you want to add special content or styling.

To switch from the rich text editor to the Text editor, click on the **Text** tab next to the **Visual** tab at the top of the content box:

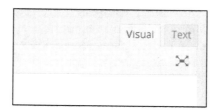

You'll see your post in all its raw HTML glory, and you'll get a new set of buttons that let you quickly bold and italicize text, as well as add link code, image code, and so on. You can make changes, and swap back and forth between the tabs to see the result.

For example, going back to the post we were building just a minute ago – the one with the embedded podcast episode – when we switch between **Visual** and **Text**, we'll see that in the Visual editor mode, the link to the audio file has already been turned into a live audio player, while in the Text editor mode, we can still see the URL in its raw form. The next screenshot presents this side by side:

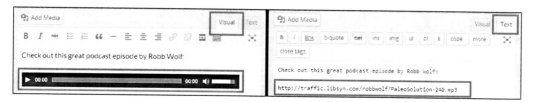

Even though the Text editor allows you to use any HTML element in existence, it's not a fully-fledged HTML support. For instance, using <p> tags is not necessary in the Text editor, as they will be stripped by default. In order to create a new paragraph in the Text editor, all you need to do is press the *Enter* key twice. That being said, at the same time, the Text editor is currently the only way to use HTML tables in WordPress (within posts and pages).

You can easily place your table content inside `<table>`, `<tr>`, and `<td>` tags and WordPress won't alter it in any way, effectively allowing you to create the exact table you want. Another thing the Text editor is most commonly used for, is introducing custom HTML parameters in `<img/>` and `<a>` tags, and also custom CSS classes in other popular tags. Some content creators actually prefer working with the Text editor, rather than the Visual editor because it gives them much more control, and more certainty regarding the way their content is going to be presented on the frontend.

Lead and body

One of the many interesting publishing features WordPress has to offer is the concept of the lead, and the body of the post. This may sound like a strange thing, but it's actually quite simple. When you're publishing a new post, you don't necessarily want to display its whole contents right away on the front page. A much more user-friendly approach is to display only the lead, and then display the complete post under its individual URL. Achieving this in WordPress is very simple. All you have to do is use the **Insert More Tag** button, available in the Visual editor (or the **more** button in the Text editor). Simply place your cursor exactly where you want to break your post (the text before the cursor will become the lead), and then click the **Insert More Tag** button:

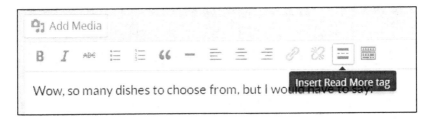

An alternative way of using this tag is to switch to the Text editor and input the tag manually, which is `<!--more-->`. Both approaches produce the same result. Clicking the main **Update** button will save the changes.

On the front page, most WordPress themes display such posts by presenting the lead along with a **Continue reading** link, and then the whole post (both the lead and the rest of the post) is displayed under the post's individual URL.

Drafts, pending articles, and timestamps

There are three additional items I'd like to cover in this section: drafts, pending articles, and timestamps.

Drafts

WordPress gives you the option to save a draft of your post, so that you don't have to publish it right away, but can still save your work. If you've started writing a post and want to save a draft, just click on the **Save Draft** button at the right (in the **Publish** box), instead of the **Publish** button. Even if you don't click on the **Save Draft** button, WordPress will attempt to save a draft of your post for you, about once a minute. You'll see this in the area just below the content box. The text will say **Saving Draft...** and then show the time of the last draft saved:

At this point, after a manual save or an auto-save, you can leave the **Edit Post** page and do other things. You'll be able to access all of your draft posts from the **Dashboard,** or from the **Edit Posts** page.

In essence, drafts are meant to hold your "work in progress", which means all articles that haven't been finished yet, or haven't even been started yet, and obviously everything in between.

Pending articles

Pending articles is a functionality that's going to be a lot more helpful to people working with multi-author blogs, rather than single-author blogs. The thing is that in a bigger publishing structure, there are individuals responsible for different areas of the publishing process. WordPress, being a quality tool, supports such a structure by providing a way to save articles as **Pending Review**. In an editor-author relationship, if an editor sees a post marked as Pending Review, they know that they should have a look at it and prepare it for the final publication.

That's it for the theory, and now how to do it. When creating a new post, click on the **Edit** link right next to the **Status: Draft** label:

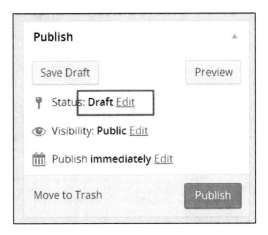

Right after doing so, you'll be presented with a new drop-down menu from which you can select **Pending Review,** and then click the **OK** button. Now, just click the **Save as Pending** button which will appear in place of the old **Save Draft** button, and you have a shiny new article that's pending review.

Timestamps

WordPress will also let you alter the timestamp of your post. This is useful if you are writing a post today that you wish you'd published yesterday, or if you're writing a post in advance and don't want it to show up until the right day. By default, the timestamp will be set to the moment you publish your post. To change it, just find the **Publish** box, and click on the **Edit** link (next to the calendar icon and **Publish immediately**), and fields will show up with the current date and time for you to change:

Change the details, click on the **OK** button, and then click on **Publish** to publish your post (or save a draft).

Advanced post options

By now, you have a handle on the most common and simple options for posts, and you may be wondering about some of the other options on the **Edit Post** page. We'll cover them all in this section.

A quick display tip

When you first visit the **Edit Post** page, some of the advanced options (**Excerpt, Send Trackbacks, Custom Fields, Discussion, Revisions, Author**, and **Format**) are "open" below the post content. If you never use them and want to clean up the look of this page, you can single-click each bar and they'll collapse. You can also rearrange them by dragging them to form a new order.

You can also use **Screen Options** (top right of the page) to uncheck certain boxes, and thus not display them at all.

Excerpt

WordPress offers theme designers the option to show a post's **excerpt** (instead of its full content) on pages within the theme:

Excerpt

Excerpts are optional hand-crafted summaries of your content that can be used in your theme. Learn more about manual excerpts.

This is how the excerpt works:

- If you enter some text into the **Excerpt** box on the **Edit Post** page, that text will be used as the post's excerpt on the theme pages that call for it.
- If you do not enter any text into the **Excerpt** box, WordPress will use the first 55 words of the post's content (which is stripped of HTML tags) followed by [...] (which is not a link).
- If you do not enter any text into the **Excerpt** box, and the theme you are using does something special, the number of words and the final text could be different.

You are never required to enter excerpt text. However, it is advisable that you do take advantage of this possibility. Excerpts can introduce big readability improvements to your site, and make your content easier to grasp for the reader, provided that your current theme uses excerpts in one way or the other.

> The more tag (`<!--more-->`), which has been described in one of the previous sections in this chapter, should not be confused with the excerpt. It is different from the excerpt because you, not the theme designer, controls its use. Additionally, the more tag is supported by every theme and it has a slightly different task than the excerpt. It's meant to present the lead of the post – the part that's going to convince the reader to visit the complete post, while the excerpt is a summary of the post's contents.

Sending pingbacks and trackbacks

Pingbacks and **trackbacks** provide you with a way to communicate with other websites, and let them know that you've published a post mentioning them in one way or the other (usually through a link). For instance, they are useful if you write a blog post that is a response to an old post on someone else's blog, and you want them to know about it.

The difference between pingbacks and trackbacks is that pingbacks are automatic, whereas trackbacks are manual. In other words, WordPress always tries to send a pingback automatically, whenever you link to another WordPress blog from any of your posts. Trackbacks are something you have to send manually, as WordPress will not do this for you. Apart from that, pingbacks and trackbacks are pretty much the same, and produce a very similar effect.

If you want to notify a given blog via trackback, just copy the trackback URL from that person's blog post, and paste it into the trackback box on your post's editing screen (this can be enabled through the **Screen Options** panel at the top). An excerpt of your blog post and a link pointing back to your site will show up as a comment on their blog post, provided that the blog has trackbacks enabled. Sending an automatic pingback will also include a link pointing back to your site, in the comments section. Again, this only works if the blog you're targeting has trackbacks and pingbacks enabled.

Quite frankly, trackbacks are becoming somewhat out-of-date with the advent of pinging. Many WordPress themes are written to essentially disable trackbacks. As it turns out, most WordPress bloggers these days don't even bother to send trackbacks when the built-in mechanism of pingbacks handles it automatically.

Discussion

The **Discussion** box on the post editing screen (sometimes needs enabling through **Screen Options**) has two checkboxes in it: one for allowing comments, and the other for trackbacks and pingbacks. When you first install WordPress, both these checkboxes will be checked by default. You have to uncheck them if you want to turn off the comments or trackbacks and pingbacks for the post:

If you uncheck the **Allow comments** box, visitors will not be able to comment on this blog post.

If you uncheck the **Allow trackbacks and pingbacks on this page** box, when other people mention your blog post and link to it on their own websites, your blog post won't notice and won't care. So, if you are using WordPress to run a non-blog website, this is the best option for you.

If the box stays checked, other people's pingbacks about this post will show up under your post along with comments, if any. If you want either or both of these boxes to be unchecked by default, go to **Settings,** and then **Discussion** in the main menu. You can uncheck either or both of the boxes labeled, **Allow link notifications from other blogs (pingbacks and trackbacks)** and **Allow people to post comments on new articles**.

If you're using WordPress to run a blog website, you'll want pingback to stay checked, at least most of the time. Every once in a while you can start experiencing something called a pingback spam. The main idea is that some bloggers attempt to ping a big number of other blogs in an attempt to get a pingback link. Once you start attracting a bigger crowd of visitors, you might have to start dealing with this issue. In such a case, disabling pingbacks altogether can be a good solution. Back in the day, no one was paying attention to what appeared in their pingback and trackback sections, so every notification went through un-moderated in any way. These days, despite the fact that online publishers are much more aware of the situation, the spamming continues, and it gets difficult to separate genuine pingbacks and trackbacks from the spammy ones, hence shutting them down altogether can make things easier in the long run. Nevertheless, the decision whether or not to support trackbacks and pingbacks on your site is entirely up to you.

Learning More

To learn more about trackbacks and pingbacks you can visit the following sites:

- `http://www.wpbeginner.com/beginners-guide/`
  `what-why-and-how-tos-of-trackbacks-and-`
  `pingbacks-in-wordpress/`

- `https://codex.wordpress.org/Introduction_`
  `to_Blogging#Trackbacks`

- `http://codex.wordpress.org/Introduction_`
  `to_Blogging#Pingbacks`

Custom Fields

Custom Fields are WordPress' way of giving you the possibility to include some additional information in your blog post (information that you don't want to display directly on the frontend). In essence, Custom Fields are a kind of semi-programming tool – they are not exactly "code" as understood by PHP programmers, yet they do give you the possibility to tweak your content in a certain, non-stock way. Many themes use various Custom Fields to style the individual aspects of posts. For example, some theme creators use Custom Fields to disable the sidebar on certain posts, or include various typographic elements.

As another example, let's say you are a gadget reviewer and every blog post is a review of some new gadget. Every time you write a review, you're writing it about a product that's made by some company, and you'd like to have that company's logo associated with the blog post. You can make a custom field called `company_logo`, and the value can be the path to the logo image:

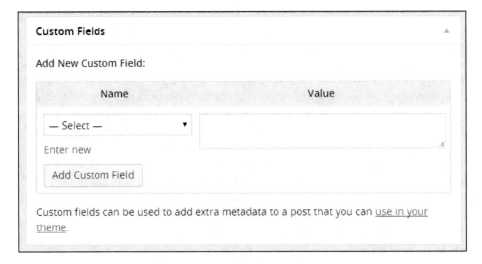

To display or make use of this Custom Field information, you either have to modify your theme files manually, or use a plugin.

Learning More

Read more about custom fields in the WordPress codex at `https://codex.wordpress.org/Using_Custom_Fields`.

Working with post revisions

Apart from many content formatting features, WordPress also allows some basic version control for your posts. What this means is that WordPress stores every subversion of your every post. Or in plain English, every time you press the **Update** button, instead of overwriting the previous version of your post, WordPress creates a completely new one. Although this feature doesn't seem like the most useful one at first, it's actually very important for sites, where the content is managed by more than one person. In such a scenario, it's easy to get the newest versions of the posts mixed up, so it's always good to have the possibility to return to the previous one.

In WordPress 3.6, the revision functionality has been completely revamped and a lot of new features have been introduced that make working with your content much more efficient. To take full advantage of this functionality, what you need to do first is enable **Revisions** in the upper slide-down **Screen Options** menu on the post editing screen. Once you do so, a small box titled **Revisions** will appear at the bottom of the screen:

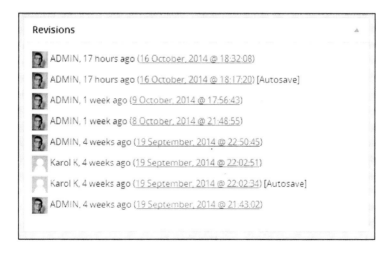

If you click on any of the links displayed inside this box, you will be taken to a page where you can compare individual revisions, and then restore the one you want to work with from now on. The interface provides a main slider that can be used to select individual revisions of the post. This is visible in the following screenshot:

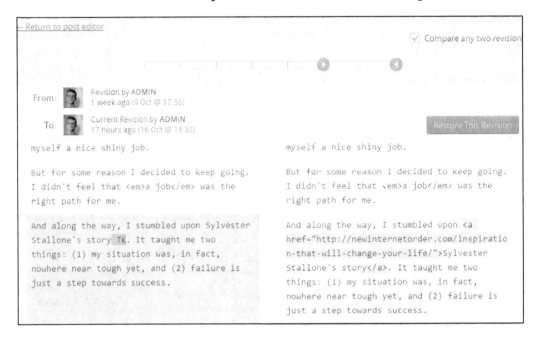

The revision functionality has two main versions. The first one is when the **Compare any two revisions** box isn't checked, and it lets you compare the revision that's currently selected (on the slider) to the revision directly preceding it. The second version is when the **Compare any two revisions** box is checked. In this case, you can select the revisions you want to compare individually which essentially allows you to compare any two revisions, just like the box suggests. The revision on the left is always the previous revision, while the one on the right is the next or current one (visible in the preceding screenshot). For every paragraph where there is a difference found, this will be highlighted in red and green, and every individual difference will have additional highlighting. Clicking on the **Restore This Revision** button will restore the revision on the right, and you will be brought back to the post editing screen automatically.

On the other hand, if you feel that revisions won't be of any particular use to your site, then you can simply choose to not pay attention to the **Revisions** box. When you work with your content normally, not worrying about the revisions, WordPress will always display the most recent versions of your posts by default.

Changing the author of the post

This is a very basic feature in WordPress, so let's only take a minute to discuss it. Basically, every post and page in WordPress has an author, which is quite obvious in itself. However, if you want to, you can change the assigned author of any given entry. In order to do it, just go to the post editing screen or the page editing screen, and scroll down until you see the **Author** box. If it's not visible, enable it from the pull-down **Screen Options** menu.

The box contains just one drop-down menu that lists every user account on your site. Just select a new author, and click on the **Update** button. That's all. If you only have one user – the admin account – on your site, then the box will only contain one name.

Protecting content

WordPress gives you the option to hide posts. You can hide a post from everyone but yourself by marking it **Private** (although the user roles of admin and editor will still see it), or you can hide it from everyone but the people with whom you share a password by marking it as **Password protected**. To implement this, look at the **Publish** box at the upper right of the **Edit Post** page. If you click on the **Edit** link next to **Visibility: Public**, a few options will appear:

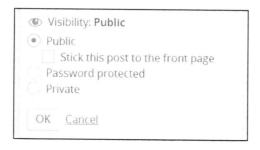

If you click on the **Password protected** radio button, you'll get a box where you can type a password (limited to 20 characters). Visitors to your blog will see the post title, along with a note that they have to type in a password to read the post.

If you click on the **Private** radio button, the post will not show up on the blog at all to any viewers, unless you are the viewer, and you are logged in. The post will also appear if the person browsing the site is a logged-in editor (having the user role of **Editor**).

If you leave the post **Public** and check the **Stick this post to the front page** checkbox, this post will be the first post on the front page, regardless of its publication date.

Be sure to click on the **OK** button, if you make any changes.

Pretty post slug

We've already talked about tuning the permalinks settings of your site in *Chapter 2, Getting Started with WordPress*. Now is a good moment to expand this knowledge, and discuss a little something called the **post slug**. One of the most accurate definitions of what a post slug is comes from the WordPress Codex itself. The one provided at `https://codex.wordpress.org/Glossary#Post_Slug` teaches us that the post slug is made from a few lowercase words separated by dashes, describing a post and usually derived from the post title to create a user-friendly permalink. In other words, the post slug is what comes after your domain name in the post's URL. For example, my post about my top three favorite dishes uses this URL: `http://localhost/wp-dev-temp/my-top-3-favorite-dishes/`, where the last part – `my-top-3-favorite-dishes` – is the slug. Just like the official definition says, WordPress chooses the slug by taking my post title, making it all lowercase, removing all punctuation, and replacing spaces with dashes. If I'd prefer it to be something else, such as `3-favorite-dishes`, I can change it in the area just below the post's title:

Just click on **Edit** to change the slug. Readable URLs are something that Google Search loves, so using them helps to optimize your site for search engines. It also helps users figure out what a post is about before clicking on the URL.

Custom post format settings

Since you will most likely start your WordPress journey with the default theme – Twenty Fifteen –, I should probably say a few words about one more box that's visible on the post editing screen – the one titled **Format**. We've already touched upon this briefly when talking about publishing videos and audio files along with your posts:

Some themes provide basic, ready-made formatting styles for certain types of posts; **Twenty Fourteen** isn't one of the most functional themes in this sense. The only thing we get is a small note near the title of the post that lets us know what format has been chosen when publishing the post. We can see this, when we take a look at our audio post and our video post (the ones we created earlier in this chapter). The audio post is this:

The video post is this:

However, there are hundreds of themes out there that support the format functionality more broadly. Here are some examples derived from the previous default theme – **Twenty Thirteen**. First we have a post saved as **Standard**:

Then the same post is saved as **Quote**:

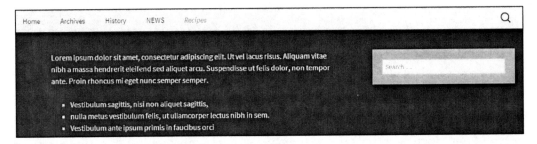

And finally it is saved as **Status**:

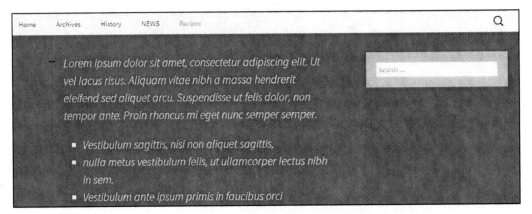

Additional writing options

In addition to simply logging into the wp-admin, you have four other choices of ways for adding posts to your blog.

Press This

WordPress offers a neat bookmarklet called **Press This**. You can put it into your browser's bookmarks or favorites, and it will let you quickly write a blog post about the website you're visiting. You may have encountered this same feature as offered by Facebook, Delicious, and other social networking sites.

You just have to add Press This to your browser once, and then you can use it anytime. To add the **Press This** link to your browser, in the wp-admin, go to the **Tools** page. At the top of the **Tools** page is the **Press This** box. Just use your mouse, and drag it up to your browser's bookmark bar.

Now you can use it! For example, if you're browsing through a website and you read an article you'd like to mention in a blog post, just click on the **Press This** bookmark. A window will pop up with the **Edit Post** page in it, and the URL of the site, at which you're looking, will already be written in as a link:

You can then write whatever additional text you want, add tags and categories, and then either save it as a draft or publish it right away.

Posting via e-mail

If you want to add a post to your blog without having to open the wp-admin and log in, you can set up your WordPress installation to accept posts sent via e-mail. First, you have to set up a special secret e-mail address that is accessible via POP. WordPress will check that e-mail address and turn any e-mails in it into posts. If you decide to set up this feature, you will have to be sure not to use this e-mail address for any other purpose!

Once you have the e-mail address set up at your mail server, go to your wp-admin and navigate to **Settings | Writing**. Scroll down a bit to the section labeled **Post via e-mail**. Now just enter the server, login name, and password into the **Writing Settings** page, and be sure to click on the **Save Changes** button. Note that on this page, WordPress provides you with three random strings you could use for the e-mail address, so you might want to visit this page first to get one, then set up your POP account, and then return to this page to set up **Post via e-mail**.

Even though posting via e-mail sounds like a good idea at first, it's actually not the safest way of doing things. As you've probably realized by now, anyone who finds out what your secret e-mail address is can easily get anything published on your site. All they have to do is send their content to that e-mail address. Spammers will quickly start capitalizing on this by publishing random-content posts containing nothing but links to their own websites (in an attempt to get some SEO benefits out of this). To be honest, posting via e-mail is a thing of the past, at least in its current form, unless WordPress comes up with some innovative way of doing it in future versions.

Learning More

Posting via e-mail in its default form is not the safest approach out there. While this is true, with just a little creativity you can do it in a way that still makes sense (safety-wise). Feel free to visit http://themefuse. com/blog/posting-to-wordpress-via-email-theres-a-safe- way-of-doing-this/ for an in-depth guide.

External blogging tools

In short, external blogging tools are specialized pieces of software that allow you to work with your blog from the desktop of your computer. The main difference between them and working with WordPress directly is that they make it possible to create content (posts) offline, and then export it directly to your WordPress site. This has some great benefits, the biggest of which being that you can write posts whenever inspiration hits you, not only when you have an internet connection at your disposal (particularly handy for creating content when travelling).

Another benefit is that your posts are stored as normal files, which you can copy wherever you want, send to someone via e-mail, or back up on Dropbox, or other similar solutions.

The first question worth answering here is: how are these tools better than writing a post in MS Word, and then copying it into WordPress manually? Well, if you've ever tried doing this, then you already know that most of your formatting, layout, as well as the graphics, are sure to go missing. There's no such problem with external blogging tools, as they are optimized for working with WordPress right from the get-go.

The only bad news in this whole story is that the best tool available – **Windows Live Writer** – works on Windows only, so Mac users will have a little harder time here. If you're on Mac, you can consider alternatives such as **MarsEdit** (`http://www.red-sweater.com/marsedit/`) or **Qumana** (`http://www.qumana.com/`).

The best thing about the Windows Live Writer is that, even though it's been created by Microsoft, it's absolutely free. You can download it at `http://explore.live.com/windows-live-writer` and then install it on any version of Windows. The tool itself is very easy to use and very efficient (when it comes to performance). Finally, Windows Live Writer doesn't require you to set up your site in any specific way before you can work with it. All you have to do is configure the Writer itself, so it can connect to the site (basically, it only needs the address of the site, your username and password). I strongly encourage you to give this a shot.

Mobile apps for iOS and Android

This final method of posting content on WordPress is growing stronger every year, or even every month. The mobile usage of the web is constantly rising, and this is reflected in the way people interact with their WordPress sites or blogs.

It's not surprising that there's a great wealth of blogging tools and apps for the two most popular mobile platforms – iOS and Android.

Both systems have the native WordPress app available. You can get these apps at `https://apps.wordpress.org/`.

The user interfaces of the apps have some minor differences depending on what device you're using to access the app with, but the core functionality remains the same. Here, we're going to use the iPad edition as an example.

The app is very user-friendly and guides you through all the crucial steps of setting up a connection with your blog. You can add a new site from the settings menu. Once you do so, you get to use a standard set of features that let you in on a variety of actions that you can perform on your site's content. You can create and edit posts, do the same with pages, moderate comments, and hop over to the site's wp-admin via a direct link. Everything is available from a clear menu in the center of the screen:

What seems to be the only downside about the native WordPress apps is that they only support the Text editor for editing content. So in order to create any kind of post you will need to have a basic understanding of working with HTML code.

Discussion on your blog – comments

Comments are an important element for most blogs. While you are the only person who can write blog posts, the visitors to your blog can add comments to your posts. This can fuel a sense of community within a blog, allow people to give you feedback on your writing, and give your visitors a way to help or talk to other visitors. The only downside of commenting is that unscrupulous people will try to misuse your blog's ability to accept comments, and will try to post spam or advertisements in your blog instead of relevant comments. It's actually reported by Akismet – one of the leaders in spam fighting on WordPress blogs – that there are 7.5 million spam comments being processed every hour. What this means is simple: whether we like it or not, spam is an integral part of our online journey. Luckily, the WordPress community is always developing more ways of fixing the problem.

Adding a comment

If you look at the front page of your blog, you'll see that every post has a link that says **Leave a Comment**. Clicking on that link will take you to the bottom of the post page, which is where comments can be added, as we saw in *Chapter 2, Getting Started with WordPress.*

If you're logged into the wp-admin, you'll see your name and a space to write your comment. If you're not logged in, you'll see a comment form that any other visitor will see. This form includes fields to fill in name, e-mail, and website, along with the commenting text area.

Once you type in the required information and click on the **Post Comment** button, the comment will be entered into the WordPress database, along with all of your other blog information. How soon it shows up on the site depends on your discussion settings:

Name *

Email *

Website

Comment

Discussion settings

In the preceding screenshot, notice that **Name** and **Email** fields are both marked required (*). As the owner of this blog/site, you can change the requirements for comments. First, log into the wp-admin and navigate to **Settings | Discussion**. We explored the first box (**Default article settings**), earlier in this chapter.

Submission, notification, and moderation settings

Let's focus on the checkboxes on this page that relate only to **submission, notification,** and **moderation**. The boxes that are checked on this page will determine how much moderation and checking a comment has to go through before it gets posted on the blog.

The default settings are relatively strict. The only way to make a more strictly controlled discussion on your blog is to check **Comment must be manually approved**. This option means that no matter what, all comments go into the moderation queue, and do not show up on the site until you manually approve them.

Let's look at the settings having to do with the comment submission that are visible under **Other comment settings**. The first two options control what the user has to do before even being able to type in a comment:

- **Comment author must fill out name and e-mail**: As you noticed in the screenshot in the *Adding a comment* section, **Name** and **Email** fields are required. If you leave this checked, then anyone posting a comment will encounter an error if they try to leave either of the fields blank. This doesn't add a huge amount of security because robots know how to fill out a name and an e-mail, and because anyone can put fake information in there. However, it does help your blog readers to keep a track of who is who if a long discussion develops, and it can slightly discourage utterly impulsive commenting. Also, visitors who have a Gravatar account (mentioned in the previous chapter), are quite willing to provide their e-mail addresses anyway. That's because using an e-mail address that's connected to Gravatar will result in their profile picture (avatar) being displayed along with the comment, making it much more personal and visible among all the other comments.

- **Users must be registered and logged in to comment**: Most bloggers do not check this box because it means that only visitors who register for the blog can comment. Most bloggers don't want random people registering, and most visitors don't want to be compelled to register for your blog. If you check this box, there's a good chance you'll get no comments (which may be what you want). Alternatively, if you're setting up a blog for a closed community of people, this setting might be useful.

- **Automatically close comments on articles older than X days**: Here, you can set any number of days, after which the comments on your content will be closed. Although this feature might not seem like a useful one at first, it can actually be valuable to various kinds of news sites or other online publications, where allowing comments on old events makes very little sense.

- **Enable threaded (nested) comments X levels deep:**: This option is enabled by default, and it's yet another way of making your site more readable and user-friendly. Sometimes commenters want to be able to respond to someone else's comments, simply as part of an ongoing discussion. This is the feature that allows them to do so. Also, it gives you – the author – a great way of interacting with your audience, through direct responses to every comment of theirs.

- **Break comments into pages [...]**: This feature won't be of any value to you unless you're getting more than 200 comments per post. So you can confidently leave it unchecked for now.

Now let's look at the settings that have to do with moderation visible under **Before a comment appears**. These two options have to do with the circumstances that allow comments to appear on the site. They are by the **Before a comment appears** header:

- **Comment must be manually approved**: As I mentioned before, if this box is checked, every comment has to be manually approved by you before it appears on the site.

- **Comment author must have a previously approved comment**: If you uncheck the box above this, but check this one, then you've relaxed your settings a little bit. This means that if the person commenting has commented before and had his or her comment approved, then the person's future comments don't have to be verified by you; they'll just appear on the website immediately. The person just has to enter the same name and e-mail as the one in the previously approved comment.

Now let's look at the settings that have to do with notification. These two options are under the **E-mail me whenever** header. These options are related to the circumstances of receiving an e-mail notification about the comment activity:

- **Anyone posts a comment**: This is generally a good setting to keep. You'll get an e-mail whenever anyone posts a comment—whether or not it needs to be moderated. This will make it easier for you to follow the discussion on your blog, and to be aware of a comment that is not moderated, and requires deletion quickly.

- **A comment is held for moderation**: If you're not particularly interested in following every comment on your blog, you can uncheck the **Anyone posts a comment** checkbox, and only leave this one checked. You will only get an e-mail about legitimate-looking comments that appear to need moderation and need your approval.

When to moderate or blacklist a comment

If you scroll down the page a bit, you'll see the **Comment Moderation** area:

Comment Moderation

Hold a comment in the queue if it contains 2   or more links. (A common characteristic of comment spam is a large number of hyperlinks.)

When a comment contains any of these words in its content, name, URL, e-mail, or IP, it will be held in the moderation queue. One word or IP per line. It will match inside words, so "press" will match "WordPress".

This is an extension of the moderation settings from the top of the page. Note that if you've checked the **Comment must be manually approved** checkbox, you can safely ignore this **Comment Moderation** box. Otherwise, you can use this box to help WordPress figure out which comments are probably okay, and which might be spam or inappropriate for your blog. You can tell WordPress to suspect a comment if it has more than a certain number of links, as spam comments often are just a list of URLs.

The larger box is for you to enter suspect words and IP addresses:

- Here, you can type words that are commonly found in spam (you can figure this out by looking in your junk mail in your e-mail), or just uncouth words in general.

- The IP addresses you will enter into this box would be those of any comments you've gotten in the past from someone who comments inappropriately, or adds actual spam. Whenever WordPress receives a comment on your blog, it captures the IP address for you so that you'll have them handy.

Scroll down a bit more, and you'll see the **Comment Blacklist** box:

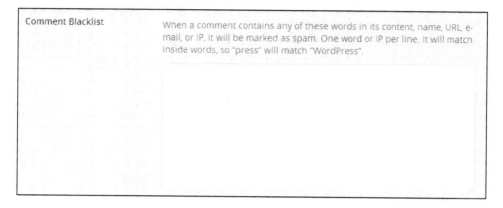

Unlike the **Comment Moderation** box we just saw, which tells WordPress how to identify the comments to suspect, the **Comment Blacklist** box tells WordPress how to identify comments that are almost definitely bad. These comments won't be added to the moderation queue, and you won't get an e-mail about them; they'll be marked right away as spam.

Avatar display settings

The final box on this page is the **Avatars** box. Just as I mentioned in the previous chapter, an avatar is an image that is a person's personal icon. Avatars in WordPress are provided through Gravatar – a service available at `http://gravatar.com/` that lets you create your personal online profile, which is going to then be consistently used on other websites across the web. By default, avatars will show up on your blog if you leave the **Show Avatars** radio button checked, which is visible near the bottom of the discussion settings page.

The second box, **Maximum Rating**, will tell WordPress if it should not show avatars that have been rated too highly. Remember the rating we were setting when uploading a new picture to Gravatar? This setting here is the place where you can choose which pictures you want to allow on your own site (selecting the **G** rating is advisable).

The third box, **Default Avatar**, tells WordPress what avatar to use for visitors who do not come with their own gravatar. When you installed WordPress, it created a comment for you on the first post, and also created a default avatar for you. You can see the default avatar, Mystery Man, in use on the Hello World! post:

Moderating comments

Now that we've thoroughly explored the settings for which comments need to be moderated, let's discuss what you actually need to do to moderate comments. 'Moderating' means that you look over a comment that is in limbo and decide whether it's insightful enough that it can be published on your site. If it's good, it gets to appear on the frontend of your website; and if it is bad, it's either marked as spam, or is deleted and is never seen by anyone but you, and the person who wrote it.

To view comments waiting for moderation, log in to your wp-admin and navigate to **Comments** in the main menu.

If you have any comments waiting for moderation, there will be a little number in the main menu telling you how many comments await moderation:

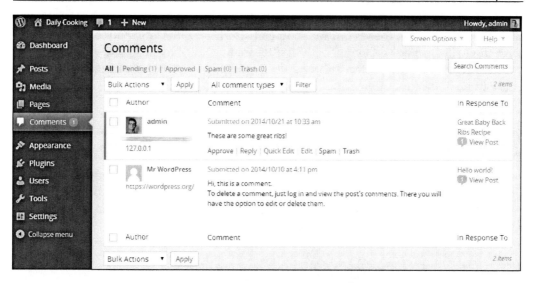

This main **Comments** page is fully featured, just like the **Posts** page. For each comment, you see the following information from left to right:

- Commenter avatar, name, website address (if there was any given), e-mail address (if there was any given), and IP (if there was any given)

- Comment text, along with links to approve it so that it shows up on the site (the links appear when you hover your mouse over the comment), you can also mark it as **Spam**, **Trash it**, **Edit it**, **Quick Edit it**, or **Reply** to it

- Comment submission time and date

- The title of the post on which the comment was made (which is also a link to edit that post), a number in parentheses indicating how many approved comments are already there on that post (which is also a link that will filter the comments list so that it shows only comments on this page), and a link to the post itself (labeled **View Post**)

Comments that are awaiting moderation have a red-ish background, like the first comment in the preceding screenshot (you can also see my Gravatar).

You can click on the **Quick Edit** link for any comment to open form fields right within this list. This will allow you to edit the text of the comment and the commenter's name, e-mail, and URL.

You can use the links at the top – **All**, **Pending**, **Approved**, **Spam**, and **Trash** – to filter the list based on those statuses. You can also filter either pings or comments with the **All comment types** pull-down filter menu. You can check one or more comments to apply any of the bulk actions available in the **Bulk Actions** menus at the top and bottom of the list.

Another quick way to get to this page, or to apply an action to a comment, is to use the links in the e-mail that WordPress sends you when a comment is held for moderation (provided you've selected this option in the **Settings | Discussion** section).

Additionally, this listing is where all pingbacks appear for your moderation. From a blog owner's point of view, pingbacks look just like any other comments, which means that you can edit them, mark them as spam, or trash them like you normally would with standard comments.

How to eliminate comment spam

Comment spam is one of the most annoying things on the Internet if you're an online publisher. Basically, a spam comment is a comment that has been submitted for the sole purpose of getting a link back to a specific website. The main reason why people submit spam comments is Search Engine Optimization – the number of links pointing to a site is a known SEO factor, and website owners around the world do whatever they can to get as many links as possible. Unfortunately for us, sometimes it means using various spam methods as well.

The way WordPress comments are set up by default makes it possible for anyone to get a link from your site just by submitting a comment, and providing a website address in one of the comment fields. If they do so and the comment gets approved, whatever was typed into the **Name** field of the comment becomes the text of the link, and the **Website** becomes the link's destination.

The worst thing about comment spam is that once your site gets even remotely popular, you can start getting hundreds of spam comments a day; hence dealing with them by hand becomes almost impossible.

Unfortunately, fighting comment spam is not something built into WordPress by default. This means that you have to get some plugin(s) to enable this functionality. For now let's focus on the most popular spam protection plugin at the moment – **Akismet**. The good thing about it is that it comes along with the standard WordPress installation, so you should be able to find it in the **Plugins** section in your wp-admin. We will cover plugins in detail later in this book, for now let's just review how to get Akismet working on your blog. If your blog is built on WordPress.com, then Akismet is already activated by default. For a standard, standalone blog, you'll have to activate it first.

Learning more

You can learn more about the Akismet spam-fighting service at http://akismet.com/. Also, if you're interested in some alternative solutions then please visit https://wordpress.org/plugins/antispam-bee/ and https://wordpress.org/plugins/growmap-anti-spambot-plugin/

Getting an Akismet API key

The Akismet plugin requires that you have a special API key. Getting this API key isn't something particularly difficult, but we still need to go through a couple of steps. First of all, you need to go to https://wordpress.com/, and create a new account. Once you have it, you can navigate to https://akismet.com/signup/, and click the link labeled **I already have a WordPress.com account!** On the next screen, you will be asked to simply input your login details (for the WordPress.com account). Finally, what you have to do to complete the process is click the blue **Authorize** button:

At this point, Akismet will attempt to sell you some of their premium services, but luckily this isn't mandatory. Click on the **Sign Up** button, under the plan labeled **Personal**:

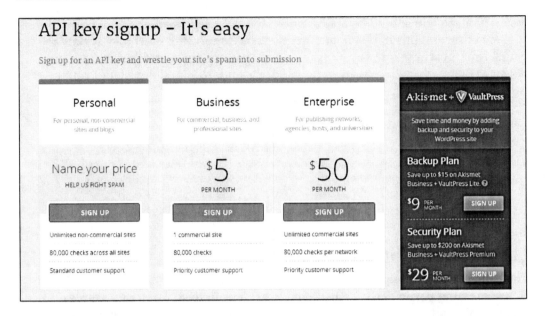

Now, this is tricky. The plan you've selected is based on voluntary donations. If you're not willing to spend any money, just take the slider that's in the center and slide it to the left, all the way to **$0.00/yr**. Apart from that, you just have to provide standard details like your first and last name:

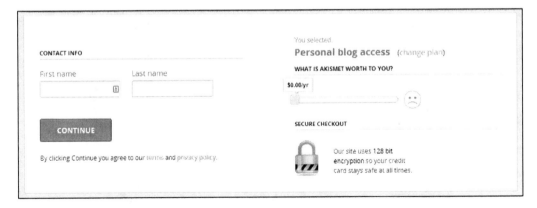

Your API key will arrive via e-mail to the address specified during registration. Select and copy that text. You may want to paste it into a text file to be sure you have it.

Activating Akismet

Now go back to your WordPress installation, and navigate to **Plugins** in the main menu:

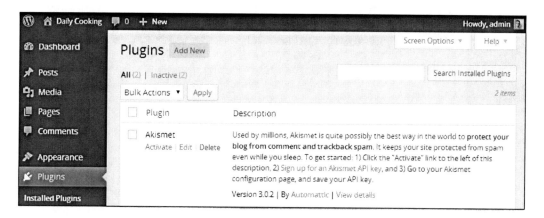

You'll see Akismet listed as the first plugin. Click on the **Activate** link. A green message bar will appear at the top of the page that says **Activate your Akismet account**. Click on that button, and you'll be taken to a page where you can enter the API key you copied from WordPress.com. Paste your API key into the box, and click the button:

In the next step, if you're feeling confident, you can check the box labeled **Silently discard the worst and most pervasive spam so I never see it**. Akismet is relatively good at identifying which comment is actually spam, and checking this box will make those comments disappear. However, if you're concerned about Akismet misidentifying comments, leave this unchecked.

Now click on **Save Changes,** and your blog is protected from comment spam!

Adding and managing categories

Earlier in this chapter, you learned how to add a category quickly when adding a post. Now, let's talk about how to manage your categories in a bigger way. First, navigate to **Posts | Categories** in your wp-admin. You'll see the **Categories** page:

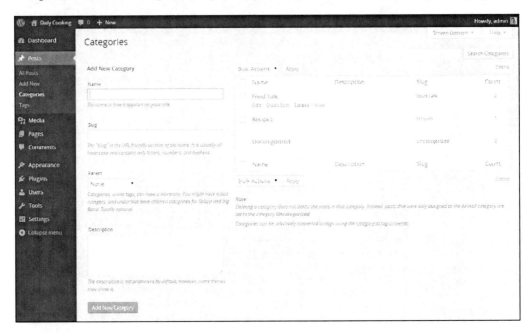

This is a useful page that combines the ability to add, edit, and review all of your categories. As you can see, any category that you've added via the **Edit Post** page is listed. You can edit, quick edit, or delete any category by clicking on the appropriate link in the list.

If you add a category on this page, you can also choose its slug. The **slug** is the short bit of text that shows up in the URL of your site, if you have pretty permalinks enabled. If you don't choose a slug, WordPress will create one for you by taking the category name, reducing it to all lowercase, replacing spaces with dashes, and removing any other punctuation mark (similarly to what's being done with slugs for posts).

Another thing you can do on this page is to choose a parent category for any category. Some themes support displaying categories hierarchically, but not all do. In a good, modern theme (we'll talk about those in *Chapter 7, Developing Your Own Theme*), if you create a custom menu for categories, all child categories will be displayed as submenus.

The ability to create a hierarchy of categories is actually the main technical thing that separates categories from tags. Other than that, both elements are quite similar in construction, although they still have different purposes.

Summary

In this chapter, you learned everything you need to know in order to add content to your blog, and then manage that content. You learned about posts, categories, and comments. You discovered tags, spam (unfortunately), and excerpts. You also learned about adding and editing images, working with video and audio content, using the Visual editor (and the Text editor), changing timestamps, customizing excerpts, and the different ways of posting (for example through e-mail or external blogging tools).

Your control of your blog content is complete, and you are well equipped to set your blog on fire!

In the next chapter, you'll learn about all the other types of content that you can manage on your website with WordPress.

4
Pages, Menus, Media Library, and More

You now have the blog part of your website fully under control. By now, you've probably noticed that WordPress offers you a lot more than simply posts, comments, tags, and categories.

In this chapter, we will explore and control all the other types of content that WordPress already has. You'll be able to create static pages that aren't a part of your ongoing blog, add various types of media to your posts, and create appealing image galleries to display photos and other images (working with the new media library). You'll also learn how to manage navigation menus and work with the basic layout customization features to further enhance the capabilities of your entire website.

Pages

At first glance, pages look very similar to posts. Both pages and posts have a title and a content area in which we can write extended text. However, pages are handled quite differently from posts. First of all, pages don't have categories, or tags (pages don't need to be categorized since on most websites there's a lot less pages than posts). Moreover, posts belong to your blog and are meant to be a part of an ongoing, expanding section of your website. Posts are added regularly, whereas pages are more static and aren't generally expected to change that much.

In short, I would advise you to think of pages as pieces of static content, and posts as a series of articles published in a timely manner. In other words, pages are meant to hold content that is equally up to date, no matter when someone reads it. Posts are often very time-sensitive and present advice/news that's important today/now. For most blogs, posts are the pillars of their content and make up more than 90 percent of the whole content. Furthermore, posts appear in the RSS feed of a WordPress blog, while pages don't.

When you installed WordPress, a page was automatically created for you (along with the first post and the first comment). You can see this by going to `http://YOURSITE.com/sample-page/`:

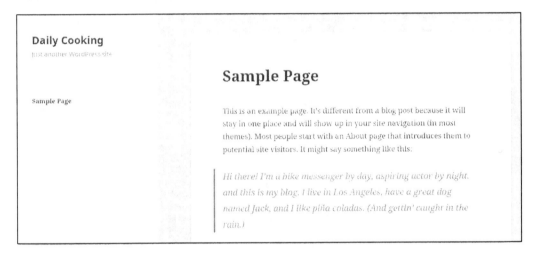

Adding a page

To add a new page, go to your wp-admin, and navigate to **Pages | Add New**, or use the drop-down menu in the top dark menu by clicking on **New** and then **Page**. This will take you to the **Add New Page** screen:

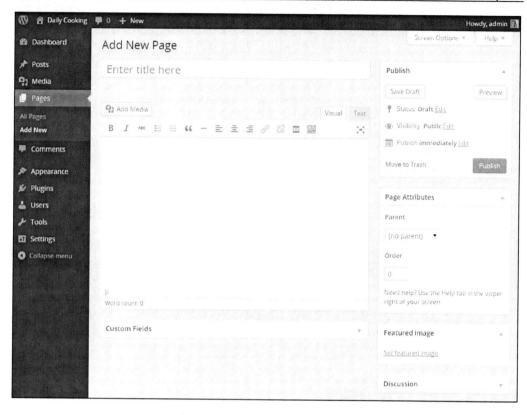

The minimum you need to do in order to create a new page is type in a title and some content. Then, click on the blue **Publish** button, just as you would for a post, and your new page will become available under its unique URL.

You'll recognize most of the fields on this page from the **Add New Post** page. They work the same for pages as they do for posts. Let's talk about the one section that's new: The box called **Page Attributes**, consisting of elements such as **Parent** and **Order**:

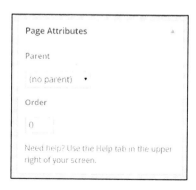

Parent

WordPress allows you to structure your pages hierarchically. This way, you can organize your website's pages into main pages and subpages, which is useful if you're going to have a lot of pages on your site. For example, if I was to write a blog along with three other authors, we would each have one page about us on the site, but those would be subpages of the main **About** page. If I was adding one of these pages, I'd first create a new **About** page, then create another page just for me, called **About Karol**, and finally choose **About** as the parent page for this new page.

Order

By default, the pages on your page list in the sidebar or the main navigation menu of your blog will be in alphabetical order by page title. If you want them in some other order, you can specify it by entering numbers in the **Order** box for all your pages. Pages with lower numbers (for example, 0) will be listed before pages with higher numbers (for example, 5). You can easily test this by editing some of your pages and assigning various numbers to them. That being said, to be honest, this isn't a very clear method of rearranging pages inside menus. You can do it much more easily with a functionality called **Custom Menus** (described later in this chapter). In the end, I would advise you to save all of your pages with the order of 0.

Managing pages

To see a list of all the pages on your website in the wp-admin, navigate to **Pages | Edit** in the main menu. You'll see the **Pages** screen, as shown in the following screenshot:

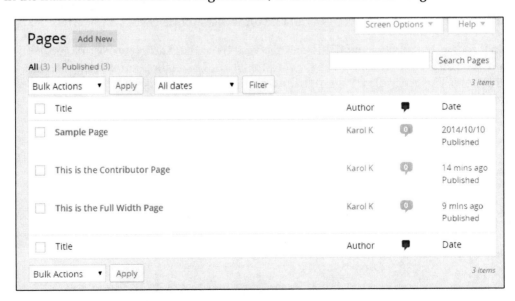

By now, this list format should begin to look familiar to you. You've got your list of pages and in each row there are a number of useful links allowing you to edit, quick edit, trash, or view the page. You can click on an author's name to filter the list by that author. You can use the two links at the top, **All** and **Published**, to filter the pages by status (if you have pages saved as **Drafts** or **Pending Review**, then they will also appear here). There's also filtering by date through the drop-down menu just above the list of pages. Additionally, you can check certain boxes and mass-edit pages by using the **Bulk Actions** menu at the top and bottom of the list. You can also search your pages with the search box at the top.

Menus

As of WordPress 3.0, custom menus are now available within the wp-admin. This wasn't always the case, but these days, all modern themes support custom menus, and so does the default theme: Twenty Fifteen.

The **Custom Menus** feature lets you create menus with links to pages, category archives, and even arbitrary links to any URL (which also allows you to link to your individual posts). Then you can place your custom menu into your theme.

Adding a Menu

Let's take a look at the menus management screen. To get there, just navigate to **Appearance | Menus**:

To create your first menu, enter a title (for example, Main) where it says **Enter menu name here**. After doing so, you can select individual pages from the panel on the left and click on the **Add to Menu** button to confirm:

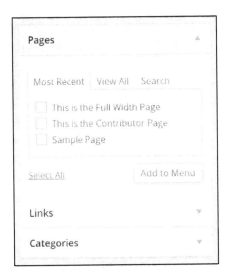

You can add some custom links to the menu if you want to. This can be done after clicking on the **Links** heading on the left and then filling out the required link information. To confirm, click on **Add to Menu**:

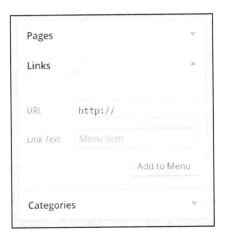

Finally, you can add some category links. Click on the **Categories** heading on the left and then proceed to clicking on the checkboxes next to the categories you want to include. Click on **Add to Menu** to confirm:

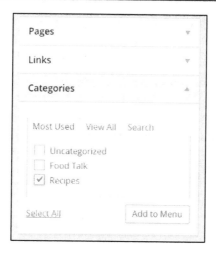

Finally, be sure to click on **Save Menu** in the upper-right corner. The following is what my new menu looks like now:

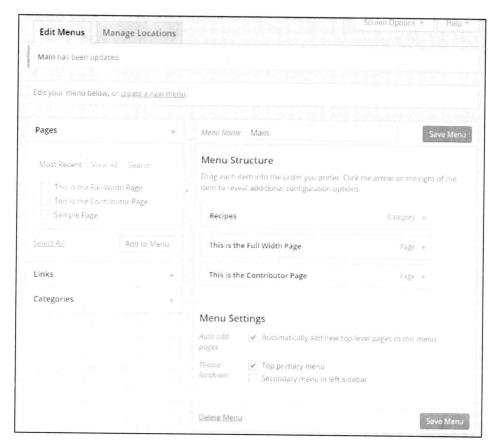

You can also drag items to the right to make them subitems of the item immediately above. For example, I'll drag one of my pages as a subitem under the other page. Now, my menu looks like the following screenshot:

You can make more menus by clicking on the **create a new menu** link at the top and repeating the process. Now you might ask: I created my new menu, but how do I make it show up on my site?

Displaying a Menu

If you have a menu-enabled theme, then once you have one menu, a new box will appear on the **Menus** page showing you the menu locations. Twenty Fifteen has two menu locations, and they're named **Primary Menu** and **Social Links Menu**:

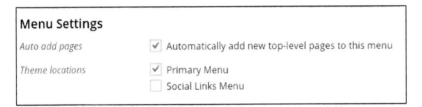

All you have to do to assign your newly created menu to the predefined menu area in Twenty Fifteen is to check one of the boxes, as shown in the preceding screenshot. Right now, my primary navigation on the website looks like the following screenshot:

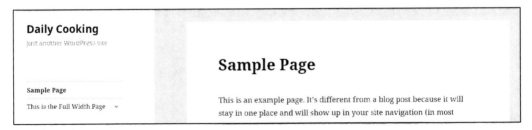

And when I click on the down arrow next to **This is the Full Width Page**, I will also see my other page that was saved as a subpage, as shown in the next screenshot. Twenty Fifteen displays subitems in a rollover menu.

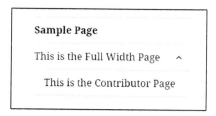

Header

The functionality I'm about to describe is highly dependent upon your current theme. Not all themes support header functionality, and even the ones that do can provide you with different set of features related to this topic. However, most modern themes these days do support header customizations in some form. So learning a few things about this feature will definitely come in handy for you sooner rather than later.

If you're starting your WordPress adventure with the default theme Twenty Fifteen, then in the **Appearance** section, you will see one link labeled **Header**. This is where you can adjust the design of your site's header:

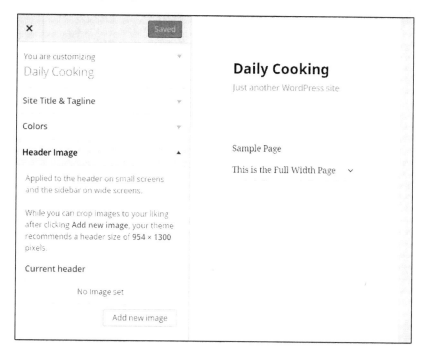

As you can see, my header doesn't feature anything fancy at the moment. However, with just a little effort, this can be changed in no time. Most themes will allow you to select any image to be placed inside the header. Twenty Fifteen has some specific requirements for this image, which you can see in the preceding screenshot. The suggested size is 954 pixels wide by 1300 pixels high, but you don't have to worry all that much about this because WordPress also provides some handy image editing tools. All you have to do here is use the **Choose Image** button and select one of the pictures from the media library, or upload a new one. WordPress will immediately redirect you to the aforementioned image editing tools, where you can adjust and crop your image, as shown next:

After clicking on the **Crop Image** button and then **Save & Publish**, we're done with setting up the header image. Here's what my site looks like now:

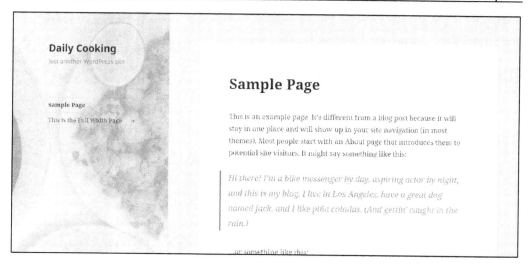

This looks much better, right?

Background

Now let's take a look at the other visual setting in the **Appearance** section called **Background**. When you navigate to **Appearance | Background** for the first time, there's nothing visually appealing there, but we can change this with just a couple of clicks, as shown in the following screenshot:

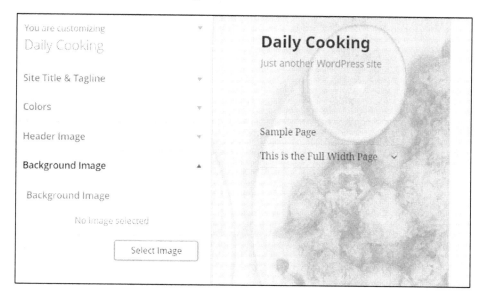

The first thing we have to do is select an image we want to place in the background of our whole site. Let me say that again—our whole site. As an example, I will try using the same picture that I used for the header image; only this time, it will be displayed in its original resolution. Right after selecting the image (just click on **Select Image** visible in the preceding screenshot), the **Preview** block will get refreshed, and you will be able to see what your background looks like at the moment.

Immediately, there are some new options visible at the bottom of the block:

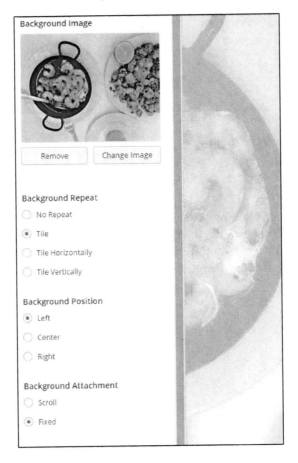

The various options are as follows:

- **Background Repeat**: This can be **No Repeat**, **Tile**, **Tile Horizontally**, or **Tile Vertically**:
  - **No Repeat**: This means that your background image will be displayed only once, and after the visitor scrolls down, they will simply "run out" of the background image.

- ° **Tile**: This is the most popular setting and actually the default one as well. This means that WordPress will repeat your image in both dimensions (width and height). So, no matter what part of your site the visitor is browsing, the background image will always be visible.
- ° **Tile Horizontally**: This tiles your image horizontally.
- ° **Tile Vertically**: This tiles your image vertically.

- **Background Position**: This can be **Left**, **Center**, or **Right**. This decides whether the background image should be aligned to the left, center, or right.
- **Background Attachment**: This can be either **Scroll** or **Fixed**:
  - ° **Scroll**: In this, your image scrolls along with the content.
  - ° **Fixed**: In this, your image remains in a fixed position. In other words, it stands still in the background at all times.

I encourage you to play around with these settings for a while when adjusting your site. In the meantime, you can see the exact settings I've selected in the preceding screenshot. And finally, here's what my site looks like now:

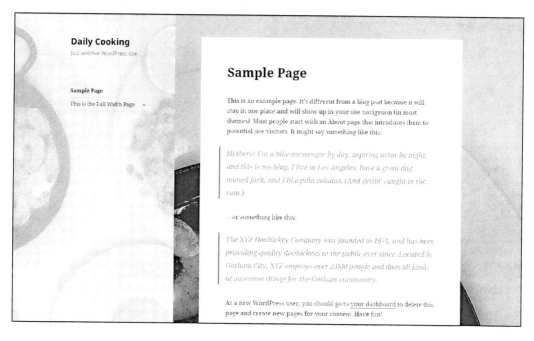

I'm sure you can agree that setting a custom header image and a custom background has given my site a much more attractive appearance.

Advanced site customization

Yet another feature in WordPress that's highly dependent upon your theme is the Customize Your Site module. If you still have the Welcome box enabled in your Dashboard's screen settings, you can access this module by clicking the big **Customize Your Site** button, as shown in the following screenshot:

Another way of accessing this module is by visiting `http://yoursite.com/wp-admin/customize.php`. This is what you'll see (provided you're working with the default theme):

This module doesn't deliver any new functionality. It simply takes all the customization features and displays them in one, easy to grasp place.

By going through the individual tabs on the left, you can adjust various aspects of your site that we've already talked about in this and the previous chapters. These aspects are as follows:

- **Site Title & Tagline**
- **Colors**

- **Header Image**
- **Background Image**
- **Navigation** (you can choose which menu you want to assign as the top primary menu and secondary menu in the left sidebar)
- **Widgets** (more on this later)
- **Static Front Page**

The best thing about this module is that it provides a live preview, which makes editing the basic aspects of your design much quicker. When you're done, you can click on either the **Cancel** button or the **Save** button.

Media library

The media library is where WordPress stores all of your uploaded files such as images, PDFs, music, videos, and so on. To see your media library, navigate to **Media** in the main menu (there probably isn't a lot of media in there at the moment):

The content layout we're seeing here is a new type of presentation introduced in WordPress 4.0. Previously, the media library could be browsed only via the now-familiar management table/listing. This new grid layout makes looking through media much more user-friendly. This is mostly due to larger thumbnails and the lack of distracting text data.

My media library has three photos in it at the moment. Once I click on any of them, I will see the **Attachment Details** screen that we talked about in *Chapter 3, Creating Blog Content*. On this screen, there are a lot of options to modify the file that's been selected. We can edit details, such as **Title**, **Caption**, **Alt Text**, and **Description**, and also delete the file permanently, or view it on the front page of the site:

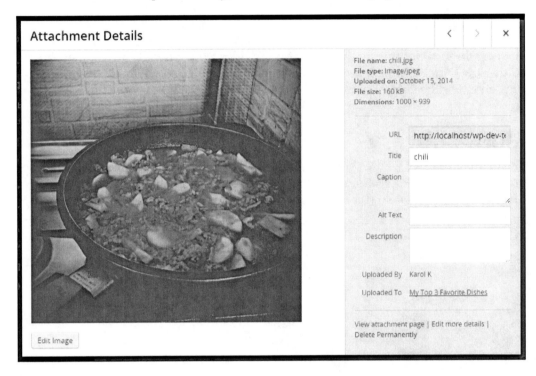

You can also add a new file to your media library. Navigate to **Media** | **Add New** to get a page similar to the upload media page that you got while uploading a file for a post. When you click on the **Select Files** button and select the file to be uploaded, or drag and drop it directly from your desktop, it will upload the file and then display it along with the rest of the media files in the library. Your new item will be unattached to any post or page at this point.

To include it somewhere (in a post or page), just go to the **Add/Edit Post** or **Add/Edit Page** screen and click on the **Add Media** button as you did previously. However, instead of uploading a new file, just select it from the media library (the default screen after clicking on the **Add Media** button):

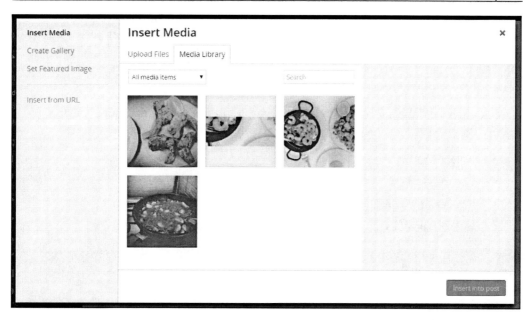

When you click on any image displayed on this **Insert Media** screen, you'll see the same set of options you got after uploading an image. Now you can click on the **Insert into post** button. The media item will now appear as **Uploaded To** that post or page:

By the way, as you can see, I've created a whole new post for that image and titled it **Some Spanish Dishes**.

Media Manager

The aforementioned **Insert Media** screen that's visible in the preceding screenshots is also known as the **Media Manager**. This Media Manager is a relatively new feature in WordPress as it was introduced in version 3.5. Its interface is a lot different than it was in the previous versions of the platform. It's certainly more visually attractive and, at the same time, much easier to use.

You can always access the Media Manager from within the **Add/Edit Post** or **Add/Edit Page** screen by clicking on the **Add Media** button. We've already discussed two ways of using it—uploading new media and attaching media that has been previously uploaded—but that's not all. The Media Manager has a lot more interesting stuff under the hood.

First of all, if we take a look at the left sidebar, there are four links there (please review the preceding screenshots). Starting from the top, these are as follows:

- **Insert Media**
- **Create Gallery**
- **Set Featured Image**
- **Insert from URL**

Also, later on, when you have some third-party plugins installed, you might find even more links in that sidebar, but for now, four it is.

Clicking on any of them will reload the center part of the screen to present a new range of features. We've already mostly covered the **Insert Media** tab, that is, the default one. This is where you can either upload new files or select existing ones from the media library. This tab also provides a handy search box and a filtering dropdown:

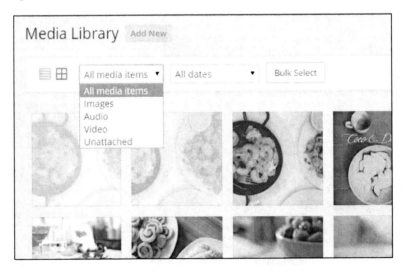

The filtering dropdown won't be of much use right now, but once you have hundreds of different media in the media library, being able to sort through them will become invaluable. The filtering dropdown simply lets you display media only of a specific type (the types are **Images**, **Audio**, **Video**, and **All media items**). Also, the dropdown right next to it delivers the possibility to filter by date. The search field is simply a "search field", and works immediately as you type (there's no submit button).

The second tab is **Create Gallery**. This is a completely new gallery creation mechanism. The number of things we can do in this module are truly impressive. It's all explained in the section ahead.

The third tab in the Media Manager is **Set Featured Image**. This offers you yet another way to assign a featured image to your posts (the first method was from within the box on the post editing screen itself). This is a very simple task. All you need to do is click on the image you want to save as the featured one and then click the **Set Featured Image** button in the bottom-right corner.

Finally, we have the last tab called **Insert from URL**. Apart from the possibility to upload your own images, WordPress also allows you to pick an image from the Web and have it displayed on your site. As always in such situations, you have to be careful not to take a copyrighted image, but from the technical point of view, WordPress is capable of importing any image that you input into the main field, as shown in the following screenshot:

As you can see, I've used a link to an image on Flickr (an image from my personal account, actually). There are some additional settings here that you should use. Apart from the **Caption** and the **Alt Text** options (this is the text that gets displayed in case the image fails to load for whatever reason), there are also settings for the alignment and the URL destination of the link (if you want to link your image to something).

The important thing worth pointing out here is that WordPress doesn't import this external image into your media library. Instead, it hot-links the image from the source. In other words, the image is still on another server. What this means for you is that you don't have any actual control over this image. It can be removed overnight or replaced with another image without your knowledge. That's why in 90 percent of the cases, it's actually better to download the image you want to use and then upload it to your media library, instead of hot-linking it.

Adding an image gallery

As mentioned in the previous section, the gallery module that you can find inside the Media Manager provides a completely redesigned, modern way of working with image galleries. Just to remind you, this new gallery module can be accessed by clicking on the **Add Media** button when editing a post or a page, and then clicking on the **Create Gallery** link in the left sidebar.

One of the most user-friendly aspects about creating image galleries in WordPress is that you can drag and drop multiple images at once, and WordPress will immediately start turning them into a gallery. However, before you can do this, you have to choose where you want to display your new gallery, and that's what we're going to do next.

Choosing a post or page

This is a very simple step, and we've been doing this previously, so here we go. You can add a gallery (or multiple galleries) to any new or existing page or post. I, for example, went with one of my existing posts, which you can see in the following screenshot:

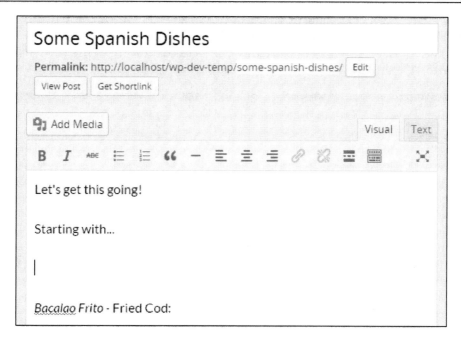

Note where I have left my cursor (it's right in the middle if you can't see it). I made sure to leave it in a spot on the page where I want my gallery to appear, that is, underneath my introductory paragraphs.

Selecting or uploading images

You can start either by uploading some new images or selecting the ones already in your media library. If it's the former you're after, then simply click on the **Create Gallery** link on the left, grab some images from your desktop, and drag and drop them onto the upload area.

If you want to work with some of your existing images that are already in the media library, then just click on the **Media Library** link as shown in the following screenshot. As an example, I've selected two images that I want to use (they have a checkbox in the upper-right corner):

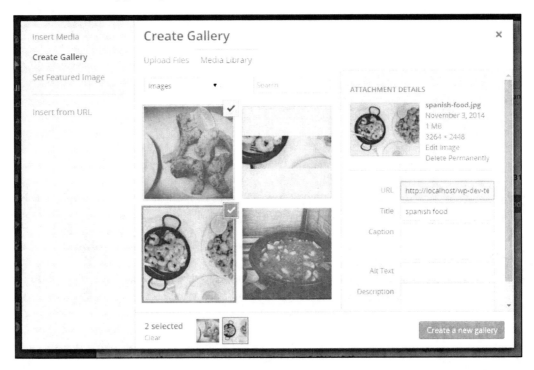

At this stage, you can adjust the titles and descriptions of the images if you want to, and then click on the **Create a new gallery** button. In the next step, you have the opportunity to rearrange your images by dragging them around the display area. You can also adjust the captions (the captions will be saved so that they can be reused later on if you're creating a gallery using the same images). On the right side, under **Link To**, there's a drop-down menu where you can change the link destination for each image. The way a gallery works in WordPress is that when visitors click on any image, they will be redirected either to the media file itself, to the attachment page (an individual page created for each image by default), or nowhere at all. Going with the default value of **Media File** is the recommended choice.

The other two options on this page—the number of columns, and the **Random Order** checkbox—are pretty self-explanatory. When you're done, just click on the **Insert gallery** button:

On the post editing screen, the gallery block itself has a nice preview. There's a small space, and in it we can see the images that will appear as part of the gallery:

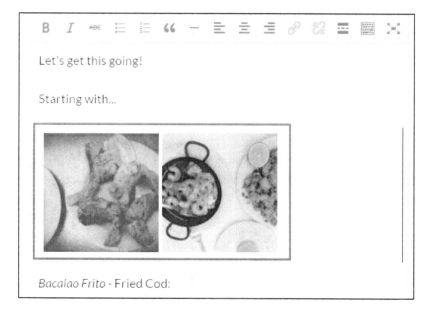

However, when you view the gallery on the frontend of your site, it's going to look great. The degree of its greatness depends closely on the theme you're using, though. When you click on any of the images, you'll be taken to a larger version of the image.

Also, while on the post editing screen, you can edit any image and any gallery by clicking on the preview and then on one of the buttons that will appear:

One more note, if you're in the text view, you'll see the gallery shortcode instead of the visual gallery block:

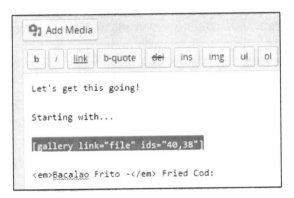

In this case, the gallery is inserted through a simple shortcode, which is `[gallery link="file" ids="40,38"]`. These IDs are the individual IDs of the media files that are a part of the gallery. What this means is that you can also edit your gallery by hand, simply by replacing the IDs or adding some new ones.

> We're going to talk about shortcodes in more detail in *Chapter 9, Developing Plugins and Widgets*. For now, all you need to know is that they allow you to sometimes use quite complex functionality just by using short trigger codes; hence the name "shortcodes".

Note that because I'm uploading the photos while editing this particular post, all of these photos will be attached to this post, which is a nice way of indicating which images go where.

The [gallery] shortcode is quite powerful! Take a look at the codex to get all of its parameters, at https://codex.wordpress.org/ Gallery_Shortcode.

Importing/exporting your content

The final thing I want to describe in this chapter is the feature of importing and exporting your content. By default, WordPress allows you to "take" content from other places and publish it on your site. There are a number of platforms supported, including Blogger, LiveJournal, Tumblr blogs, and more. You can see the complete list by navigating to **Tools** | **Import** (it's also the starting point when importing content):

Import

Help ▾

If you have posts or comments in another system, WordPress can import those into this site. To get started, choose a system to import from below:

Blogger	Install the Blogger importer to import posts, comments, and users from a Blogger blog.
Blogroll	Install the blogroll importer to import links in OPML format.
Categories and Tags Converter	Install the category/tag converter to convert existing categories to tags or tags to categories, selectively.
LiveJournal	Install the LiveJournal importer to import posts from LiveJournal using their API.
Movable Type and TypePad	Install the Movable Type importer to import posts and comments from a Movable Type or TypePad blog.
RSS	Install the RSS importer to import posts from an RSS feed
Tumblr	Install the Tumblr importer to import posts & media from Tumblr using their API.
WordPress	Install the WordPress importer to import posts, pages, comments, custom fields, categories, and tags from a WordPress export file.

If the importer you need is not listed, search the plugin directory to see if an importer is available.

Importing content

If you want to import content from any source, after you click on any of the links visible in the preceding screenshot, WordPress will prompt you to install some plugins to fully enable the feature. Plugins are the topic of the next chapter, but the way WordPress uses them for importing is really a hands-off approach, so you don't need to know much about plugins themselves in order to be able to import content.

Now, importing content from each of the available platforms is a bit different, but the general process looks similar, so we're going to use another WordPress site as an example here (that is, we're going to import content from another WordPress site). The first step is to click on the **WordPress** link visible in the preceding screenshot. Immediately, you'll see a prompt to install the **WordPress Importer** plugin:

You can just click on the blue **Install Now** button at the bottom and the process will start automatically. When it finishes, you can click on the **Activate Plugin & Run Importer** link, which will take you straight to the importer panel:

Import WordPress

Howdy! Upload your WordPress eXtended RSS (WXR) file and we'll import the posts, pages, comments, custom fields, categories, and tags into this site.

Choose a WXR (.xml) file to upload, then click Upload file and import.

Choose a file from your computer: (Maximum size: 8 MB)

Choose File   No file chosen

Upload file and import

It's a very simple interface where all you have to do is take a **WordPress export file** and upload it to your site. The platform will take care of extracting the archive and importing the content in it. As a result, your site is going to be filled with new posts, pages, even comments, custom fields, and navigation menus.

The main purpose of this feature is to help anyone who's migrating their sites from platforms such as Blogger or LiveJournal. Imagine if someone had a Blogger blog with over a hundred posts in it. Going through each one individually and inputting it to WordPress by hand would be too time-consuming. With this feature, it can be done in minutes.

Exporting content

Exporting content is even simpler than importing. To start, navigate to **Tools | Export**:

Export

When you click the button below WordPress will create an XML file for you to save to your computer.

This format, which we call WordPress eXtended RSS or WXR, will contain your posts, pages, comments, custom fields, categories, and tags.

Once you've saved the download file, you can use the Import function in another WordPress installation to import the content from this site.

Choose what to export

● All content

This will contain all of your posts, pages, comments, custom fields, terms, navigation menus and custom posts.

○ Posts

○ Pages

Download Export File

There's not much you can do here except select what you want to export and then click the big button to download the **WordPress export file**.

Selecting **All content** will export your posts, pages, comments, custom fields, terms, navigation menus, and custom posts. Selecting just **Posts** or **Pages** is pretty self-explanatory.

When you click on the **Download Export File** button, you will end up with a file that's just like the one we used when importing. This means that you can take that file and create a mirror copy of your site somewhere else under another domain name. Keep in mind though that the mirror file doesn't include your media files; these you will need to import separately. The export file is only for the content that sits in the database.

Summary

In this chapter, we explored the content that WordPress can handle that's not directly about blogging. You learned about static pages, menus, the media library (and the Media Manager), image galleries, header and background settings, and more.

You are now fully equipped to use the WordPress Admin panel to control all of your website's content. Next, you'll learn how to expand your site's functionality by installing new plugins, which we'll be discussing in the following chapter.

5
Plugins and Widgets

The topic of plugins and widgets has grown a lot in recent years. Nowadays, it's hard to imagine any WordPress site that could operate without at least a handful of (essential) plugins or widgets.

In this chapter, you will get to know what plugins are, why to use them, how to use them, where to get them, and how to be up to date and take notice of any new useful plugin that gets released to the community. We will also talk about some of the most basic and popular plugins in the WordPress world, and why getting them might be a good idea. Finally, you'll learn how to work with widgets to make your sidebars even more functional and reader-friendly. Okay, let's get on with it!

Breaking down plugins – what are they?

Simply speaking, plugins are small scripts (files with executable PHP code) that allow you to include new functionality in your WordPress site – functionality that is *not* available or enabled by default. One of the best advantages of WordPress is that it's quite an optimized platform. It makes your site load fast and doesn't contain much redundant code. However, WordPress itself only offers the absolute essential range of features – the features that are useful to everyone. However, the platform does provide a straightforward way of expanding the abilities of your site by introducing, you guessed it, plugins. The idea is simple: if you want your site to be able to handle a specific new task, there's surely a plugin for that. Much like in the Apple world and the popular expression, "there's an app for that."

Why use plugins

The best thing about plugins is that you don't need any specific programming knowledge in order to use them. Essentially, they are just like standard applications for iOS or Android—you can install them and enjoy the things they have to offer without knowing what's going on inside. This being said, not all plugins are safe to use in terms of data security or code quality. We will discuss this topic later in this chapter.

Furthermore, the right combination of plugins can make your site more optimized, more user-friendly, more attractive, more social-media-friendly, properly backed up, protected against spam, and, ultimately, unique. Plugins are really one of the best things about WordPress.

You see, before content management systems like WordPress were popularized, there was no easy way for site owners to introduce new functionalities on their sites. Doing so always required hiring a professional programmer and investing in the whole development process. Nowadays, this is no longer the case, and virtually anyone can have an impressive site without losing the shirt off their back.

Where to get plugins from

The community behind WordPress plugins is a huge one. There's no one central plugin-building company. Developers all over the world create plugins and then distribute them across the Internet. And, very often, they receive no direct compensation whatsoever. The best place to visit for WordPress plugins is the official directory at `https://wordpress.org/plugins/`.

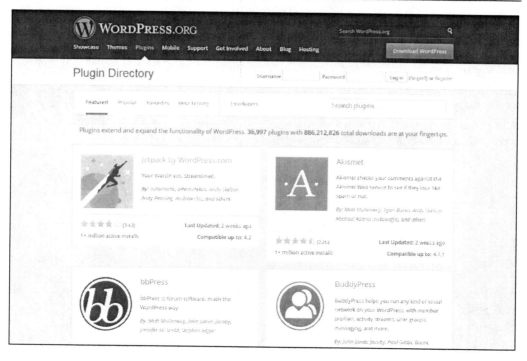

There are over 37,000 different plugins available in the directory at the time of writing this book, and this number is constantly expanding with around 110 new plugins being added every week. This really is an impressive number considering that many of these plugins are very advanced pieces of web software and not just simple, one-script add-ons.

There's a search field available in the center of the page in the directory (visible in the preceding screenshot), which allows you to search plugins by topic and by tag. You can also view a list of the most popular plugins as well as featured plugins. In short, the official plugin directory is where you should always go first when looking for a plugin.

It's also a good habit to always check how popular the plugins you're interested in are. Getting plugins that already have a proven track record of happy users will improve your chances of getting a quality product that you'll enjoy using.

You can also do Google searches. I recommend searching for the problem you're trying to solve and see what plugins other users recommend and why. Often, there are multiple plugins that perform similar functions, and you will find the feedback of other WordPress users valuable in choosing between them. However, as you do this, be sure to keep an eye out for malicious or poorly coded plugins that could break your website or allow someone to hack into it. Be careful when installing new plugins with no reviews, comments, or feedback from users, in addition to those plugins that have bad feedback about them on the Internet.

To get even more in-depth with your plugin investigation, you can also check out the changelogs and support forums for each plugin you're considering for your site (every plugin page inside the official plugin directory has a tab named **Changelog** and **Support**). They should give you an idea of how well or how poorly a given plugin is coded, supported, and so on.

Apart from free plugins, there's also a big set of premium plugins (paid ones) available. However, you won't find them in the official directory. Most of those plugins have their own websites handling sales, customer support, and usage tutorials. If you're interested, one of the more popular premium plugin directories can be found at `http://codecanyon.net/category/wordpress`.

Finding new plugins

Generally speaking, if a given plugin proves that it's a quality solution and gains some popularity, it will be showcased on the home page of the official directory in the **Featured Plugins** section. But if you want to be up to date with things as they happen, you can pay attention to what's going on at `https://wordpress.org/plugins/browse/new/`.

Additionally, a great way to discover new plugins is to become a regular visitor to one of the popular blogs about WordPress. Although these blogs are not official creations (they are run by independent owners), they do provide an impressive range of tips and advice, not only on plugins but also on other aspects related to WordPress. The list includes the following:

- `http://wptavern.com/`
- `http://www.wpbeginner.com/`
- `http://www.codeinwp.com/blog/`
- `https://yoast.com/`
- `http://premium.wpmudev.org/blog/`

- `http://bobwp.com/bobwp-wordpress-blog/`
- `http://themefuse.com/blog/`

Installing a plugin – the how-to

The steps for installing a plugin are simple:

1. Find your plugin.
2. Download it to your WordPress site, either manually or through the automatic installer.
3. Install and activate it.
4. Configure and/or implement it (if necessary).

There are two ways to get the plugin into your WordPress installation:

- Install manually
- Install from within the wp-admin

The first option – installing plugins manually – generally requires a bit more effort than the second one, but sometimes it's the only way to work with some specific plugins (mostly premium ones). The second option – installing from within the wp-admin – is generally quicker and easier, but it's not possible in all cases. You need to be on a server that's configured correctly, in a way that allows WordPress to add files (we talked about installing WordPress and server configuration in *Chapter 2, Getting Started with WordPress*). Plus, the plugin you want to install has to be available in the WordPress plugin repository, that is, the official plugin directory.

In the following section, we'll go over the manual method first, and then handle auto-installation.

Manual plugin installation

As an example here, I will install a popular plugin called **Jetpack** by WordPress.com. It's quite a large plugin, offering a range of features and effectively making your WordPress site more functional and easier to use at the same time. We'll discuss it in more detail later in this chapter. That being said, the following procedure allows you to install any WordPress plugin you can get your hands on, not only Jetpack.

To install a plugin manually, you must start by downloading the plugin archive either from the official directory at `https://wordpress.org/plugins/` or from some other website or source (usually when dealing with premium plugins).

In this case, the Jetpack plugin is available in the official directory at
`https://wordpress.org/plugins/jetpack/`.

Just click on the orange **Download Version 3.2** button, and save the resulting ZIP file
on your computer in a place where you can find it easily.

An important point to note is that before downloading any plugin, check the plugin
compatibility. You can do so by looking at the parameter labeled **Compatible up to**
that's visible on the plugin page (preceding screenshot). You can check which version
of WordPress you are using on your site by taking a look into the **Updates** section of
the **Dashboard** (available at `http://yoursite.com/wp-admin/update-core.php`),
as shown in the following screenshot:

Once you have the plugin downloaded, and if your server is set up correctly, you should be able to upload the ZIP file directly via the **Plugins | Add New** page. Just click on the **Upload Plugin** button at the top and choose the ZIP file of the plugin, as shown in the following screenshot:

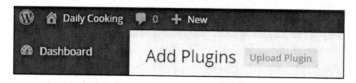

 If this automatic uploader doesn't work for you, you can do this the old-fashioned way. First unzip, that is, extract the ZIP file you downloaded so that it's a folder, probably named `jetpack` (at least in this case). Then, using your FTP client, upload this folder inside the `wp-content/plugins/` folder of your WordPress installation. You'll also see the two plugins in that folder that WordPress came with—`akismet` and `hello.php`.

If you need some assistance with FTP software, please review *Chapter 2, Getting Started with WordPress*, where we talked about the topic of installing WordPress.

After the uploading finishes, you will be able to activate the plugin. This is required to effectively "turn the plugin on". This can be done simply by clicking on the **Activate Plugin** link, as shown in the following screenshot. At this point, you're done and the Jetpack plugin is working.

Now you are ready for the final step—configuring and ultimately making use of the plugin. But, before we shift our attention to this, let's discuss an easier method of dealing with plugin installation, which is also the recommended way.

Auto-installation

If the plugin you want to install is available in the official plugin directory at `https://wordpress.org/plugins/` and your server configuration meets the requirements for auto-installation (your webhost has to grant you the read/write/ modify directory and file permissions: this is usually the case with the majority of serious hosting companies), then you can search for and install a new plugin from within the wp-admin. Just navigate to **Plugins | Add New**. It just so happens that the plugin I'm using here as the example—Jetpack—is one of the most popular plugins in the directory at the moment. Therefore, you will actually see it right on the main screen in the **Plugins | Add New** section. If the plugin you want to install is not in this featured plugins area, you can type its name in the search box to the right (the following screenshot):

Once you see a plugin that seems interesting, you can click on the **More Details** link to see some more information about the features it has to offer:

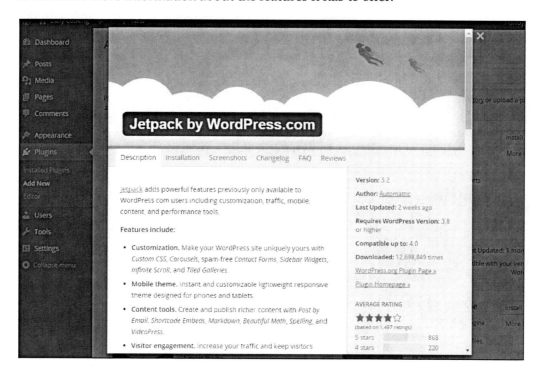

I recommend you always look at this information carefully. Be sure to watch for version compatibility. Just like with the manual installation method, there's a parameter labeled **Compatible up to** here as well. In some cases, you can risk installing a plugin that's a little outdated, but you should proceed with caution.

After the installation, you need to test the plugin carefully and verify that it's behaving correctly. Most of the time, if the **Compatible up to** parameter indicates an older version of WordPress, it doesn't necessarily mean that the plugin will fail to work with a newer version. It just means that it hasn't been thoroughly tested, hence the importance of performing your own tests. However, I strongly advise against installing any plugins that haven't been updated in more than two years. Luckily, whenever you encounter such a plugin, WordPress itself will warn you either through this message on the official plugin page, as shown in the following screenshot:

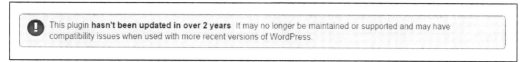

Or, alternatively, inside the plugin details section in the wp-admin, there's a parameter labeled **Last Updated**, as shown in the following screenshot:

Last Updated: 3 years ago

Requires WordPress Version: 2.2
or higher

If everything is fine, you can proceed by clicking on the **Install Now** button. The next screen you see will invite you to activate the plugin (just like when installing a plugin manually), as shown in the following screenshot:

Installing Plugin from uploaded file: jetpack.3.2.zip

Unpacking the package...

Installing the plugin...

Plugin installed successfully.

Activate Plugin | Return to Plugins page

At this point, the plugin has been installed and activated. In other words, it should be fully operational.

There's just one more thing. Some plugins are perfectly functional right after activation, while others require some additional tuning up. The following are the four most likely scenarios:

- You may not have to do anything. Some plugins simply change the way WordPress does some things, and activating them is all you have to do.
- You may have to configure the plugin before it begins to work. Some plugins need you to make choices and set new settings.
- You may also get a set of shortcodes or other elements that you can use to include additional content that the plugin provides inside your posts or pages.
- There may not be a configuration page, but you may have to add some code to one of your theme's template files.

If you're unsure of what to do after you've uploaded and activated your plugin, be sure to read the `readme` file that came with the plugin, or look at the FAQ on the plugin's website.

Many plugin authors accept donations. I strongly recommend giving donations to the authors of the plugins that you find useful. It helps to encourage everyone in the community to continue writing great plugins that everyone can use.

 If, for some reason, the auto-installation process has failed, then you will need to switch to the manual installation described in the previous section.

The must-have pack of plugins

Even though there are over 37,000 plugins available in the official directory, you obviously don't need all of them on your WordPress site at the same time! There is, therefore, a small set that we might call the "must-have pack". And, obviously, my list of must-have plugins can be different from the next guy's, so please treat the following information more as guidance rather than as a written-in-stone necessity. That being said, I am being honest here, and despite the fact that some of my blogs feature more than 25 plugins, all working at the same moment, the essential must-have list consists of only seven plugins. All these plugins handle a specific task geared toward making a WordPress site better and more functional.

Backing up

Backing up is probably the most important task for any website owner, and I'm saying this in all seriousness. For instance, can you imagine a situation in which you lose your whole site overnight with no ability to restore it? This might sound a bit hard to believe right now, but it does happen. If it's a personal blog you've been running, then it's not that tragic. But for a business website, it's a completely different story.

So, one of the main problems with backing up is that it's only effective if it's done regularly. In other words, you need to create backups often and keep them somewhere safe. While that's all fine, who has the time to do this manually? No one, honestly. That's why we'll be using a plugin that does its magic in the background without any supervision required on our part: introducing **WordPress Backup to Dropbox**, available at `https://wordpress.org/plugins/wordpress-backup-to-dropbox/`.

This plugin allows you to handle website backups in an easy to grasp and hassle-free way. It connects with your Dropbox account and then backs up your site regularly on autopilot. It requires only minimal initial setup. After installing and activating it, you need to integrate it with your Dropbox account by going to the **WPB2D** section in your wp-admin.

 If you don't have an account yet, you can sign up to Dropbox for free at https://www.dropbox.com/. As part of the free package, you get 2 GB disk space, which will be more than enough to keep your site backed up.

The activation is done with one click on the orange **Authorize** button, as shown in the following screenshot:

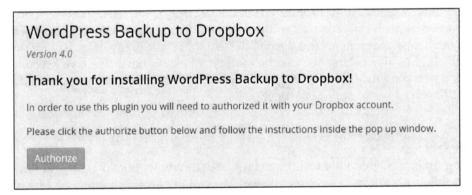

After you're done with that, you get to pick the things you want to back up and also select the directory where you want your backups to sit within your Dropbox. The way I have my site set up is to handle the backups on Sunday at 5 A.M., and to do them weekly (for a busy site, you can even go as far as setting up daily backups) On the **Settings** screen, you can also pick the files and directories that you want excluded from the backups.

Once you click on the main **Save Changes** button your site is integrated with Dropbox and backups will be done automatically, as shown in the following screenshot:

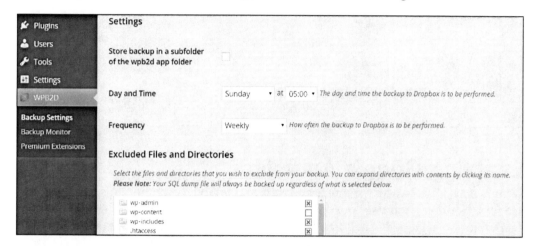

With this plugin, you can also trigger backups manually (on top of the backup scheduling feature). Doing so is a good idea when you first install the plugin, just to check that everything's working fine and to have your initial backup done. You can start the backup in **WPB2D** | **Backup Monitor**. You will be presented with the following screen:

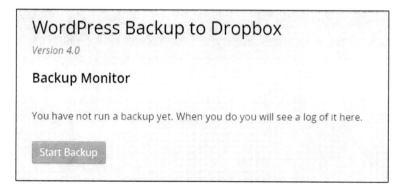

When the backup finishes, you will be able to see everything in your Dropbox account, as shown in the following screenshot:

Enabling Google Analytics

Google Analytics is a very popular site stats and analytics solution. It's free, easy to use for a beginner, and very powerful for anyone willing to get into it a little more deeply. In short, Google Analytics lets you in on a set of stats and data regarding the web traffic your site is getting, including things such as the exact number of visitors (daily, monthly, and so on), traffic sources, your most popular content, and virtually myriads of other statistics. Google Analytics is available at https://www.google. com/analytics/.

To enable Google Analytics on your site, you have to sign up for a Google account first, then enable Analytics, then add your site in the control panel (all available on the official Google Analytics page, along with extensive tutorial documentation), and then take the tracking code that Google gives you and include it in your site. This last step is where the **Google Analytics by Yoast** plugin comes into play and makes the whole thing a lot simpler. You can get it at https://wordpress.org/ plugins/google-analytics-for-wordpress/.

Once you download and activate it, proceed to **Analytics | Settings** (in the wp-admin). Although the plugin has a lot of settings, the only thing you must do in order to make it work is to authenticate the plugin to enable a connection with your Analytics account. Just click on the **Authenticate with your Google account** button. This will redirect you to a page on Google where you have to click on another button, **Grant access**, and then you'll be taken back to your wp-admin. Now you can select your UA-profile that you want to use for monitoring the site.

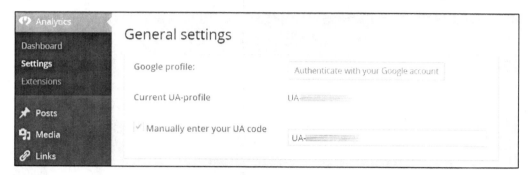

If you're having problems with this semi-automatic way of authentication, you can simply input your Analytics code (called the UA code) manually. This code is visible in your profile at Google Analytics (usually starts with "UA-" and is followed by nine numbers).

Once you're done with the authentication procedure, your site is fully connected to Google Analytics and the traffic stats are being collected. After a while, you can navigate to your profile in Google Analytics and see how your site's been doing in terms of visitor popularity. Also, to get a more immediate indication whether the tracking code has been set correctly or not, you can navigate to the **Real-Time** traffic section inside Google Analytics.

Caching

To be honest, caching is a pretty complicated concept. If you speak "Engineering," then here's the definition: *in computer science, a cache is a component that transparently stores data so that future requests for that data can be served faster.* What it means in plain English is that if you have caching enabled on your site, it will load faster and be much more accessible to your audience/visitors. Luckily, even though the concept itself is not that straightforward, the plugin that enables you to "cache" is. Currently, the top of the line plugin is called **W3 Total Cache**, available at `https://wordpress.org/plugins/w3-total-cache/`.

And it's not just me recommending it. Actually, a number of major hosting companies and experts say that it provides *the* way to get your site optimized fast. More than that, this plugin is also in use on some major blogs around the web.

The installation procedure is the same as with any WordPress plugin. But right after you activate it, you'll see that the usage is quite different. For one thing, it's accessible through a completely new section in the left sidebar.

It's labeled **Performance** and it's placed right below **Settings**. Less than a second after you click on it, you will realize that this plugin is a huge one. It could probably have a completely separate book written about it. So here, I will only share the quick-start guide, so to speak.

Go to **Performance | General Settings** and browse through the page. There's a number of checkboxes labeled **Enable**. Just to get started with the plugin, I advise you to enable (check the checkbox below) the following blocks:

- **Page Cache**
- **Database Cache**
- **Object Cache**
- **Browser Cache**

And, then, click on any of the **Save all settings** buttons. From now on, caching will be fully enabled on your site and your visitors should start experiencing performance improvements right away. Obviously, we've only touched on the possibilities and customizations that this plugin brings to the table, so I encourage you to give it a closer look in your spare time.

Search engine optimization (SEO)

SEO is one of the most popular topics online (at least among website owners). The simple truth is that working on your site's SEO, if done right, will raise its position in search engines (like Google) and will bring you more visitors on a daily basis. The concept is pretty simple in theory, but the work involved in order to achieve this can become a full-time job. If you're not interested in devoting a big chunk of your time to SEO, then at least get the **WordPress SEO** plugin, available at `https://wordpress.org/plugins/wordpress-seo/`, and have the basics handled. The plugin is very popular in the blogosphere. Among others, it's being used by blogs like `http://css-tricks.com/` and `http://www.viperchill.com/`.

Similar to the previous plugin—W3 Total Cache—this one has a custom section within the wp-admin too. It's visible right below **Settings** and it's called **SEO**, as shown in the following screenshot:

The best way to get the core how-to on this plugin is to click on the **Start Tour** button visible at the top of the settings page, as shown in the following screenshot:

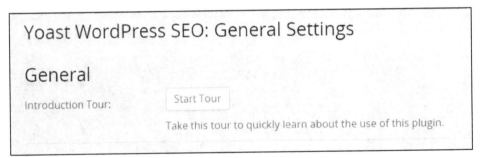

This tour will guide you through the most basic settings and features of the plugin. I really encourage you to spend a while optimizing your site with this plugin because this work will definitely pay off in the long run, or maybe even much sooner.

 There's a separate resource published by the author of the WordPress SEO plugin—Joost de Valk. It's where you should go to get true, in-depth information on how to set up the plugin and also what other things you can do to make your site SEO-friendly. You can find it at `https://yoast.com/articles/wordpress-seo/`.

Securing your site

The issue of site security and hacker attacks is a really serious thing online these days. You might be thinking that no one will try to harm your site because you're not that popular yet, right? Well, the reality can be harsh in this case. Most hacker attacks are not about stealing your revenue or taking over your site as a whole. Usually, they are about including a small piece of code on your site that will link out to other external sites (most of the time either fraudulent sites or "naughty" content). The idea of such an attack is that you won't find out that it ever took place, which is the biggest danger.

Don't sweat though, there's a plugin that will help you with that—**Wordfence Security**, available at `https://wordpress.org/plugins/wordfence/`.

Getting started with this plugin requires only basic setting up. First of all, download and activate it (the usual procedure). Immediately afterward, you will see an invitation to take the tour and input your admin e-mail to get notifications about your site's security, as shown in the following screenshot:

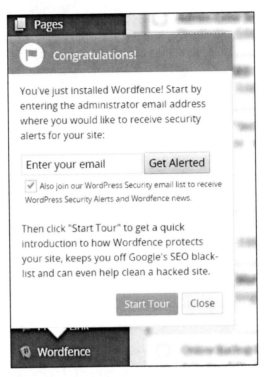

This tour, although short, will present all of the most important features to you and tell you how to work with the plugin effectively. For the most part, the plugin doesn't require any supervision, and thanks to the notification e-mails, you can just sit back, relax, and wait for the plugin to reach out to you, so to speak.

The best way to get started with the plugin is to click on the orange **Start a Wordfence Scan** button, as shown in the following screenshot:

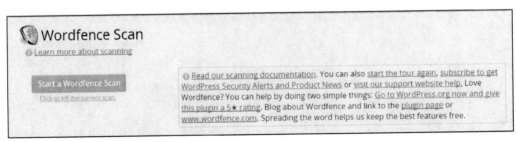

Right after doing so, you will see the scan running (inside the two blocks visible below the scan button you've just clicked). When the scan is done and everything is okay, you will see a success message, as shown in the following screenshot:

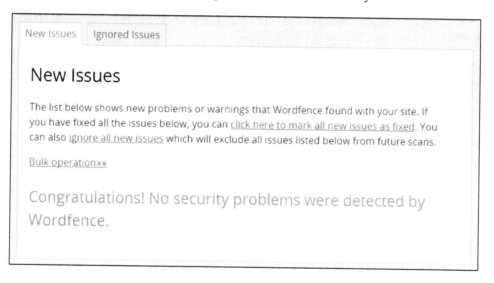

In case there are any problems, Wordfence will display them to you further down the page inside the **New Issues** block, as shown in the following screenshot, and will also give you tips on how to solve them. Unfortunately, or rather fortunately, I don't have a screenshot with actual problems inside to show you.

Apart from the basic scanning functionality, this plugin also gives you the ability to block certain IP addresses from accessing your site, improving your site's performance with caching, and even making your site inaccessible to whole countries (in case some geographical area causes you serious problems).

So, now your site is fully protected against various hacker attacks. As usual, there are a lot more settings available in this plugin. However, I wouldn't advise playing around with them without reading the official documentation first. This type of protection is a very powerful mechanism and it's easy to make a mess if you're not careful.

Social media integration

Social media has taken the online world by storm, and these days we can hardly imagine a website existing without at least some level of social media integration. The benefits of such integration are clearly visible. With a good social media WordPress plugin, you will be able to share your posts with friends and family on all of the most popular social platforms online. More than this, your readers will be able to do so too, effectively growing your audience and making your site more popular. Ultimately, publishing content that goes viral on social media can skyrocket your traffic and make your site visible to thousands of new people every week or even day.

So, the way we're going to make it easier for your readers (and you) to share your content is by displaying some social media buttons on your site or, more accurately, on each post and page that your site consists of.

But there's a problem here. Most social media plugins out there, while doing a great job of enabling your audience to share the content, also display a lot of negative social proof. In short, when you first publish a new post, the share counters on them always say **0 shares** — this simply doesn't look good.

To solve this problem, I've developed a plugin of my own and I'm making it available to you for free since you've already invested money in this book. It's called the **Social Share Starter**. To get the full description on what makes this plugin unique, feel free to visit http://bit.ly/sss-plugin.

The main feature of this plugin is displaying social media share buttons to your visitors, nothing unusual there. However, instead of showing an individual share number for each service, it shows a cumulative number for all of them. Plus, it also allows you to set the minimal displayed number of shares.

Right after downloading and installing the plugin (via manual plugin installation explained earlier in this chapter) you can go to **Settings | Social Share Starter by KK** to set it up.

Settings (all optional):

Minimal displayed number of shares: 10

Maximum width of the whole share buttons block: 560   px

Your Twitter name: @ carlosinho   ⊞

The story source parameter for LinkedIn: newInternetOrder.com

Where to display the buttons: ○ Above the post

⦿ Above + below the post

○ Below the post

Buttons to use: ✓ Facebook

✓ Twitter

✓ Google +

☐ LinkedIn

☐ Pinterest *(Note. the Pinterest button will only appear if there's a featured image assigned to the post.)*

The post IDs you don't want to show the buttons on (comma-separated):

Save Changes

The following are the options you can see in the preceding screenshot:

- **Minimal displayed number of shares**: This is the number of total shares that a given piece of content has to achieve in order for that number to be displayed.

- **Maximum width of the whole share buttons block**: This is just a typical design setting. You can experiment with this pixel value to get the right presentation for your theme.

- **Your Twitter name**: This will be used to construct custom tweets.

- **The story source parameter for LinkedIn**: Just place the name of your site here.

- **Where to display the buttons**: There are three display options available here. You can choose whichever makes the most sense to you.

- **Buttons to use**: The plugin displays buttons for Facebook and Twitter by default. You can also enable three more buttons for Google+, LinkedIn, and Pinterest.

- **The post IDs you don't want to show the buttons on (comma-separated)**: To see an individual post's ID, just go to **Posts** in the wp-admin and then proceed to edit the post. The ID is going to be visible in the URL, right next to `post=`.

After clicking on the **Save Changes** button, you've successfully enabled social media integration on your site. Just to give you an example, the following is what the buttons look like on one of my more popular blog posts:

And the following is what they look like on my **Daily Cooking** blog on a completely new post:

Jetpack

This mysterious name is what one of the most popular plugins of today is called (it's being used by some mainstream blogs on the web, such as Tim Ferriss' `http://www.fourhourworkweek.com/`). Jetpack, by the guys behind WordPress.com, offers a truly exceptional range of features and functionalities. The plugin consists of a number of modules that can be enabled or disabled one by one. This gives you full control over the features you want and don't want to use. Jetpack is available at `https://wordpress.org/plugins/jetpack/`.

After downloading and activating it, you'll see a new section in the wp-admin, but this time, it's right below the **Dashboard**, as shown in the following screenshot:

Inside, you can see all of the available modules and functionalities. First, you should navigate to **Jetpack | Settings** to enable or disable the modules you need/don't need. There are over 30 modules there, so you have a lot to choose from.

In the current version, the modules are Beautiful Math, Carousel, Contact Form, Custom CSS, Custom Content Types, Enhanced Distribution, Extra Sidebar Widgets, Gravatar Hovercards, Infinite Scroll, JSON API, Jetpack Comments, Jetpack Single Sign On, Likes, Markdown, Mobile Theme, Monitor, Notifications, Omnisearch, Phonon, Post By Email, Publicize, Related Posts, Sharing, Shortcode Embeds, Site Icon, Site Verification, Spelling and Grammar, Subscriptions, Tiled Galleries, VideoPress, WP.me Shortlinks, Widget Visibility, WordPress.com Stats, and VaultPress.

As you can see, the list is impressive to say the least. I won't go over each of the modules here in detail because it would probably require a chapter of its own. Instead, I encourage you to click on the name of each module you'd like to look into. Right away, a pop-up window will appear with the description.

That being said, the modules that you will quite possibly find the most useful are Publicize (allows you to share your content automatically with various social media platforms), WordPress.com Stats (gives accessible stats), Spelling and Grammar (an advanced spelling and grammar checker), Contact Form (lets your visitors contact you directly), Monitor (checks if your site is online and sends you an e-mail notification in case it isn't), and Shortcode Embeds (an easy way of including YouTube videos and other external media in your content).

Widgets

Widgets are one of the native mechanisms in WordPress. Their main purpose is to provide us with an easy-to-use way of customizing the sidebars, footers, and headers of our site, with the addition of extra content. Even though the most common placement for widgets is indeed the sidebar, the only actual rule is that a widget can be displayed inside a **widget area**. And, a widget area can be anywhere a theme developer wants it to be. Common widgets contain the following:

- A monthly archive of blog posts
- A clickable list of pages
- A clickable list of recent posts
- A metadata box (containing log in/out links, RSS feed links, and other WordPress links)
- Recent comments posted on the blog
- A clickable list of categories
- A tag cloud
- A block of text and HTML
- A search box

These days, most themes are widget-enabled with one or more widget areas available for use. If I were to simplify this a bit, I'd say that widget areas behave like locations for menus. To control the widgets on your new website, navigate to **Appearance | Widgets. Twenty Fifteen** comes with one widget area. It's simply called **Widget Area**.

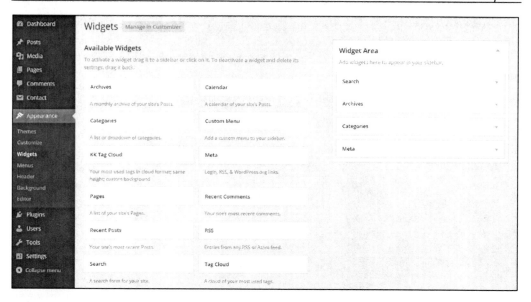

This widget area appears in the left sidebar of the site. Currently, I have a lot of stuff in there (which you can see in the preceding screenshot). Namely, there's a search field, archives, categories, and metadata.

The way you work with widgets is very simple. The only thing you have to do (on the **Appearance | Widgets** screen) is take any of the widgets visible on the left-hand side and drag and drop them into the right-hand area under **Widget Area**. For example, let's take the **Custom Menu** block and drag it all the way to **Widget Area**. The result is as shown in the following screenshot:

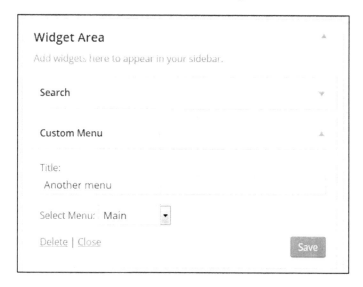

Now, we can give this block a title and also use the dropdown to select the custom menu we want to include in this widget. Currently, there's only one menu, which we created a while ago—**Main**. The following is what the site looks like with this custom menu placed in the left sidebar:

At this point, we have the main menu displayed two times on the site. There's one in the top area, and the second one is inside the left sidebar. As you can see, if you want to place your custom menu somewhere on the site, you have two ways of doing so. You can either assign it inside the **Appearance | Menus** section, or use it as a custom menu widget and place it in any widget area that your theme supports.

Enabling any other type of widget is very similar to the process just described. All you need to do is drag the widget you like and drop it onto the area where you want to have it displayed. Then, once the widget is in place, you can adjust its settings and content.

When it comes to working in the **Appearance | Widgets** section, you can click on the little down arrow to the right of any widget to expand the details and see the options. You can drag a new widget in from the collection of available widgets on the left. You can drag existing widgets up and down to change their order. You can delete a widget by expanding it and then clicking on **Delete**.

Experiment with putting widgets into different widget areas and then refresh your blog to see what they look like. Always be sure to click on **Save** if you make any changes to a widget.

Also, at the bottom of the screen, there's one more section labeled **Inactive Widgets**, as shown in the following screenshot. Many widgets have their settings and parameters. Therefore, even if you don't want to display a particular widget on your site at the moment, but don't necessarily want to lose its settings (in case you'd like to use the widget again in the future), this section is where you should put it. Just like the label says, it's where you can drag your widgets to remove them from the sidebar but keep their settings. This is also where you will find any widgets that were previously active in a sidebar, but that got deactivated automatically after switching to a theme that didn't use the same sidebar naming convention.

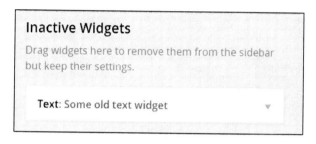

Downloading the example code

You can download the example code files from your account at `http://www.packtpub.com` for all the Packt Publishing books you have purchased. If you purchased this book elsewhere, you can visit `http://www.packtpub.com/support` and register to have the files e-mailed directly to you.

Summary

This chapter was all about expanding the features available on your site and making your content more attractive without the need to touch any source code. Basically, that's the whole idea behind plugins.

Let's face it; most developers don't actually need plugins because they can code things on their own. However, for the rest of the world, plugins are what makes WordPress easy to use and attractive for everyone.

At this point, we know how to control the content of our WordPress site, so now it's time to learn how to control the display. In the next chapter, we will start discussing themes.

6
Choosing and Installing Themes

One of the greatest advantages of using a **Content Management System (CMS)** for your website is that you are able to change the look and feel of your website without being knowledgeable about HTML and CSS. Almost every CMS allows users to customize the look of their website without having to worry about their content being changed. Those managed looks are referred to as themes. On other platforms (for example, Blogger, Joomla!, Drupal, and so on), themes are sometimes called templates or layouts.

Thousands of WordPress themes are available for download free of cost, and thousands more are available at a pretty low cost. Some of the free themes are developed by members of the WordPress community and listed on WordPress' main website at `https://wordpress.org/themes/`, while others can be found across the Web on independent sites.

But before you change the theme of your current website, you will want to know the following:

- Some basic factors about the theme you're considering
- How to find quality themes
- How to choose the theme that best suits your content and audience
- How to install a theme

In this chapter, we will discuss all of the above topics. This chapter is a ground-up guide to using themes. And, in the next chapter, we will discuss the advanced topic of developing your own themes.

If you are using WordPress.com to host your WordPress website, you cannot upload themes to your site. Instead, you have to choose from the hundred or so themes that WordPress.com makes available to you.

Finding themes

There are dozens of websites that offer WordPress themes for you to download and to implement on your own website. Many theme developers offer their themes for free, whereas some charge a small fee. Of course, if you cannot find a free theme that fits your needs, you can always hire a theme developer to create a customized theme for you, or you can be your own theme developer (see *Chapter 7, Developing Your Own Theme*).

WordPress Theme Directory

The first place you should always go to when looking for a theme is the official WordPress Theme Directory at `https://wordpress.org/themes/`. This is where everyone in the WordPress community uploads their free themes and tags them with keywords that describe the basic look, layout, and functions of their themes, as shown in the following screenshot:

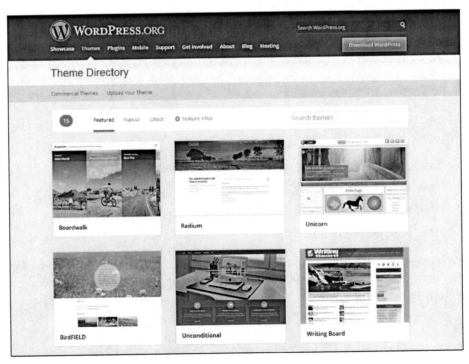

By looking at the list of popular themes on the right (the preceding screenshot), you can see which themes are chosen most often. Twenty Fifteen, as you already know, is the default theme that WordPress uses automatically when you first install it.

To get a better idea of what a theme will look like—apart from what's offered by the thumbnail—just click on the title of the theme (in my case Zerif Lite, at `https://wordpress.org/themes/zerif-lite`). You'll be taken to the theme's detail page, as shown in the following screenshot:

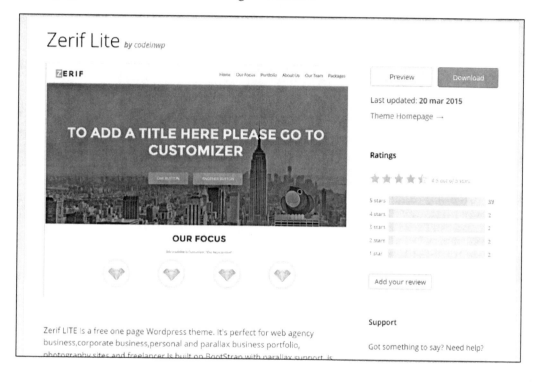

The above page shows you the theme's description, all of the tags that apply to it, the average rating given to it by other users, and some comments on the theme. If you click on the **Preview** button, you'll get to see the theme actually in action, as shown in the following screenshot:

As you browse through the Theme Directory, make sure to take note of any theme you find that you like; we'll discuss how to add it to your WordPress site later on in this chapter.

It's also worth pointing out that each theme in the official directory comes with its own **Support** section and **Ratings** section. You can view them by clicking on one of the links available in the right sidebar, as highlighted in the following screenshot:

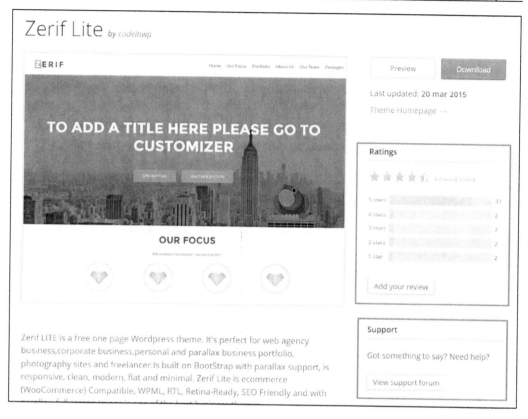

Main types of themes

As mentioned before, there are two main types of themes: free themes and premium (paid) themes. Also, if you don't consider price being a factor here, we can divide the themes into four additional groups: standard themes, child themes, starter themes, and theme frameworks.

We will discuss **child themes** in detail in the next chapter, so for now, let's say that a child theme is a theme that inherits the functionality of another theme—the parent.

Standard themes are themes meant to work in their original form while allowing some basic customizations and tuning up (just like the default theme—Twenty Fifteen).

Starter themes are a relatively new concept in the WordPress world. In short, when using them, you are encouraged to modify the theme files directly, and effectively make them the foundation of the theme you're currently building—like the name suggests, they provide a great starting point for your own theme to be built upon. They are a great solution for developers, but not so much for regular users who just want to download a great theme and be able to use it right out the box.

Theme frameworks are somewhat similar to starter themes (they are meant to be used as the base for your custom theme development), but they usually deliver a larger range of various built-in features, plus they can be used straight out the box as a standalone theme (at least to some extent). In one way, the main difference between starter themes and theme frameworks is that when you get a starter theme, you must put work into it beforehand, in order to make the theme functional. While with frameworks, you get a functional theme right away, but then you are expected to spend time tweaking its various elements to make it fit your site hand-in-glove. The thing with both theme frameworks and starter themes is that they are usually highly code-heavy products. This means that you can't really take full advantage of them if you don't possess any programming skill or don't have anyone on your payroll that does. This may not sound that clear right now, and that's okay. We will explain this concept in more depth in the next chapter.

In the end, standard themes are what most bloggers and site owners work with during their WordPress journeys, especially if they don't need any advanced customizations or don't run purpose-specific websites (such as animated sites, interactive sites, and so on).

Finding more themes

If you can't find a theme in the directory that you like, you have other options. There are other sites with free themes, and also sites that sell themes for a price. Most commercial themes are offered at two or three price points. The first price is simply the cost of buying the theme for your own use, and can be anywhere from $20 to $100. Such a license allows you to use the theme on a single site. The second price is the price you pay if you want to be able to use the theme on multiple sites (domains), or when you need the project graphics (for example, Photoshop documents) and other development files. In this case, it's usually from $60 to $200. The last price point, although not that popular nowadays, is the "exclusive license." You can get it if you want to be the only user of the theme. This can be anywhere from $500 to even $1500, or more.

Let's focus on free versus paid themes here. While every theme in the official directory is free, the rest of the Internet is split in half regarding this. Some sites provide free themes exclusively, while others offer paid ones exclusively. There are also a number of distributors who sit in between. I personally don't advise getting any free themes just from anywhere other than either the official directory or one of the respected theme stores (which offer some free themes as a promotional method). The reason is simple. Only quality themes are allowed into the official directory, and I'm not just talking about the looks or the design. What matters apart from the design is also the code structure and code quality. There's not one theme that features any mysterious blocks of code (such as encrypted code or suspicious external links) that will ever find its way into the official directory. That's what ultimately makes the official directory one of the best sources of free WordPress themes on the Internet.

When it comes to various free themes being released in theme stores, the story is much the same. The "first league" of WordPress themes, so to speak, comprises respected, serious companies. So even when they release a free theme, they can't afford it being low quality or lacking in any other way. Therefore, in most cases, they are safe to use as well.

The last thing we can see online are hundreds, if not thousands, of free themes being released on random websites, promoted through paid advertising, "top themes" lists, advertorial articles, and so on. Let me say this again: I don't advise you to get any of these, even if the designs are attractive. The fact is that you'll never know what sits on the inside and what security breaches can be taken advantage of to hack into such a theme. They are also almost never supported by their creators and there's no theme documentation or updates. In short, it is not worth it.

 If you want to learn more about why unknown-origin free themes are unsafe to use, feel free to visit the article at `http://newinternetorder.com/free-wordpress-themes-are-evil/`.

Finally, if you have some money you'd like to invest in your site and its quality, consider getting a full-blown premium theme or even a premium theme framework. As I mentioned earlier, the price range is around $20 to $100, depending on the manufacturer and the features the theme comes with.

You are welcome to check out any theme provider you wish, but just to make things quicker, the following is a go-to-first list of quality theme stores:

- **StudioPress**: `http://www.studiopress.com/`
- **ThemeIsle**: `https://themeisle.com/`

- **ThemeFuse**: http://themefuse.com/

- **WooThemes**: http://www.woothemes.com/

- **ThemeForest**: http://themeforest.net/category/wordpress

In general, most good commercial theme websites let you see a preview of the theme in action before you buy it. Some also let you customize the theme before download. As with any other online shopping experience, do some research before buying to make sure you'll be getting a quality theme with decent support. There are plenty of badly coded themes out there and even themes with malicious code. Before buying a theme, verify the source of the theme and see if you can find feedback or reviews from anyone else who has purchased it.

To find even more websites that offer themes, just do a Google search for "WordPress themes" or "premium WordPress themes" and you'll get over 70 million hits. Also, keep in mind that you can choose a basic theme now and customize it or create your own from scratch later as you build skills by reading this book.

Some not-design-related theme basics

Let's take a quick look at some factors to consider when choosing and installing themes, just so that you'll be better informed.

The structure of a theme

A WordPress theme is actually a collection of files in a folder/directory. There are no special or unusual formats, just a few requirements for those files in the theme folder. The only requirements for a folder to be a valid WordPress theme are as follows:

1. It should have a style.css file and an index.php file.

2. The style.css file must have the basic theme information in its first five lines.

There are a number of additional files that you'll find in most theme folders. They are as follows:

- A screenshot.png file that is the little thumbnail that shows what the theme looks like

- An images folder where all images associated with the theme live

- A variety of files that are used for different purposes (for example, header.php, footer.php, page.php, single.php, archive.php, and so on)

To learn more about the structure of various theme files and their hierarchy, feel free to read the article at `http://www.codeinwp.com/blog/wordpress-theme-heirarchy/`.

You don't have to worry about these details now, but knowing them will help you identify what's going on in the themes you download for now. This will also be useful in the next chapter where we will discuss making our own theme from scratch.

Also, don't worry if you download a theme and its directory structure looks very different from what's described here. Some theme developers decide to go with their own structure in order to provide some extra features and a more customizable environment. This is mostly the case with various theme frameworks and big premium themes that come with their pre-made child themes.

Factors to consider when choosing a theme

As you look through all of the available themes, you'll see that there is quite a variety when it comes to look, feel, and layout.

To be honest, picking the perfect theme involves effort and some thought. A couple of years ago, there were just a handful of quality websites and stores where you could get your hands on some themes. Now, there are hundreds to thousands of them.

All this results in a situation where there are multiple factors to consider when selecting a theme. It's best if you start with the following.

The purpose of the theme

As I've already mentioned multiple times in this and the previous chapters, nowadays, WordPress is perfectly capable of running any kind of site, and this situation is reflected in the number of available themes. Therefore, the first question to answer is: what do you need the theme for?

Depending on the kind of site you're planning to launch, you should focus on different types of themes. The following are some of the popular possibilities:

- **Traditional blogs**: These are the ones where the content is laid out in a reverse chronological order, with only several pages of static content.

- **Photo blogs**: These are very much like traditional blogs when it comes to the content organization, but in this case, the content consists mainly of photos. This is a popular type of blog among photographers and other creative individuals.

- **Video blogs**: These are very much like photo blogs except now, we're dealing with videos.

- **Small business websites and corporate websites**: Most small business sites don't feature a lot of "posts" like traditional blogs. They usually focus on static pages for providing the most important information about the business (such as contact data, offer, and so on). This type is most commonly used by local businesses such as restaurants, cafes, hotels, and other similar "physical" businesses. Corporate sites are very similar in nature, but are much bigger and feature much more content.

- **One-page micro-websites**: Some people know very well that they need only a minimal online presence, effectively treating their new website as a modern business card. In this case, a solution like a one-page site is perfect for them. In short, one-page sites are just what they sound like; they consist of only one page. However, due to the clever design and structure of that page, the visitor can still get a rich experience while browsing it.

- **Online magazines**: The main difference between traditional blogs and online magazines is that the latter feature a lot more content, with usually as many as 10 or more posts being published every day. This requires good content layout and clear presentation.

- **E-commerce stores**: Traditionally known as online stores or shops, an e-commerce store is every website that offers a shopping cart functionality and allows its visitors to buy a wide range of products, much like they'd do in a traditional store or supermarket.

- **Software/app websites**: These are websites devoted to promoting/selling one specific product. Nowadays, it's usually some kind of an app or other piece of mobile software.

The trick when choosing a theme for your site is to understand its purpose and make your decision based not only on the appearance of the theme but also on the thing you need the theme for, its capabilities, as well as options for further customization. The easiest way to do this is to pay attention to the categories of themes on the site where you're looking for them. For instance, if you go to one of the popular theme stores such as the ones at `http://www.woothemes.com/product-category/themes/`, `https://themeisle.com/allthemes`, or `http://themefuse.com/wp-themes-shop/`, you'll see that all three feature great mechanisms for filtering themes by purpose. Here's how ThemeIsle does it:

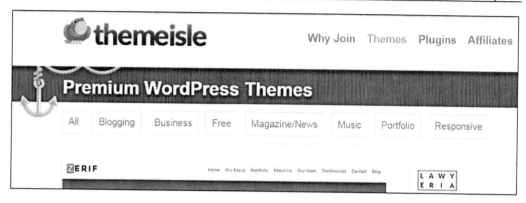

Here's WooThemes:

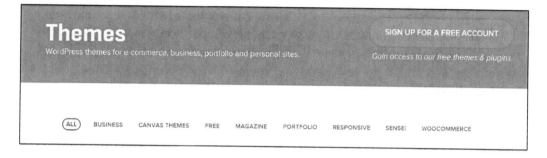

You can also do some research on the Internet and look at what the standard is when it comes to the themes being used in your niche and for your type of site. For example, if you're thinking of launching a photo blog, check what sort of themes other photo blogs use: do they feature a lot of sidebars? How big are the photos they publish? Are there a lot of static pages? And so on. The idea is this: don't reinvent the wheel. If there's a significant number of sites that are similar to the one you're planning to launch, then you should always try learning from them and then make an educated decision when choosing your theme.

Theme licensing

If you're getting a theme from the official directory, then this part doesn't concern you.

However, when getting a theme from a professional theme store, you usually have two or more options regarding the license. As I've mentioned earlier, the price range is usually $20 to $100. Now, there are many licensing models, but the following two are the most popular web-wide:

- **Standard, one-site license**: This allows you to launch one site using the theme. It's the recommended choice if you're just searching for a theme for yourself and don't need to use it on other people's sites as well. This is the cheapest kind of license.
- **Developer license**: This is targeted toward developers and people who want to launch more than one site with a theme. Additionally, the package usually includes PSD project files and other mid-development files (note that some one-site licenses include those as well). Developer licenses can be as much as two times more expensive than the standard, one-site licenses.

Up-to-date themes only

This is probably the most important parameter here. Your theme has to be up-to-date or it will fail to take advantage of all the newest features in WordPress. The only bad news is that you can't know for sure whether a theme is a modern one or not. You can only rely on the details provided by the theme seller. But as bad as it sounds, it's actually not that big of a problem, because big theme stores can't afford to lie in their marketing materials. So, whenever you see a message that the theme is compatible with WordPress version X.X, it's most likely to be true (provided you're getting a theme from a respected company).

Also, a good rule of thumb is to check when the last update took place. Depending on the theme store, this information can be displayed in various places, so I can't give you any specific advice where to look for it. Nevertheless, if you're getting your theme from the official directory at https://wordpress.org/themes/, then you can find this detail in the right sidebar on every individual theme's page (labeled **Last Updated**), as shown in the following screenshot:

Themes that are customizable

When considering a theme, make sure to find answers to the following questions:

- Are the sidebars flexible? Can I choose how many sidebars I want to display?
- Is it widget-ready?
- Does it support custom menus?
- Is it complex or simple? Which do I prefer?
- How flexible is the content and layout? Can I choose the column count and widths?
- Does it support the Customizer feature? Or does it offer a **Theme Settings** page where I can customize layout, category display, home page, and other options?

At this point in WordPress' development, I recommend rejecting any theme that does not support widgets and custom menus, or deliver good customization features. The idea behind all this is that these days, a situation where you can use a theme right out of the box rarely happens, so having at least a couple of customization possibilities goes a very long way.

Themes with responsive structure

This is one of the new parameters among modern themes. Back in the day, if you wanted to make your site mobile-friendly, you needed to get some plugins and additional mobile themes and then enable them to work at the same time. Now, with HTML5 and CSS3, you can use just one theme and be certain that it's going to look great on every possible device (from desktop computers, to laptops, to mobile devices). The keyword to all this is **responsive design/structure**.

Whenever a theme developer indicates that their theme is responsive, it means that it's compatible with all the devices people use to access the Internet these days. In a nutshell, whenever a theme is responsive, this fact will always be mentioned on the official sales/download page.

Support, reviews, and documentation

This is especially important if you're getting a paid premium theme. Quite simply, since you're paying money, you naturally want to be sure that the product you're getting is a quality one that provides good customer service and well-designed functionality, hence the importance of documentation, reviews, and customer support. It's as simple as that.

I do admit that selecting a theme can take a while, especially if you have to remember everything we just covered, but this is work that will definitely pay off. Let's not forget that you're going to be stuck with the theme you choose for at least a year or two (a common scenario), so you definitely don't want to spend money on a low-quality product.

Installing and changing themes

Now that you've chosen the theme you want to use, you'll need to install it into your WordPress website.

You'll have the following two choices, as you did when adding new plugins:

1. *If* the theme you want is in the WordPress Theme Directory, and *if* your server is set up for direct installation, you can add the theme straight from within the wp-admin.

2. If any of those two conditions are not met, you'll have to download, extract, and then upload the theme by hand.

Adding a theme within the wp-admin

As mentioned in the preceding section, you can add a theme directly from within your wp-admin if you've chosen a theme from the WordPress Theme Directory, provided you're using a current-enough version of WordPress and if your server settings allow. First, navigate to **Appearance**, and then click on the **Add New** button (visible at the top), as shown in the following screenshot:

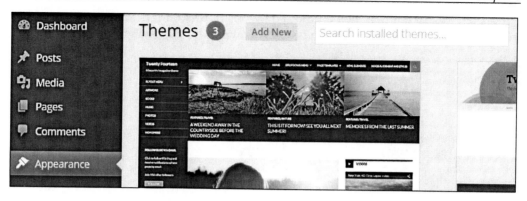

The screen that's going to appear will be very similar to the **Add New Plugins** screen. At the top, you'll see some familiar elements such as various subnavigation links (**Featured, Popular, Latest, Feature Filter**) along with a search box to the right. You can click on any theme displayed on the grid to see its details, along with a nice preview.

By using the Feature Filter (the next screenshot), you can filter out some of the themes based on the functionality they have or don't have. The Feature Filter is a great way to find a theme that offers a specific range of functionalities that you require for the site you're currently building. For instance, you can choose to display themes featuring a responsive layout only. This will make sure that your website is going to look great on all devices, and that's including all desktop computers, as well as mobiles and tablets.

Now, I've already found a theme I like, so I won't bother with filtering and just put the name of the theme in the search box, as shown in the following screenshot:

Once I hover over the theme block, I will see additional links for details, preview, and installation. Clicking on **Preview** is a great way to see how the theme is most likely going to look like in action. Note that at this point, the theme preview will be the same as the preview on the **Theme Directory** page, rather than a preview of your own site's content. Until the theme is installed, you won't see a preview of your own site. If I click on **Install**, the theme will be downloaded and added to my collection of themes automatically (and will be visible in the **Appearance** section in wp-admin), as shown in the following screenshot:

By clicking on the theme, I will see a larger block containing all the details, along with two more links to activate and see the live preview of the theme (which uses the content I currently have on my site), as shown in the following screenshot:

At this point, clicking on the **Activate** button will result in "turning the theme on" and using it as the new design on the website instead of Twenty Fifteen (which I'm using right now).

Downloading, extracting, and uploading

If you can't install a theme from within the wp-admin for whatever reason, you'll have to use the following procedure instead.

Additionally, due to the growing popularity of external theme sources such as various theme stores and independent developers, downloading and installing a theme manually becomes the default way of handling things, and gradually replaces the traditional approach of getting a theme from the official directory.

Therefore, to provide a good example when explaining the manual installation, I'm going to get a theme (a free one) from one of the premium theme stores and guide you through the process of having it installed.

It doesn't matter where you get your themes from, as the installation procedure always starts once you have the theme downloaded to your computer. When this is done, you'll see a ZIP file on your desktop (or in your Downloads folder).

The theme I'd like to try out is called Underscores, and it's a free starter theme available at http://underscores.me/.

Depending on the source of the theme, you might be required to either create a user account, make a purchase, sign up to a newsletter, and so on, in order to get the theme. Of course sometimes, there's just a direct download link. Underscores uses a pretty straightforward model. All you need to do is input the name that you want to use for your theme in the field at http://underscores.me/ (it can be whatever name you wish). After clicking on **GENERATE**, you'll get a ZIP download:

At this point, you can upload the ZIP file through the wp-admin by navigating to **Appearance | Themes** and clicking on the **Add New** button. There, you can click on the **Upload Theme** button, which will take you to the place where you can finally perform the manual installation, as shown in the following screenshot:

The only thing you need to do here is choose the ZIP file from your desktop and then click on the **Install Now** button. After a short while, you will be redirected to the success page where you will be able to activate your new theme.

If this doesn't work, continue with the following steps to extract and upload the theme files manually.

If you're using Mac, the ZIP file may have automatically been unzipped for you, in which case you'll see a folder on your desktop instead of the ZIP file or in addition to the ZIP file. If not, then just do the extraction/unzipping manually so that you do have the theme folder on your desktop.

The following screenshot shows the file contents of the Underscores theme that I downloaded:

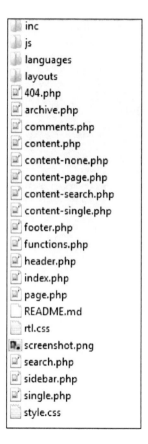

Apart from the mandatory `style.css` file and the `index.php` file, it also has a number of other files that can handle different tasks and take care of various aspects of the display and functionality of the theme.

Now you need to upload the theme folder to your WordPress website. As you did in *Chapter 2, Getting Started with WordPress,* you need to start an FTP connection with your server. Once there, navigate to your WordPress website's installation folder. Next, go to the `wp-content` folder and then to the `themes` folder. You'll see one theme folder in here already named `twentyfifteen` (and possibly others as well). These are the themes that came pre-installed with WordPress. So, the only thing you have to do here is upload the folder that you've just unzipped a minute ago, so that it sits alongside the default `twentyfifteen` folder. And that's it!

At this point, when you go back to **Appearance** in your wp-admin, you will see the new theme waiting there. All that's left to do now is to activate it and use it as the main design of your site.

Summary

This chapter described how to manage the basic look of your WordPress website. You learned where to find themes, why they are useful, what the basic differences between various themes are, how to select the perfect theme for your site, and how to install themes manually as well as through the wp-admin.

In the next chapter, you will learn, step by step, how to build your own theme from scratch.

7
Developing Your Own Theme

At this point, you know how to find themes on the web and install them for use on your WordPress website. But, there's a lot more that WordPress has to offer, particularly in the theme development department. So, in this chapter, you'll learn how to turn your own design into a fully functional WordPress theme that you'll then be able to use on your site. You'll also learn how to convert your theme folder into a ZIP file that can be shared with other WordPress users on the web.

All you will need before we get started are the following:

- Your own design
- The ability to slice and dice your design to turn it into HTML

We'll start out with tips on slicing and dicing, so that your HTML and CSS files are as WordPress-friendly as possible, and then cover the steps for turning that HTML build into a fully functional theme.

Note that I assume that you are already comfortable writing and working with HTML and CSS. You don't need to be familiar with PHP, because I'll be walking you through all of the PHP code.

 This chapter covers only the very basics of theme creation. This topic actually deserves a whole book, and it has one! I highly recommend the book *WordPress Theme Development Beginner's Guide, Rachel McCollin and Tessa Blakeley Silver, Packt Publishing*. This book covers in detail everything you can possibly want to know about creating your own theme, including details such as choosing a color scheme, considering typography, writing the best CSS, and laying out your HTML by using rapid design comping. If this chapter leaves you wanting more, go there!

Setting up your design

Just about any design in the world can be turned into a WordPress theme. However, there are some general guidelines you can follow—both regarding the design and the HTML/CSS build of your theme —that will make your job a lot easier.

Designing your theme to be WordPress-friendly

While you can design your blog any way you want, a good starting point would be with one of the standard blog layouts.

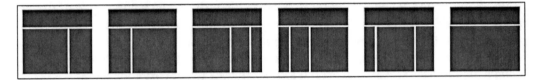

Note that while these standard layouts have differing numbers of columns, they all have these essential parts:

- Header
- Main column
- Side column(s)
- Footer

WordPress expects your theme to follow this pattern, and so, it provides functions that make your work easier. As you're designing your first blog theme, I suggest including these parts. Also, a build that stays within the same general design patterns of WordPress themes will most easily accommodate the existing plugins and widgets.

That being said, a common situation in the WordPress world is to build custom home pages or landing pages (purpose-specific pages, mostly commercial) that feature completely different designs. Therefore, you might stumble upon websites that don't look like they're built with WordPress at first glance. Also, many modern theme frameworks give us the possibility to create such custom home pages, as well as other custom page templates. This is all part of the trend to make WordPress capable of running any kind of website.

The two-column layout is the simplest and the easiest to implement as a WordPress theme, so we'll be using this layout as an example in this chapter.

Now, the example theme I will be working with isn't an ordinary one. I got it from ThemeIsle (`http://themeisle.com/`), one of the new players in the WordPress theme store market. Basically, after a brief talk, one of the co-founders was happy to help me out and agreed to provide a custom and free design for everybody to use (you can find both the HTML design and the complete WordPress theme that was built on it in the official code bundle for this chapter). Here's what it looks like:

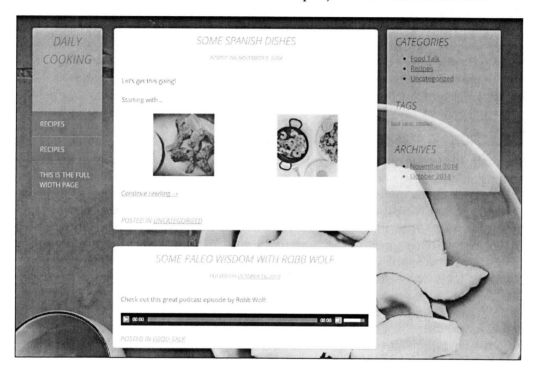

The HTML structure of the design was built on the basis of the _S starter theme (which is read as **Underscores**, `http://underscores.me/`), and the visual elements were all done through CSS, with only minimal modifications to the original HTML structure.

Three paths of theme development

Essentially, there are three paths you can follow when developing your new theme. You can either work from the ground up, by building the HTML structure and the functional structure of the theme by hand. Or, you can work on top of an existing theme framework, where you only have to adapt your design to work on the structure provided by the framework itself. Or, you can go for a solution that sits somewhere in between. All of these paths have their pros and cons though, as always.

Building a theme from the ground up

The main advantage of building a theme from the ground up is the massive educational value of this path. When you're developing a theme from scratch, you're learning the basics of theme construction and function. This kind of knowledge goes a long way for your future projects in WordPress.

On the other hand, it's also the longest of the three paths. In a professional production environment (among people designing and developing themes as a profession), creating themes from scratch is a highly time-consuming approach, making it quite ineffective. And, it's not that much about adapting the design (which always must be done with theme frameworks as well); it's more about building the core functionality of the theme.

Building a theme with a framework

The main advantage of this approach is its time efficiency and the quality of the final result. For instance, if you're building a theme from scratch, you have to make sure to keep your theme up-to-date long after the development process has been finished. The thing is that WordPress gets updated very frequently (around once every 51 days), and many features change their purpose over time and get completely erased or replaced with new ones. In such a scenario, only modern themes that are kept up-to-date can take full advantage of these features. Updating your theme will obviously take a massive amount of work. This is where theme frameworks come into play. In essence, theme frameworks are themes with a very minimalist design and no visually complicated aspects. The purpose of frameworks is to make them the base of any future theme by acting as the parent theme. So, the fact that the framework itself has no design allows every creator to introduce almost any design imaginable while taking full advantage of the features and constructions provided inside the framework. Now, the strength of quality frameworks is that they get updated almost as frequently as WordPress plugins. In short, if you're using a framework, you don't have to worry about your theme going out of date. Whenever there's an update available, you can simply perform it and forget about the whole thing.

This brings me to the main disadvantage of using theme frameworks. Most of the time theme frameworks are big and complex pieces of web software (PHP scripts). So, if you want to be able to use them effectively, you'll have to spend a significant amount of time learning the framework. On top of this, if you decide to switch to a different framework later down the road, you'll have to learn it all over again (frameworks are usually very different from each other). As you can see, reaping the benefits of using frameworks has its price.

Here are some of the popular theme frameworks (both paid and free ones):

- **Thematic** (free): `http://themeshaper.com/thematic/`
- **Gantry** (free): `http://www.gantry-framework.org/`
- **Genesis** (paid): `http://my.studiopress.com/themes/genesis/`
- **Thesis** (paid): `http://diythemes.com/`
- **Some frameworks listed by WordPress**:
  `https://codex.wordpress.org/Theme_Frameworks`

Building a theme with a starter theme

Finally, there's also a third solution, one that's somewhere in the middle between building a theme from the ground up and using a framework. What I'm talking about is using a starter theme.

A starter theme—like the one we'll be using in this chapter to create the base of our HTML structure—is a great solution to make sure that the theme you're building has the right scaffolding and that it's up-to-date with modern practices and optimized to be used for a WordPress site. Apart from this, the starter theme leaves you all the freedom in the world to adjust your creation however you wish (you have almost the same freedom as you do with from-the-ground-up theme building).

In other words, a starter theme provides us with the best of both worlds, that is, starting from scratch and using a framework. We can learn the basic structure of WordPress themes this way, and at the same time, we don't need to worry about making any silly mistakes because the core of the task is being handled by the starter theme itself.

So, in short, going with a starter theme is what we're going to do here. The main idea is to use it to learn the craft and get to know all the basic structures and mechanisms sitting inside WordPress.

Your journey with theme development starts once you have a graphic design prepared in Photoshop or some other similar tool. You can also take the code bundle for this chapter and work with the design from there. Either way, the next step is to turn it into some HTML code.

Converting your design into code

The next step towards turning your ideal design into a WordPress theme is to slice images out of your design and write HTML and CSS files that put it all together. For the purpose of this chapter, I assume that you already know basically how to do this. We'll cover some pointers on how to do your slicing and dicing in a way that will fit best into WordPress.

Let's get down to business and take a look at the HTML structure that was generated (by the _S starter theme) for the purpose of the theme we're building here. Just to remind you, the starter theme can be generated at http://underscores.me/.

Examining the HTML structure

The following is the very basic layout of the HTML file for my food blog design; I'm showing it just to give you a general understanding of what we're going to be working on:

```
<!DOCTYPE html>
<html lang="en-US">
<head>
<meta charset="UTF-8">
<meta name="viewport" content="width=device-width, initial-
    scale=1">
<link rel="profile" href="http://gmpg.org/xfn/11">
<link rel="stylesheet" id="open-sans-css"
    href="//fonts.googleapis.com/css?family=Open+Sans%3A300italic
    %2C400italic%2C600italic%2C300%2C400%2C600&#038;subset=latin%2
    Clatin-ext&#038;ver=4.0.1" type="text/css" media="all" /> <!--
embedding Google Fonts -->
<link rel="stylesheet" id="daily-cooking-custom-style-css"
    href="style.css" type="text/css" media="all" /> <!--
    embedding the style sheet for the design -->
<title>Daily Cooking</title>
</head>

<body>
<div id="page">
  <header id="masthead" class="site-header" role="banner">
    <div class="site-branding">
      <h1 class="site-title">Daily Cooking</h1>
    </div>
    <nav id="site-navigation" class="main-navigation"
      role="navigation">
      <!-- placeholder for site navigation -->
```

```
      </nav>
    </header>

    <div id="content" class="site-content">
      <div id="primary" class="content-area"><main id="main"
        class="site-main" role="main">
      <article>
        <header class="entry-header">
          <h1 class="entry-title">Hello world!</h1>
        </header>

        <div class="entry-content">
          <p>Welcome!</p>
          <!-- main content block -->
        </div>

        <footer class="entry-footer">
          <!-- footer of the content block -->
        </footer>
      </article>
      </main></div>

      <div id="secondary" role="complementary">
        <!-- sidebar -->
      </div>
    </div>

    <footer class="site-footer" role="contentinfo">
      <!-- main footer of the page -->
    </footer>
  </div>

  </body>
  </html>
```

You can see that I've separated out these major parts:

- The header is in an HTML5 `<header>` tag

- As part of it, there's the main site navigation—also an HTML5 tag `<nav>`

- Next, we have the main content block: `<div id="content" class="site-content">`; each individual post will be displayed inside separate HTML5 `<article>` tags

- After this, we have a section that handles the sidebar: `<div id="secondary" role="complementary">`. The sidebar is set with the `role="complementary"` attribute. Roles are one of the relatively new HTML parameters. Essentially, a role attribute describes the role that the element plays in the context of the document. In this case, the sidebar is complementary to the main content (and if you pay close attention, you'll notice that the main part, that is, the content, is indeed set to `role="main"`). In general, such attributes are meant to explain the purpose of elements in the HTML structure.

- Finally, there's the footer using the `<footer>` tag. Keep in mind that this is HTML5 and it may not work on older web browsers.

Now that I've got my basic layout, I'm going to add a few more HTML elements to flesh it out a bit, including more information in `<head>` as well as in the main content box, plus some additional CSS. Then, I'll fill up the sidebar, header, content, and footer.

Examining the CSS

Generally, a very good practice in web development is to start your CSS design by resetting all the default styles used by various web browsers. The main issue and the reason why this is an important step is that most popular web browsers, or should I say every single one of them, have their own *default* set of CSS styles. And, if you want your theme to look exactly the same in every browser, you have to start your work by resetting these styles, whatever they might actually be. The good thing about it is that you don't have to do it by hand. You can just use one of the reset scripts available on the Internet. For the purpose of this description, I'm using the reset script that's part of our starter theme. Keep in mind that every piece of code that's listed in this chapter is also available in the official code bundle that came with your book. So, what we're doing first is just having the following CSS at the beginning of our new `style.css` file:

```
/* setting up the basic elements - starter setup */
html, body, div, span, applet, object, iframe,
h1, h2, h3, h4, h5, h6, p, blockquote, pre,
a, abbr, acronym, address, big, cite, code,
del, dfn, em, font, ins, kbd, q, s, samp,
small, strike, strong, sub, sup, tt, var,
dl, dt, dd, ol, ul, li,
fieldset, form, label, legend,
table, caption, tbody, tfoot, thead, tr, th, td {
  border: 0;
  font-family: inherit;
```

```css
    font-size: 100%;
    font-style: inherit;
    font-weight: inherit;
    margin: 0;
    outline: 0;
    padding: 0;
    vertical-align: baseline;
}

html {
    font-size: 62.5%;
    overflow-y: scroll;
    -webkit-text-size-adjust: 100%;
    -ms-text-size-adjust: 100%;
    box-sizing: border-box;
}
*, *:before, *:after {
    box-sizing: inherit;
}

body {
    background: #fff;
}

/* resetting the basic content blocks */
article, aside, details, figcaption, figure, footer, header, main,
    nav, section {
    display: block;
}

/* resetting the lists */
ol, ul {
    list-style: none;
}

table {
    border-collapse: separate;
    border-spacing: 0;
}
caption, th, td {
    font-weight: normal;
    text-align: left;
}
```

```
blockquote:before, blockquote:after, q:before, q:after {
  content: "";
}
blockquote, q {
  quotes: " "";
}

a:focus {
  outline: thin dotted;
}

a:hover, a:active {
  outline: 0;
}

a img {
  border: 0;
}
```

Let's now take a look at the actual CSS — the things that build our design and not just *reset* it. First, we'll review the CSS that displays everything you see in the design. Note that I've got styles for all of the key elements such as header, sidebar, main content area, and footer.

Also, please notice that this is just the *scaffolding*, so to speak. It only indicates the individual areas of the final CSS stylesheet. Listing the complete version here wouldn't be very helpful as I'm sure that you're much more likely to copy and paste the code from the official bundle rather than rewriting it straight from here. Besides, talking about CSS isn't the main thing we're focusing on in this book anyway. Therefore, I'm including the complete version in the aforementioned code bundle, and right now, I'm only presenting the individual areas of the CSS. This is just to make the whole thing easier to grasp once you look at the complete stylesheet. To be honest, the final CSS isn't actually that complex from a CSS design point of view, but it is quite lengthy. Here's the simplified version.

Let's start with the typography settings and various standard content elements. I'm not showcasing the individual styles here as they are kind of basic and don't have a huge role in our WordPress site structure:

```
/*---------
Typography
-----------*/
body, button, input, select, textarea {}
h1, h2, h3, h4, h5, h6 {}
```

```
h1 a, h2 a, h3 a, h4 a, h5 a, h6 a {}
p {}
b, strong {}
dfn, cite, em, i {}
blockquote {}
address {}
pre {}
code, kbd, tt, var {}
abbr, acronym {}
mark, ins {}
sup, sub {}
small {}
big {}
/*--------
Elements
--------*/
hr {}
ul, ol {}
dt {}
dd {}
img {}
figure {}
table {}
button, input, select, textarea {}
```

What follows next is a set of rules that will take care of the alignment, general design structure, the headers, and other typical HTML elements:

```
.site-header {
  width: 15%;
  float: left;
  height: auto;
  background: #279090;
  margin-right: 2.5%;
  border-radius: 6px;
}

#page {
  width: 1160px;
  margin: 0 auto;
  margin-top: 50px;
  position: relative;
  overflow: auto;
}
```

```
#primary {
  width: 56%;
  float: left;
}

/* Navigation */
.main-navigation {
  clear: both;
  display: block;
  float: left;
  width: 100%;
}

/* Alignments */
.alignleft {
  display: inline;
  float: left;
  margin-right: 1.5em;
}
.alignright {
  display: inline;
  float: right;
  margin-left: 1.5em;
}
.aligncenter {
  clear: both;
  display: block;
  margin: 0 auto;
}
```

The center part of the site structure is where the posts and pages will be displayed. The code for it is as follows:

```
.site-content .page, .site-content .post {
  margin-bottom: 40px;
  background-color: white;
  border-radius: 6px;
}

.entry-header h1.entry-title {
  text-align: center;
}

.site-content .entry-content {
  padding: 10px 20px;
}
```

The code for the main sidebar is this:

```css
#secondary {
  width: 24.5%;
  float: left;
  height: auto;
  margin-left: 2%;
  opacity: 0.6;
  background-color: white;
  border-radius: 3px;
  padding: 0 10px;
}
```

And finally, the code for the footer is as follows:

```css
.site-footer {
  float: right;
  padding: 20px;
}
```

Inside this stylesheet, you will find many specific classes that aren't just my own creations but rather come from WordPress itself. Here's what I mean. When WordPress spits out items that include page lists, category lists, archive lists, images, and galleries, it gives many of these items a particular class name. If you know these class names, you can prepare your stylesheet to take advantage of them. This is one more reason why we're using a starter theme here. With it, we don't have to worry about any of this.

 To learn more about this, feel free to check out `http://css-tricks.com/back-basics-wordpress-css-understanding-native-classes/` for an in-depth post on one of the top websites about CSS on the web.

For example, when you add an image to a post or page, WordPress gives you the option to have it to the right or left, or at the center of the text. Depending on what you choose, WordPress will give the image the `alignleft`, `alignright`, or `aligncenter` class. These classes, for example, are handled in the `Alignments` section of our CSS stylesheet. Another thing is that when you add an image with a caption, WordPress gives it the `wp-caption` class. This particular thing is handled in the `Captions` section of the stylesheet we're using. WordPress uses many other classes that you can take advantage of when building your stylesheet. I've listed a few of them in *Chapter 12, Creating a Non-blog Website Part 2 – Community Websites and Custom Content Elements*.

Now that you've got your HTML and CSS lined up, you're ready for the next step: turning the HTML build into a WordPress theme.

Converting your build into a theme

You'll be turning your HTML build into a theme, which is composed of a number of template files and other scripts. We are going to first dig into the inner workings of a theme so as to get familiar with how it's put together. Then, we'll actually turn the HTML build into a theme folder that WordPress can use. Finally, we'll include WordPress functions that spit out content. As I mentioned in an earlier chapter, doing development for your WordPress website in a local environment can make the whole process much smoother. Consider getting a server up and running on your home computer by using WAMP, MAMP, or some other way to install Apache and MySQL.

Creating the theme folder

The first step to turning your HTML build into a theme is to create your theme folder and give it everything it needs to be recognized as a theme by WordPress. Let's look at an overview of the steps and then take them one by one:

1. Name your folder and create backup copies of your build files.
2. Prepare the essential files.
3. Add a screenshot of your theme named `screenshot.png`.
4. Upload your folder.
5. Activate your theme.

Let's take these steps one by one now:

1. Name your folder and create backup copies of your build files.

    You'll want to give your build folder a sensible name. I'm naming my theme Daily Cooking Custom because it's a custom version of a theme provided by the ThemeIsle team, and since it is meant to run my cooking blog, the new name kind of makes sense. I'll name the folder `daily-cooking-custom`.

    Now, I suggest creating backup copies of your HTML and CSS files. As you'll eventually be breaking up your build into template files, you can easily lose track of where your code came from. By keeping a copy of your original build, you'll be able to go back to it for reference.

2. Prepare the essential files.

    WordPress has only the following two requirements to recognize your folder as a theme:

    ◦ A file called `index.php`

    ◦ A file called `style.css` with an introductory comment

Just rename your main design's HTML file to `index.php`, and this takes care of the first requirement.

To satisfy the second requirement, your stylesheet needs to have an introductory comment that describes the basic information for the whole theme: title, author, and so on. Also, it has to be at the very top of the stylesheet. I've added this comment to my `style.css` file:

```
/*
Theme Name: Daily Cooking Custom
Theme URI: http://newinternetorder.com/
Author: Karol K & ThemeIsle
Author URI: http://themeIsle.com/
Description: Daily Cooking Custom is a custom theme created
   for the buyers of "WordPress Complete"
Version: 1.0
License: GNU General Public License v2 or later
License URI: http://www.gnu.org/licenses/gpl-2.0.html
Text Domain: daily-cooking-custom
Tags: brown, orange, tan, white, yellow, two-columns,
   right-sidebar, flexible-width, custom-header, custom-
   menu, translation-ready
*/
```

The preceding structure has been created on the basis of the template available at `https://codex.wordpress.org/Theme_Development#Theme_Stylesheet`. Whenever you're creating a new theme, it's always good to check the current recommended template beforehand. When you add this comment section to your stylesheet, just replace all of the details with those that are relevant to your theme.

3. Add a screenshot.

    Remember when we first learned how to activate a new theme that there were thumbnail versions of the themes in your **Appearance** tab? You'll want a thumbnail of your own design. It has to be a PNG file with the name `screenshot.png`. Just do the following:

    1. Flatten a copy of your design in Photoshop.
    2. Change the image width to 880 px and the height to 660 px.
    3. Save it for the web as a PNG-8 file.

    The preceding requirements (880 x 660 px) are the current ones at the time of writing. To get the latest guidelines at any point in time, please revisit the official codex at `https://codex.wordpress.org/Theme_Development#Screenshot`

4. Name your file `screenshot.png` and save it in your build folder.

5. Upload your folder.

   Using your FTP software, upload your template folder to `wp-content/ themes/` in your WordPress build. It will share the themes folder with `twentyfifteen` and any other theme you've added as you installed WordPress. In the following screenshot, you can see my `daily-cooking-custom` theme living in the `themes` folder:

   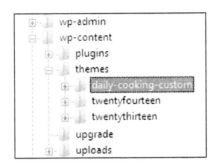

6. Activate your theme.

   You've got the absolute basic necessities in there now, so you can activate your theme (although it won't look like much yet). Log in to your wp-admin and navigate to **Appearance**. There you'll see your theme waiting for you. As you can see, I've created a nice screenshot for my theme, with the name of the theme on it for easier identification:

At this point, you can activate your new theme and continue working on it to include WordPress-generated content and make it into a full-fledged WordPress theme in general. Don't be alarmed if the theme doesn't look perfectly right after activation though. There's still a lot of work to do. This is another good reason to have a development server. You wouldn't want to have this incomplete theme active on a live site while you finish the final pieces in the background.

Note that not every theme installation goes as expected, and sometimes, you have to deal with an error. In most cases, WordPress will let you know what went wrong through a notification. Every once in a while, however, the activation can end up in a critical error and your whole site can go blank. If that happens, simply rename the new theme's folder or delete it completely. This will force WordPress to switch to the default theme, and things should get back to normal. From there, you can start looking for the issue that caused the crash in the first place.

Speaking of final pieces, your theme is now ready to have all of the WordPress content added, so let's do just that!

How to create basic WordPress content

Right now, your `index.php` file is your only theme file. We'll be breaking it up into template files a bit later. First, we need to include WordPress functions that will spit out your actual content into your theme.

The functions.php file

In short, the `functions.php` file is meant to set up your theme and provide some helper functions and settings to make the usage of the theme easier. Apart from this, the functions file also has many other applications that we're not going to be discussing here, as it is beyond the scope of this book. In essence, `functions.php` is a kind of file that allows you to perform a very wide scope of modifications. Even though there is a set of standard things that should always be taken care of when dealing with a functions file, no one restricts you from doing virtually anything you wish. For instance, you can create a classic PHP function such as `my_function_name()` and then call it from within one of your template files (such as `index.php`) through `<?php my_function_name(); ?>`, but this is just one of the possible scenarios.

Although this isn't a requirement, it's always good to start your functions file with the following lines of code (just as a good reference point):

```php
<?php
/**
 * Daily Cooking Custom functions and definitions.
 *
 * @package Daily Cooking Custom
 */
```

The preceding lines of code provide the essential information about the theme.

Next in line is the $content_width variable. Here's how to use it:

```php
if(!isset($content_width))
    $content_width = 610; //pixels
```

This parameter is often overlooked by many theme developers despite the fact that it can mean a lot to the final form of the theme. It's simply the maximum width of the content area allowed in your theme (in pixels). For example, if you ever upload a picture that massively exceeds this value, it will always be scaled down to prevent messing up your site's layout. The exact value you should set depends on your CSS and design. The value 610 in the preceding example is just that—an example.

The next part in our functions.php file is the setup of the default features that the theme is going to enable:

```php
if(!function_exists('daily_cooking_custom_setup')) :
function daily_cooking_custom_setup() {

    //Make theme available for translation.
    //Translations can be filed in the /languages/ folder.
    load_theme_textdomain('daily-cooking-custom',
        get_template_directory().'/languages');

    //Adds RSS feed links to <head> for posts and comments.
    add_theme_support('automatic-feed-links');

    //Let WordPress manage the document title.
    /* By adding theme support, we declare that this theme does not
       use a hard-coded <title> tag in the document head, and expect
       WordPress to provide it for us. */
    add_theme_support('title-tag');

    //This theme uses wp_nav_menu() in one location.
    register_nav_menus(array(
```

```
    'primary' => __('Primary Menu', 'daily-cooking-custom'),
));

//Switch default core markup for search form, comment form, and
    comments to output valid HTML5.
add_theme_support('html5', array(
    'search-form', 'comment-form', 'comment-list',
        'gallery', 'caption',
));

//Enable support for Post Formats.
add_theme_support('post-formats', array(
    'aside', 'image', 'video', 'quote', 'link',
));

//Set up the WordPress core custom background feature.
add_theme_support('custom-background', apply_filters(
    'daily_cooking_custom_custom_background_args', array(
    'default-color' => 'ffffff',
    'default-image' => '',
)));
}
endif; //daily_cooking_custom_setup
add_action('after_setup_theme', 'daily_cooking_custom_setup');
```

The preceding function—`daily_cooking_custom_setup()`—is going to be executed at just the right time, triggered by the `after_setup_theme` action called at the end to set up the basic features of our theme properly. Most of the code is pretty self-explanatory due to the comments, but there's just one thing I'd like to mention individually, which is this part (registering the menu):

```
register_nav_menus(array(
    'primary' => __('Primary Menu', 'daily-cooking-custom'),
));
```

This is a small piece of code that will let us assign any custom menu to appear as the primary menu later on. It is also what we'll use to set in our new theme. In addition, the preceding function allows you to register even more menu areas if you wish so, and all you'd have to do is add the following line: `'secondary' => 'Secondary Menu'`.

Next, let's enable our stylesheet CSS file to load with our theme, or more accurately, to be "enqueued" and then load in precisely at the right moment. Here's how to do so:

```
function daily_cooking_custom_scripts() {
  wp_enqueue_style('daily-cooking-custom-style', get_stylesheet_
uri());
}
add_action('wp_enqueue_scripts', 'daily_cooking_custom_scripts');
```

As you can see, there's only one stylesheet here. It is enabled by the very first line in the function.

Nowadays, the preceding code is the best practice for including various CSS styles and JS scripts into our themes. You can still go with the traditional (alternative) approach by placing `<link rel="stylesheet" href="<?php bloginfo('stylesheet_url'); ?>" type="text/css" media="screen" />` inside the header section of your design, but it will lower the performance of your site as CSS styles and various JS scripts tend to take a long time to load. So, it's always better to deal with them through the modern `wp_enqueue_scripts` handle.

The preceding code closes our first template-like `functions.php` file. Later, we will add new lines to it to make it even more functional. Now, the interesting part is that there is no closing PHP tag in the functions file (no `?>`). This is not a typo or anything. It's intentional. Since most of the file is pure PHP, we don't need this tag for anything.

The complete file is as follows:

```php
<?php
/**
 * Daily Cooking Custom functions and definitions
 *
 * @package Daily Cooking Custom
 */

/**
 * Set the content width based on the theme's design and stylesheet.
 */
if(!isset($content_width))
  $content_width = 610; //pixels

if(!function_exists('daily_cooking_custom_setup')) :
/**
 * Sets up theme defaults and registers support for various WordPress
features.
 */
function daily_cooking_custom_setup() {
```

```
//Make theme available for translation.
load_theme_textdomain('daily-cooking-custom',
  get_template_directory().'/languages');

//Adds RSS feed links to <head> for posts and comments.
add_theme_support('automatic-feed-links');

//Let WordPress manage the document title.
add_theme_support('title-tag');

//This theme uses wp_nav_menu() in one location.
register_nav_menus(array(
  'primary' => __('Primary Menu', 'daily-cooking-custom'),
));

//Switch default core markup for search form, comment form, and
  comments to output valid HTML5.
add_theme_support('html5', array(
  'search-form', 'comment-form', 'comment-list', 'gallery',
    'caption',
));

//Enable support for Post Formats.
add_theme_support('post-formats', array(
  'aside', 'image', 'video', 'quote', 'link',
));

//Set up the WordPress core custom background feature.
add_theme_support('custom-background', apply_filters(
  'daily_cooking_custom_custom_background_args', array(
  'default-color' => 'ffffff',
  'default-image' => '',
)));
}
endif; //daily_cooking_custom_setup
add_action('after_setup_theme', 'daily_cooking_custom_setup');

/**
 * Enqueue scripts and styles.
 */
function daily_cooking_custom_scripts() {
  wp_enqueue_style('daily-cooking-custom-style',
    get_stylesheet_uri());}
add_action('wp_enqueue_scripts', 'daily_cooking_custom_scripts');
```

Just to remind you, this whole `functions.php` file can be found inside the code bundle for this chapter.

The <head> tag

Okay, let's move on to our index.php file and the things we can do inside of it. In the following section of the chapter, we're going to be altering specific lines of code from the original HTML structure.

First, we'll set up the <head></head> section of your HTML file. Let's start with charset and the device width parameter. Simply, here are the two lines to begin with right after the opening <head> tag:

```
<meta charset="<?php bloginfo('charset'); ?>">
<meta name="viewport" content="width=device-width, initial-
    scale=1">
```

The first one holds the character set that your blog uses. The other defines the width of the viewport used. Here, it's set to the width of the device being used (this allows everyone to view the site correctly, including desktop computer users, iPad users, and Android phone users).

Next, you need to add another important chunk of code: First, to put header tags into your theme for the pingback URL; second, other miscellaneous WordPress stuff. Add the following lines in your <head> section:

```
<link rel="profile" href="http://gmpg.org/xfn/11">
<link rel="pingback" href="<?php bloginfo('pingback_url'); ?>">
```

Finally, add the following line right before the closing </head> tag (it takes care of displaying your site's title and enabling a number of WordPress-specific functionalities):

```
<?php wp_head(); ?>
```

Now, add the body_class() function to the body tag, so it looks like this:

```
<body <?php body_class() ?>>
```

Your header now looks something like this:

```
<!DOCTYPE html>
<html <?php language_attributes(); ?>>
<head>
<meta charset="<?php bloginfo('charset'); ?>">
<meta name="viewport" content="width=device-width, initial-
    scale=1">
<link rel="profile" href="http://gmpg.org/xfn/11">
<link rel="pingback" href="<?php bloginfo('pingback_url'); ?>">
```

```
<?php wp_head(); ?>
</head>

<body <?php body_class(); ?>>
```

The header and footer

It's time to start adding some content. Here, we'll take care of things such as displaying a link to the blog's home page, displaying the blog's title, displaying the tagline, and displaying the main navigation.

All these operations are pretty simple, so let's just take a look at the lines of code that take care of them. Then, we'll put these lines of code in just the right place within our HTML structure.

First, we have the code that displays the site's main URL:

```
<?php echo esc_url(home_url('/')); ?>
```

Next, the code that displays the site's title is as follows:

```
<?php bloginfo('name'); ?>
```

Here's the code for displaying the tagline:

```
<?php bloginfo('description'); ?>
```

The preceding two lines pull information from where you set the blog name and description in wp-admin, and you can simply change them from the **Settings | General** page.

Lastly, displaying the main navigation is done through the following code:

```
<?php wp_nav_menu(array('theme_location' => 'primary')); ?>
```

The wp_nav_menu() function is a built-in way of displaying the navigation menu. It will take care of the proper HTML structure of the menu and all its elements. In other words, you don't have to worry about anything else other than using this one line of code.

Now, the part of your HTML that describes the header looks like what the following listing presents. As you can see, additionally, we're linking the logo to the home page—a standard practice in modern website design:

```
<div id="page" class="hfeed site">
  <a class="skip-link screen-reader-text" href="#content"><?php
    _e( 'Skip to content', 'daily-cooking-custom' ); ?></a>
```

```
<header id="masthead" class="site-header" role="banner">
  <div class="site-branding">
    <h1 class="site-title"><a href="<?php echo esc_url
      (home_url('/')); ?>" rel="home"><?php bloginfo('name');
      ?></a></h1>
    <h2 class="site-description"><?php bloginfo('description');
      ?></h2>
  </div><!-- .site-branding -->

  <nav id="site-navigation" class="main-navigation" role=
    "navigation">
    <button class="menu-toggle" aria-controls="menu" aria-
      expanded="false"><?php _e( 'Primary Menu', 'daily-cooking-
      custom' ); ?></button>
    <?php wp_nav_menu(array('theme_location' => 'primary')); ?>
  </nav><!-- #site-navigation -->
</header><!-- #masthead -->

<div id="content" class="site-content">
```

Are you wondering why you should bother with some of this when you could have just typed your blog title, URL, and description to the theme? One reason is that if you ever want to change your blog's title, you can just do it in one quick step in wp-admin and it will change all over your site. The other reason is that if you want to share your theme with others, you'll need to give them the ability to easily change the name through their own wp-admin panels. Keep in mind, anything, anything at all, that will change from site to site based on the site's purpose and content, should not be hardcoded into the theme but should be dynamically generated.

Now, when I refresh the site, there's the actual blog title in the header:

The three links visible in the header are live links coming from one of my custom menus. Just to tie things up, I'm going to add some code to my footer to display the **Proudly powered by WordPress** message, and to include the wp_footer() function/hook that's often used by many plugins in one way or the other, so every theme should feature it. The code for my footer section now looks like the following:

```
</div><!-- #content -->

<footer id="colophon" class="site-footer" role="contentinfo">
```

```
<div class="site-info">
  <a href="<?php echo esc_url( __( 'http://wordpress.org/',
    'daily-cooking-custom' ) ); ?>"><?php printf( __( 'Proudly
    powered by %s', 'daily-cooking-custom' ), 'WordPress' );
    ?></a>
  <span class="sep"> | </span>
  <?php printf( __( 'Theme: %1$s by %2$s.', 'daily-cooking-
    custom' ), 'Daily Cooking Custom', '<a
    href="http://karol.cc/" rel="designer">Karol K.</a>, <a
    href="https://themeisle.com/" rel="designer">ThemeIsle</a>
    , and <a href="http://underscores.me/"
    rel="designer">_S</a>' ); ?>
</div><!-- .site-info -->
</footer><!-- #colophon -->
</div><!-- #page -->

<?php wp_footer(); ?>

</body>
</html>
```

One thing you might have noticed inside the previous listing is the mysterious
function __(). It's a native WordPress function that retrieves the translated string
corresponding to the parameters given in the function. It's a feature meant for
internationalization of your site. More details about the function can be found
at https://codex.wordpress.org/Function_Reference/_2.

The sidebar

Now, we can move along to adding WordPress-generated content in the sidebar.
Essentially, this part of our work is pretty simple. All we have to do is include some
WordPress functions that will handle displaying various bits of dynamic content.
In this case, it is the categories, tags, and archives.

Starting at the top, include the following piece of code in the sidebar area:

```
<div id="secondary" class="widget-area" role="complementary">
  <?php if(is_active_sidebar('sidebar-1')) dynamic_sidebar(
    'sidebar-1' ); ?>
</div><!-- #secondary -->
```

This code takes care of displaying whatever widgets have been assigned to that particular widget area. Placing widgets in the sidebar of your HTML structure is the easiest and probably the most usable way of widget-enabling your theme. Also, WordPress will take care of actually displaying everything properly, so you don't have to worry about any weird-looking elements on your site. For instance, every menu is displayed as an `<ul>` list, and every menu element is inside `<li>`. This is as in tune with the standards as it can be.

Main column – the loop

The most important part of the WordPress code comes next. It's called the **loop**, and it's an essential part of your theme. The loop's job is to display your posts in a reverse chronological order, choosing only those posts that are appropriate. You need to put all of your other post tags inside the loop. The basic loop text, which has to surround your post information, is displayed using the following code:

```php
<?php if (have_posts()) : ?>
<?php while (have_posts()) : the_post(); ?>
  <?php get_template_part('content', get_post_format()); ?>
<?php endwhile; else: ?>
  <?php get_template_part('content', 'none'); ?>
<?php endif; ?>
```

The `get_template_part()` function call that's right in the middle fetches another file that contains the rest of the loop, but for now, let's just focus on the main section here.

There are two basic parts of the loop:

- Individual post information
- What to do if there are no appropriate posts

The first part is handled by a standard PHP `while` loop that goes through every post and for each element calls the appropriate `content-[TYPE].php` file. The second part is similar, as it calls the `content-none.php` file, in case there are no posts that can be displayed. The use of these various `content-[TYPE].php` files is currently the standard for handling different types of content that WordPress displays. It's a lot more effective and clear than working with individual `if` or `switch` clauses.

So, in order to get started with this, let's create a basic `content.php` file that will serve the role of a placeholder for the default type of content. In this file, let's place the following code that handles the loop:

```php
<article id="post-<?php the_ID(); ?>" <?php post_class(); ?>>
  <header class="entry-header">
```

```php
<?php the_title(sprintf('<h1 class="entry-title"><a href="%s"
    rel="bookmark">', esc_url(get_permalink())), '</a></h1>');
    ?>

    <?php if('post' == get_post_type()) : ?>
    <div class="entry-meta">
        <?php daily_cooking_custom_posted_on(); ?>
    </div>
    <?php endif; ?>
</header>

<div class="entry-content">
    <?php
    the_content(sprintf(
        __('Continue reading %s <span class="meta-nav">
        &rarr;</span>', 'daily-cooking-custom'),
        the_title('<span class="screen-reader-text">"', '"</span>',
        false)
    ));

    wp_link_pages(array(
        'before' => '<div class="page-links">' . __('Pages:',
        'daily-cooking-custom'),
        'after'  => '</div>',
    ));
    ?>
</div>

<footer class="entry-footer">
    <?php daily_cooking_custom_entry_footer(); ?>
</footer>
</article><!-- #post-## -->
```

If you give it a closer look, you'll notice that it's very similar to the static HTML version I shared earlier in this chapter. The only difference is that instead of the dummy text, there are calls to specific WordPress functions and custom-made functions that we'll discuss in a minute.

Let's take it from the top; the file starts with these two lines:

```php
<article id="post-<?php the_ID(); ?>" <?php post_class(); ?>>
    <header class="entry-header">
```

This is just some standard HTML and basic WordPress function calls to display proper element IDs and CSS classes. For instance, the `the_ID()` function displays the ID of the post. Next, we have the following line:

```
<?php the_title(sprintf('<h1 class="entry-title"><a href="%s"
   rel="bookmark">', esc_url(get_permalink())), '</a></h1>'); ?>
```

It displays the link and the title of the current content element (usually a post), instead of using the dummy text. The `the_title()` function takes three parameters (all optional). Right here, we're using just two. The first one defines the text to place before the title (in this case, we're making a `sprintf()` function call), and the second one defines the text to place after the title. Right below this line, there's a piece of code that displays various types of meta information about the current content element:

```
<?php if('post' == get_post_type()) : ?>
<div class="entry-meta">
  <?php daily_cooking_custom_posted_on(); ?>
</div>
<?php endif; ?>
```

If what we're dealing with is a standard post, a custom function is called to display the details. This way of handling things — through an additional function — makes everything much clearer, in comparison to placing the code right there. Here's what the function looks like (we can place it in our main `functions.php` file, or inside a new file in a separate subdirectory called `inc` — indicating that it holds additional functions):

```
function daily_cooking_custom_posted_on() {
  $time_string = '<time class="entry-date published updated"
    datetime="%1$s">%2$s</time>';
  if ( get_the_time( 'U' ) !== get_the_modified_time( 'U' ) ) {
    $time_string = '<time class="entry-date published"
      datetime="%1$s">%2$s</time><time class="updated"
      datetime="%3$s">%4$s</time>';
  }

  $time_string = sprintf( $time_string,
    esc_attr( get_the_date( 'c' ) ),
    esc_html( get_the_date() ),
    esc_attr( get_the_modified_date( 'c' ) ),
    esc_html( get_the_modified_date() )
  );
```

```php
$posted_on = sprintf(
  _x( 'Posted on %s', 'post date', 'daily-cooking-custom' ),
  '<a href="' . esc_url( get_permalink() ) . '" rel="bookmark">'
    . $time_string . '</a>'
);

$byline = sprintf(
  _x( 'by %s', 'post author', 'daily-cooking-custom' ),
  '<span class="author vcard"><a class="url fn n" href="' .
    esc_url( get_author_posts_url( get_the_author_meta( 'ID' ) )
    ) . '">' . esc_html( get_the_author() ) . '</a></span>'
);

echo '<span class="posted-on">' . $posted_on . '</span><span
  class="byline"> ' . $byline . '</span>';

}
```

As you can see, this is quite a long function, but the thing to remember is that it's just meant to display the date of when the post was published and the byline of the author. Also, there are language functions (_e() and _x()) used here to fetch translated data from the database. You can learn more about these functions at https://codex.wordpress.org/Function_Reference/_e and https://codex.wordpress.org/Function_Reference/_x.

Going back to our content.php file, we have the following:

```php
<div class="entry-content">
  <?php
  the_content(sprintf(
    __('Continue reading %s <span class="meta-nav">&rarr;</span>',
      'daily-cooking-custom'),
    the_title('<span class="screen-reader-text">"', '"</span>',
      false)
  ));

  wp_link_pages(array(
    'before' => '<div class="page-links">' . __('Pages:', 'daily-
      cooking-custom'),
    'after'  => '</div>',
  ));
  ?>
</div>
```

The first part (the_content ()) takes care of displaying the contents of the current post, along with a Continue reading link. This is actually the most important part of the whole file. Next, the second part (wp_link_pages ()) is meant to display page links for paginated posts (WordPress allows you to divide your content into individual subpages; this can be useful when dealing with an overly long piece of text). Finally, we have the code for the footer section for the entry:

```
<footer class="entry-footer">
  <?php daily_cooking_custom_entry_footer(); ?>
</footer>
```

There's another call to a custom-made function there. Here's what the function looks like:

```
function daily_cooking_custom_entry_footer() {
  // Hide category and tag text for pages.
  if ( 'post' == get_post_type() ) {
    $categories_list = get_the_category_list( __( ', ', 'daily-
      cooking-custom' ) );
    if ( $categories_list &&
      daily_cooking_custom_categorized_blog() ) {
      printf( '<span class="cat-links">' . __( 'Posted in %1$s',
        'daily-cooking-custom' ) . '</span>', $categories_list );
    }

    $tags_list = get_the_tag_list( '', __( ', ', 'daily-cooking-
      custom' ) );
    if ( $tags_list ) {
      printf( '<span class="tags-links">' . __( 'Tagged %1$s',
        'daily-cooking-custom' ) . '</span>', $tags_list );
    }
  }

  if ( ! is_single() && ! post_password_required() && (
    comments_open() || get_comments_number() ) ) {
    echo '<span class="comments-link">';
    comments_popup_link(__('Leave a comment', 'daily-cooking-
      custom'), __('1 Comment', 'daily-cooking-custom'), __('%
      Comments', 'daily-cooking-custom'));
    echo '</span>';
  }

  edit_post_link( __( 'Edit', 'daily-cooking-custom' ), '<span
    class="edit-link">', '</span>' );
}
```

All this code handles the post details such as the categories and tags, and the comment links (which other visitors can click to submit their own opinion about the post). One interesting thing I'd like to point out here is the call to the comments_popup_link() function:

```
comments_popup_link(__('Leave a comment', 'daily-cooking-custom'),
    __('1 Comment', 'daily-cooking-custom'), __('% Comments',
    'daily-cooking-custom'));
```

Here, you can see that there are three arguments passed, separated by commas:

- The first option tells WordPress the text that it has to display when there are no comments.

- The second option tells WordPress the text that it has to display when there is just one comment.

- The third option tells WordPress the text that it has to display for more than one comment. The percent symbol (%) gets replaced with the actual number of existing comments.

I'm happy to say that this is it when it comes to the basic understanding of the loop. Of course, its structure allows you to do many more things and include many custom features. But for now, we are good with what we have here. Once you save your index.php and reload your website, you will see your new theme in action.

 This version of the index.php file is available in the code bundle for this chapter—inside a subdirectory labeled phase 2. Our theme files will go through a couple of phases before we have the final version (phase 1 was the raw HTML).

Later in the chapter, I will show you how to create a custom page template, which will take advantage of the loop and use it for a slightly different purpose.

Creating template files within your theme

You've now got a functional basic template for your theme. It works great on the main blog page and successfully loads content for anything you can click on in your site. However, we want slightly different templates for other types of content on our site. For example, a *single post* page needs to have a comments form where visitors can post comments; the *page* page doesn't need to show the date, category, or tags; and the *category* page should show the category name.

Before we can create other templates, we need to break up the main `index.php` file into parts so that these different templates can share the common elements. I've mentioned many times the importance of the header, sidebar, and footer. We're going to break them up now. First, let's take a quick look at how it works.

Understanding the WordPress theme

Usually, WordPress themes are composed of a number of template files. This allows the different parts of the site (such as the frontend, blog archive, pages, single posts, and search results) to have different purposes. Breaking the `index.php` file into template files allows us to not only share some common parts of the design but also have different code in the different parts.

As I mentioned earlier, we'll soon be breaking up the four main pieces of the design (header, sidebar, main column, and footer) so that WordPress can make good use of them. That's because while the header and footer are probably shared by all pages, the content in the main column will be different. Also, you may want the sidebar on some pages, but not on others.

We'll first create these template files and then, move on to other, more optional template files.

Breaking it up

We're going to break up the `index.php` file by removing some of the code into three new files:

- `header.php`
- `footer.php`
- `sidebar.php`

The header.php file

First, cut out the entire top of your `index.php` file. This means cutting the `doctype` declaration, the `<head>` tag, any miscellaneous opening tags, and the `<header>` tag. In my case, I'm cutting out all the way from this initial line:

```
<!DOCTYPE html>
```

I'm cutting through to and including these lines:

```
</header><!-- #masthead -->
<div id="content" class="site-content">
```

Then, paste this text into a new file named `header.php` that you created within your `theme` folder.

Now, at the very top of the `index.php` file (that is, where you just cut the header text from) write in the following line of WordPress PHP code:

```
<?php get_header(); ?>
```

This is a WordPress function that includes the `header.php` file you just created. If you save everything and reload your website now, nothing should change. The important part here is to make sure that the call to the preceding PHP function sits right at the very top of your `index.php` file.

The footer.php file

Next, we will create the footer file. To create this, first cut out all of the text at the very bottom of the `index.php` file, from the following code:

```
</div><!-- #content -->
<footer id="colophon" class="site-footer" role="contentinfo">
```

Cut all the way through to the `</html>` tag. Paste the text you just cut into a new `footer.php` file that you create within your `theme` folder.

Now, at the very bottom of the `index.php` file (from where you just cut the footer text), write in the following line of WordPress PHP code:

```
<?php get_footer(); ?>
```

This is a special WordPress function that includes the `footer.php` file you just created. Again, you should save everything and reload your website to make sure nothing changes.

The sidebar.php file

There is just one more essential template file to create. For this one, cut out the entire `div` element containing your sidebar. In my case, it's the following text:

```
<div id="secondary" class="widget-area" role="complementary">
  <?php if(is_active_sidebar('sidebar-1')) dynamic_sidebar(
    'sidebar-1' ); ?>
</div>
```

Paste this text into a new file in your `theme` folder named `sidebar.php`.

Now, in `index.php`, add this function in the place you just cut your sidebar from:

```php
<?php get_sidebar(); ?>
```

This will include the sidebar. In the case of my design, I will want the sidebar on every page. So, it's not very crucial for it to be a separate file. I could have included it in the `footer.php` file. However, in some templates, including the default template that came with your WordPress installation, the designer prefers to not include the sidebar in some views such as the Page view and single posts.

Your four template files

You've now got four template files in your theme folder, namely `header.php`, `footer.php`, `sidebar.php`, and the now-much-shorter `index.php`. By the way, my `index.php` file now has only a handful of WordPress functions and the loop. The following is the entire file:

```php
<?php get_header(); ?>

    <div id="primary" class="content-area">
      <main id="main" class="site-main" role="main">

    <?php if (have_posts()) : ?>

      <?php /* Start the Loop */ ?>
      <?php while (have_posts()) : the_post(); ?>

        <?php
        get_template_part('content', get_post_format());
        ?>

      <?php endwhile; ?>

      <?php daily_cooking_custom_paging_nav(); ?>

    <?php else : ?>

      <?php get_template_part('content', 'none'); ?>

    <?php endif; ?>

      </main><!-- #main -->
    </div><!-- #primary -->
```

```
<?php get_sidebar(); ?>
<?php get_footer(); ?>
```

This whole cutting-and-pasting process to create these four files was just to set the scene for the real goal of making alternative template files.

 This version of the index.php file, as well as header.php, footer.php, and sidebar.php, is available in the code bundle for this chapter—inside a subfolder labeled phase 3.

Archive template

WordPress is now using the index.php template file for every view on your site. Let's make a new file—one that will be used when viewing a monthly archive, category archive, or tag archive.

 To learn even more about how WordPress utilizes different files to display its content, feel free to read the guide at http://www.codeinwp.com/blog/wordpress-theme-heirarchy/.

To create your archive template, make a copy of index.php and name this copy archive.php.

Now, navigate to a monthly archive on the site by clicking on one of the month names in the sidebar. At this point, it looks exactly like the main listing—the one handled by index.php.

Let's make one more change to the archive template. I'd like it to display a message that lets the users know what type of archive page they are on. Currently, the archive looks the same as the main index listing and this isn't the most optimized situation. To fix it, just add this code below the `<?php if (have_posts()) : ?>` line:

```
<header class="page-header">
  <?php
  the_archive_title('<h1 class="page-title">', '</h1>');
  the_archive_description('<div class="taxonomy-description">',
    '</div>');
  ?>
</header>
```

Now, when I click on a month, category, or tag, I see a new heading at the top of the page that lets me know where I am:

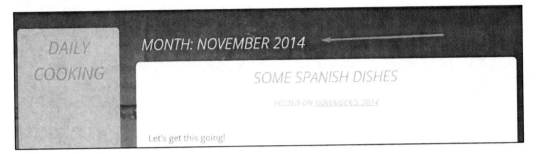

[This version of the `archive.php` file is available in the code bundle for this chapter—inside a subfolder labeled `phase 4`.]

Single template

The next template we need to create is for the single post view. To view a single post, you can usually just click on the post title. Right now, the single post looks like the site's front page (because it's using `index.php`)—except with just one post.

To get started, again make a copy of `index.php`, and name the copy `single.php`. This is the template that WordPress will look for first when it's serving a single post. If it doesn't find `single.php`, it'll use `index.php`.

Without further delay, here's my `single.php` file. You should notice that the file features almost exactly the same elements as the `index.php`. The only difference is that the `get_template_part()` function call fetches a different element. In this case, it's single.

```php
<?php get_header(); ?>

  <div id="primary" class="content-area">
    <main id="main" class="site-main" role="main">

    <?php while (have_posts()) : the_post(); ?>

      <?php get_template_part('content', 'single'); ?>

      <?php daily_cooking_custom_post_nav(); ?>
```

```php
<?php
if (comments_open() || get_comments_number())
    comments_template();
?>

<?php endwhile; // end of the loop. ?>

</main><!-- #main -->
</div><!-- #primary -->

<?php get_sidebar(); ?>
<?php get_footer(); ?>
```

The aforementioned `get_template_part('content', 'single')` call will fetch the `content-single.php` file. Here's what the file looks like:

```php
<article id="post-<?php the_ID(); ?>" <?php post_class(); ?>>
    <header class="entry-header">
        <?php the_title('<h1 class="entry-title">', '</h1>'); ?>

        <div class="entry-meta">
            <?php daily_cooking_custom_posted_on(); ?>
        </div>
    </header>

    <div class="entry-content">
        <?php the_content(); ?>
        <?php
        wp_link_pages( array(
            'before' => '<div class="page-links">' . __( 'Pages:',
                'daily-cooking-custom' ),
            'after'  => '</div>',
        ) );
        ?>
    </div>

    <footer class="entry-footer">
        <?php daily_cooking_custom_entry_footer(); ?>
    </footer>
</article><!-- #post-## -->
```

This file's structure is almost exactly the same as the one we've discussed a couple of pages ago—content.php—with only minor differences. Also, the following are three specific things that are worth pointing out:

- The presence of the `<article>` tag. The individual post's content is displayed inside this tag.
- The call to the `the_content()` function. This time, we're displaying the whole content of the post, not just the excerpt.
- The call to the `comments_template()` function in `single.php`. It displays the comment form and the individual comments that have been submitted for this post.

 These versions of the `single.php` file and the `content-single.php` file are available in the code bundle for this chapter—inside a subfolder labeled phase 4.

Page template

The last template we're going to create is for the static page view. On my food blog site, this would be the Sample Page, for example. The easiest way to go about this is to start with the `single.php` file this time. So, just make a copy of this file and name it `page.php`. Now, we'll be simplifying the file so that only the essential information about a given page is displayed. In the end, this is what my `page.php` file looks like:

```php
<?php get_header(); ?>

    <div id="primary" class="content-area">
    <main id="main" class="site-main" role="main">

      <?php while (have_posts()) : the_post(); ?>

        <?php get_template_part('content', 'page'); ?>

      <?php endwhile; // end of the loop. ?>

    </main><!-- #main -->
    </div><!-- #primary -->

<?php get_sidebar(); ?>
<?php get_footer(); ?>
```

I did just a few of modifications here. They are as follows:

- I changed the last parameter of the `get_template_part()` function to `page`, instead of `single`.

- I erased the call to `daily_cooking_custom_post_nav()`, which handled the display of post navigation.

- I erased the whole block of code that handled the comments. We don't need those on pages.

Next, we need a custom `content-page.php` file. The easiest way to build it is to make a copy of the `content-single.php` file and tune it up a bit. Here's my final `content-page.php` file:

```php
<article id="post-<?php the_ID(); ?>" <?php post_class(); ?>>
  <header class="entry-header">
    <?php the_title('<h1 class="entry-title">', '</h1>'); ?>
  </header>

  <div class="entry-content">
    <?php the_content(); ?>
    <?php
      wp_link_pages(array(
        'before' => '<div class="page-links">' . __( 'Pages:',
          'daily-cooking-custom' ),
        'after'  => '</div>',
      ));
    ?>
  </div>

  <footer class="entry-footer">
  </footer>
</article><!-- #post-## -->
```

Here's what I did here in terms of simplifying:

- I got rid of the whole code displaying meta data.

- I erased the entry footer, which was meant to display categories and tags. We don't use those with WordPress pages.

Now, my Sample Page looks much cleaner:

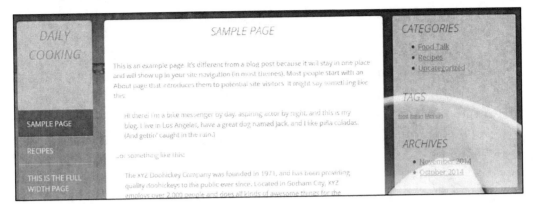

> These versions of the page.php file and the content-page. php file are available in the code bundle for this chapter—inside a subfolder labeled phase 4.

Generated classes for body and post

As you're modifying your theme to make accommodations for different types of pages, you should also know about the CSS classes that WordPress will put into your theme. If you look carefully at the code we've been using, you'll see these two functions:

- body_class(): For example, in the header.php file, the exact line is
  `<body <?php body_class(); ?>>`
- post_class(): For example, in the content-page.php file, the exact line is
  `<article id="post-<?php the_ID(); ?>" <?php post_class(); ?>>`

The body_class() function adds a whole bunch of classes to the body tag, depending on the page you're viewing. For example, the main page of my site has the following class in the body:

```
<body class=" home blog custom-background">
```

My *Some Spanish Dishes* single post page's body tag looks like the following:

```
<body class=" single single-post postid-41 single-format-standard
    custom-background">
```

If I wanted to style anything differently on different pages, I could do it largely with CSS, without having to create another template.

The `post_class()` function does something similar with the individual post's `div`, giving it different classes depending on the characteristics of the post itself. For example, my *Some Spanish Dishes* post's tag has the following class:

```
<article id="post-41" class="post-41 post type-post status-publish
    format-standard hentry category-uncategorized">
```

Further, my *Sample Page* post tag has the following class:

```
<article id="post-2" class="post-2 page type-page status-publish
    hentry">
```

By using these classes in my stylesheet, I could style every post differently depending on its category, tag, post type, and so on. Keep this in mind as you design your next theme. This becomes extremely important when working with theme frameworks further down the road. Although modifications inside PHP files are allowed, most of the time, you can customize the design of your whole site just by working in the CSS and tweaking various classes (both the native ones in WordPress and the new ones that the framework uses). Situations where a whole new site working on a theme framework gets built purely in the CSS files are not uncommon.

Other WordPress templates

In addition to `archive.php`, `single.php`, and `page.php`, there are a number of other standard template files that WordPress looks for before using `index.php` for particular views. We're not going to create these files here, but you should feel free to experiment on your own WordPress installation. To learn about the complete file hierarchy for WordPress themes, feel free to visit `http://www.codeinwp.com/blog/wordpress-theme-heirarchy/`. There's a great graph there that presents the hierarchy visually. It's very easy to follow and does a much better job at explaining this than I would do here through just words. In addition, when you browse the official code bundle for this chapter, you'll see that many additional files have been created and are actually available inside the bundle. We're not covering them here, however, as it would probably be too much information at this point.

Learning more
You can also find a detailed flow chart of the template hierarchy at `https://codex.wordpress.org/Template_Hierarchy`.

In this chapter, we've experimented with the uses of quite a number of WordPress template tags. In *Chapter 12, Creating a Non-blog Website Part 2 – Community Websites and Custom Content Elements*, I have listed more of the most useful template tags.

Next, we'll explore making custom templates for pages.

Creating and using a custom page template

WordPress allows you to create custom templates. These can be used only for pages (not for posts). A custom template allows you to display the content differently or easily use built-in WordPress functions within a template.

Just to give you a good example of what custom page templates are and how they can benefit your site (no matter what theme you're using), let's create a custom version of the archives template. This is also what we will use to create a custom archives page that should be much more useful to our readers than the standard one. Here's what the archives look like on my blog right now:

There are just a couple of small links in the sidebar that redirect the visitors to a standard monthly archive. Of course, later on, when there are more posts on your site, there will be many more links shown (exactly one link for each month of your site's existence).

Now, as far as the idea of **archives** goes, I have to admit, somewhat reluctantly, that WordPress was never good at this. One of the few problems with the platform as a web publishing solution was the fact that posts usually have very short life spans. Whenever you publish a post, it sits on the front page for a while and then it vanishes in the archives never to be seen again, irrespective of whether it's still relevant or not. In the end, it's really hard for a new visitor to find these old posts on your site.

One of the few chances you have at reviving those old posts is mastering the art of **search engine optimization (SEO)** and driving some new traffic to your old posts through your SEO efforts only (it's the most popular solution). But luckily, it's not the only way around to fix this issue. Again, custom page templates are an interesting remedy here.

In the preceding screenshot, you can see that the default version of the archives is just a sidebar widget with some links to the individual months. The problem with such content organization is that it provides a rather bad user experience. Archives, in general, are not about listing everything in one place; they are about providing a hub where the visitor can go and find some specific piece of content. For example, think about how archives work in your local library. This is what you want to eventually have on your site as well. So, what we're going to do here is say no to the traditional archives template in WordPress and create a custom page template to handle the archives manually. Then, we're going to link to this archive from one of the menus. Here's how to do it.

On our new archives page, we want to achieve the following things:

- Display a piece of custom text. For instance, as a form of introduction or a notification message explaining what's in the archives

- Display a categories archive—a list all the categories in use on the site.

- Display a tag cloud—a form of tag archive where all of the tags in use on the site are displayed one after the other (inline, not in a list format), and the font size increases for the tags that have been used more often than others.

- Display a list of 15 latest posts or whatever other number you wish.

- Display a monthly archives block. The fact that it's displayed at the bottom is not accidental, as this block is not particularly useful for a typical visitor.

To do this, we need to create a template. The following are the steps we'll take:

1. Create the template file.

   Make a copy of `page.php` within your theme, and give it a new name. I like to prepend all of my custom template files with `tmpl_` so that they are sorted separately from all the WordPress template files that I will create. I'll name this file `tmpl_archives.php`.

   In order for WordPress to be able to identify this file as a template file, we need to add a specially styled comment to the top of the page (just as we did with `style.css`). The comment needs to be formatted as follows:

   ```php
   <?php
   /* Template Name: Blog Archives Custom */
   ?>
   ```

   In the wp-admin panel, the template will be identified by this template name, so make sure the name signals to you for what the template is used.

2. Add WordPress functions.

This is a crucial part of the process, but thankfully not a complicated one at this stage. Look over your new template file and find the occurrence of this line:

```php
<?php get_template_part('content', 'page'); ?>
```

Now, erase it and put this in its place:

```php
<?php get_template_part('content', 'tmpl_archives'); ?>
```

This is the result we're after; the middle part of your `tmpl_archives.php` file should now look like the following:

```php
<?php while (have_posts()) : the_post(); ?>

  <?php get_template_part( 'content', 'tmpl_archives' ); ?>

<?php endwhile; // end of the loop. ?>
```

Next, create a completely new file called `content-tmpl_archives.php` and put the following code in it:

```php
<article id="post-<?php the_ID(); ?>" <?php post_class();
  ?>>
  <header class="entry-header">
    <?php the_title('<h1 class="entry-title">', '</h1>');
    ?>
  </header>

  <div class="entry-content">
    <?php the_content(); ?>

    <div style="float: left; width: 50%;">
      <h2>Categories</h2>
      <ul>
      <?php wp_list_categories('orderby=name&title_li=');
      ?>
      </ul>
    </div>
    <div style="float: left; width: 50%;">
      <h2>Tags</h2>
      <?php wp_tag_cloud('smallest=8&largest=20'); ?>
    </div>
    <div style="clear: both;"></div><!-- clears the
      floating -->
```

```php
<?php
$how_many_last_posts = 15;
echo '<h2>Last '.$how_many_last_posts.' Posts</h2>';
$my_query = new WP_Query('post_type=post&nopaging=1');
if($my_query->have_posts())
{
  echo '<ul>';
  $counter = 1;
  while($my_query->have_posts() &&
    $counter<=$how_many_last_posts)
  {
    $my_query->the_post();
    ?>
    <li><a href="<?php the_permalink() ?>"
      rel="bookmark" title="Permanent Link to <?php
      the_title_attribute(); ?>"><?php the_title();
      ?></a></li>
    <?php
    $counter++;
  }
  echo '</ul>';
  wp_reset_postdata();
}
?>

<h2>By Month</h2>
<p><?php wp_get_archives('type=monthly
  &format=custom&after= |'); ?></p>
</div>

<footer class="entry-footer">
</footer>
</article><!-- #post-## -->
```

The preceding code includes some additional functionality on our new archives template. Actually, because we are creating a custom template, we can add any of the WordPress functions we discovered earlier in the chapter, as well as any other WordPress function in existence (see *Chapter 12, Creating a Non-blog Website Part 2 – Community Websites and Custom Content Elements*).

What we did here is the following. Here are some of the more interesting parts of the code. Starting with the following:

```html
<div style="float: left; width: 50%;">
  <h2>Categories</h2>
  <ul>
```

```
<?php wp_list_categories('orderby=name'); ?>
</ul>
</div>
```

It's about adding a complete list of categories that are present on the site. The `div` elements are responsible for displaying this block on the left side and allowing the next block—tags—to be placed next to it (it's a more effective way of achieving such an effect than using HTML tables because it's a more cross-device-friendly approach).

The next part of the code is the following:

```
<div style="float: left; width: 50%;">
  <h2>Tags</h2>
  <?php wp_tag_cloud('smallest=8&largest=20'); ?>
</div>
<div style="clear: both;"></div><!-- clears the floating --
  >
```

It has a very similar purpose, only this time we're displaying the aforementioned tag cloud. The last `div` element visible here is meant to clear the float parameter used in the previous `div` elements.

Next, we have the part responsible for displaying the latest posts:

```
<?php
$how_many_last_posts = 15;
echo '<h2>Last '.$how_many_last_posts.' Posts</h2>'; $my_query =
new WP_Query('post_type=post&nopaging=1');
if($my_query->have_posts()) {
  echo '<ul>';
  $counter = 1;
  while($my_query->have_posts() &&
    $counter<=$how_many_last_posts)        {
    $my_query->the_post();
    ?>
    <li><a href="<?php the_permalink() ?>" rel="bookmark"
      title="Permanent Link to <?php the_title_attribute();
      ?>"><?php the_title(); ?></a></li>
    <?php
    $counter++;
  }
  echo '</ul>';
  wp_reset_postdata();
}
?>
```

Currently, the code displays 15 latest posts, but this can be adjusted if you just change the value of the $how_many_last_posts variable.

Finally, there's the block that displays a traditional monthly archive, where every month is represented as a standard link:

```
<h2>By Month</h2>
<p><?php wp_get_archives('type=monthly&format=custom&after=
    |'); ?></p>
```

At this point, you can save the file and proceed to the next step.

3. Apply the template to a page.

   Leave your HTML editor, and log in to your wp-admin. You need to edit or create the page in which you want to use this template. In this case, I will create a page and name it Archives.

   On the **Edit Page** page, look for the **Template** menu within the **Page Attributes** box (on the right, by default):

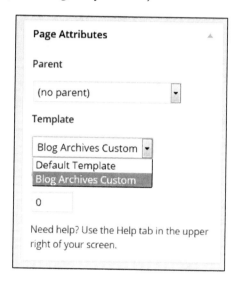

Change it from **Default Template** to **Blog Archives Custom,** and click on **Update** (Note that you can also change a page's template using **Quick Edit** on **Pages | Edit Page**). Now, in order to see the page somewhere, you have to add it to one of the menus. We already covered this in *Chapter 4, Pages, Menus, Media Library, and More,* so I'm sure you can get it done quickly. Once you have this handled, you can return to the frontend of your website and click on the **Archives** page. However, because your site is not that content-heavy at this point, you won't get a staggering effect, but there's still some nice presentation of the most recent posts:

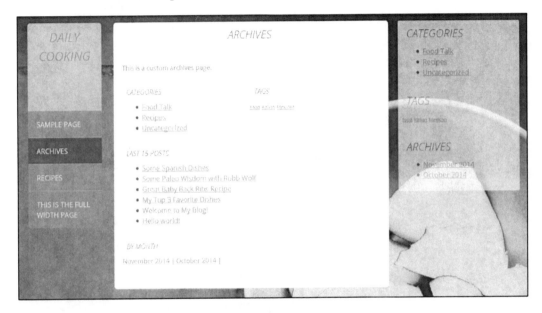

There is no limit to the number of custom templates you can make in your WordPress theme. And now that we are done making templates for the `daily-cooking-custom` theme, the `theme` folder has grown quite a lot.

 These versions of the `tmpl_archives.php` file and the `content-tmpl_archives.php` file are available in the code bundle for this chapter — inside a subfolder labeled `phase 5`.

Making your theme widget-friendly

If you want to be able to use the widgets in your theme, you will need to make your theme widget-friendly (also known as **widgetizing** your theme). Widgetizing is actually pretty easy, and to be honest with you, we already took care of that when constructing our sidebar. I hadn't discussed much back then, but now let's go back to this topic and explain how widgetizing works.

Going back to our sidebar

Back in the old days, it was very common for a WordPress site to use statically placed content blocks in the sidebar. In other words, the only way to place dynamic content in the sidebar of our sites was to use handmade code that would fetch whatever data we wanted and then display it. This solution wasn't very usable for the everyday user who might not be familiar with the PHP source code. So, a better solution needed to be found. Hence, widgets.

Widgets give us the ability to set the sidebars in a way so they fetch the data that's been set in **Appearance | Widgets**. Therefore, the only thing the user has to do is go to **Appearance | Widgets** and pick whatever type of content they want to feature in the sidebar (or any other widget area for that matter; it can be in the footer as well).

Just to give you an example of old versus new, here's what a standard piece of code might look like that handles displaying blog archives the old way (this can be placed in `sidebar.php`):

```
<div id="secondary" class="widget-area" role="complementary">
  <aside>
    <h1>Archives</h1>
    <ul>
      <?php wp_get_archives(); ?>
    </ul>
  </aside>
</div><!-- #secondary -->
```

However, this code is not customizable in any way, so a much better solution to display the archives is to use the code that we already have in our `sidebar.php`, which is as follows:

```
<div id="secondary" class="widget-area" role="complementary">
  <?php if(is_active_sidebar('sidebar-1')) dynamic_sidebar(
    'sidebar-1' ); ?>
</div><!-- #secondary -->
```

And then, just assign a new Archives widget to this sidebar in the **Appearance | Widgets** section of wp-admin.

Working with the functions.php file

Okay, so right now, let's examine how all this actually works. As I said earlier, the functions.php file can contain many different elements, so now, it's about time to focus on how to actually enable dynamic sidebars also known as widgets. So, in the functions.php file, we place the following code:

```
function daily_cooking_custom_widgets_init() {
  register_sidebar(array(
     'name'           => __('Sidebar', 'daily-cooking-custom'),
     'id'             => 'sidebar-1',
     'description'    => '',
     'before_widget'  => '<aside id="%1$s" class="widget %2$s">',
     'after_widget'   => '</aside>',
     'before_title'   => '<h1 class="widget-title">',
     'after_title'    => '</h1>',
  ));
}
add_action('widgets_init', 'daily_cooking_custom_widgets_init');
```

In this code, I'm using one new function to register a new widget area. As you can see, the widget area is simply called Sidebar (the name parameter).

Now, the final add_action('widgets_init', 'daily_cooking_custom_widgets_ init') function call is what actually registers the widget areas (it's the most important line of code here; it lets WordPress know when to enable the widget areas).

Adding some widgets

At this point, your theme is ready for widgets! You can now go to wp-admin, navigate to **Appearance** | **Widgets**, and add widgets. For example, as you can see in the following screenshot, I've added three widgets to one of the widget areas:

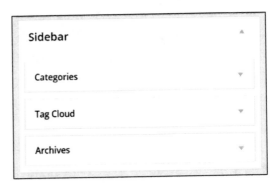

Be sure to click on **Save**, and then return to your website and reload the page. The default items you had placed in the sidebar have been replaced with widgets, as shown in the following screenshot:

Additional widgetizing options

What we just covered is the simplest way to widgetize a theme. There are actually a lot of other possibilities that you could utilize when adding the code to your `sidebar.php` and `functions.php` pages. For example, there are options that allow you to do the following:

- Widgetize more than one sidebar, giving each a name
- Widgetize a part of your sidebar, but leave in some default items
- Widgetize the footer
- Customize the search form widget
- And much more

Learning more

To learn about the variety of options available and how to take advantage of them, take a look at the codex at `https://codex.wordpress.org/Widgetizing_Themes`.

Enabling a menu in your theme

As of WordPress 3, users can now more easily control what appears in menus. Instead of having to show "all pages" in the menu, you can choose to show a selection of pages and/or categories, and/or other options (as we saw in *Chapter 4*, *Pages, Menus, Media Library, and More*).

The good news I have for you right now is that menus are already enabled in the structure of the theme we're creating here. Because we used the `wp_nav_menu()` function in the header of the site (in the `header.php` file), if the user creates a menu in **Appearance** | **Menus** and then assigns it to the area indicated as **Primary Menu**, it will show up in this spot.

Menu Settings

| Auto add pages | ☐ Automatically add new top-level pages to this menu |
| Theme locations | ☑ Primary Menu |

If you want to have more than one navigation menu in your theme, you can register multiple navigation menu locations and let the user create multiple menus and choose which menu goes in which location. To learn more about this, check out the codex at `https://codex.wordpress.org/Navigation_Menus`.

Learning more

The `wp_nav_menu()` function is quite powerful and can take a number of parameters that will let you control the classes and IDs, the name of the menu, and more. Take a look at the codex at `http://codex.wordpress.org/Function_Reference/wp_nav_menu`.

Creating a child theme

If you've found an existing theme or theme framework that you like, and you just want to adjust it a bit to fit your requirements hand-in-glove, you can create a child theme on top this existing theme. A child theme uses the parent theme as a starting point and, without changing the theme itself, alters just the bits you want to alter.

As a matter of fact, using child themes is the recommended way of making modifications to any theme. The rule of thumb is simple: if you want to change anything at all about a stock theme (either inside the source code, graphics, or template files), do it through a new child theme.

In plain English, a child theme inherits the functionality and features of the parent theme. The biggest value of creating child themes is that you can introduce any bells and whistles you wish without altering the structure of the parent theme. I know that this sounds like some additional work, because if you just want to change a couple of lines of code, then it's always going to be quicker to do it directly within the theme. However, taking the longer "child theme" way has its benefits.

The main one is that if you were to modify the original theme directly, all your modifications would vanish the minute you updated the theme. However, if you're using child themes, you can take full advantage of any update that the original theme's authors release. Let me say this again, preserving your modifications after performing a theme update is impossible unless you're using a child theme.

Another benefit of working with child themes is that you have a very clear view over the modifications that you've introduced into your theme. Basically, every new thing that you're implementing through a child theme has to be placed in a new file, so even when you come back to review your child theme after a while, you can still easily identify every piece of your work.

The final benefit, actually, there's probably a lot more of them, but the final one on this short list is that it's very easy to revert every modification you've introduced through a child theme. In short, if something is causing any serious problems and you have to fix your site quickly (you know—an emergency), then you can simply delete the files responsible. If you were modifying your original theme directly, going through every file individually would surely take much more time and would make any sort of quick recovery very difficult to achieve.

Let's take a quick look at how to make a child theme.

Creating the new theme folder

Just to make things easier to understand here, we'll take the theme that we've been creating in this chapter and build a child theme for it. The starting point is really simple. Create a new folder in `wp-content/themes/`, and name it `daily-cooking-child`.

Creating the style sheet

The only file you need to start with in this folder is the stylesheet (`style.css`).
The stylesheet needs the usual header, plus a new line:

```
/*
Theme Name: Daily Cooking Child Theme
Description: Child theme for the Daily Cooking Custom theme.
Theme URI: http://newinternetorder.com/
Author: Karol K
Author URI: http://karol.cc/
Template: daily-cooking-custom
*/
```

The key line in that code is `Template: daily-cooking-custom`. This tells
WordPress that your new theme is a child theme of `daily-cooking-custom`.
To make your child theme start out with the CSS from the parent theme, add
the following code below the comment:

```
@import url("../daily-cooking-custom/style.css");
```

If you don't use the preceding line, your child theme will begin its existence on
a blank stylesheet. In most cases, this is not a desirable scenario.

Using your child theme

That's it! Your new theme now shows up on the **Appearance** page (the new child
theme doesn't have a screenshot icon yet), as shown in the following screenshot:

Granted, the theme is not really useful at this point, but it does exist and we can use
it as the base for further modifications. By default, it will use all of the main theme's
styles, template files, functions, and everything else. If you activate it, it will present
your site as if you were using your main theme.

If you want to change anything, do so in your child theme's folder. You will override the main theme's original template file if you create a new template file (for example, `single.php`, `index.php`, and `archive.php`). The `functions.php` file works a little differently, however. If you create a `functions.php` file, it will be in addition to the main theme's original `functions.php` file; it will not override. In fact, your new file will be loaded first, right before the original file. If you want to override a specific function in the original `functions.php` file, just create a function with the same name. You can also create completely new functions that are not present in the parent theme.

Like I said, every other template file you create inside the child theme (such as `page.php` and `single.php`) will override its namesake, so it's the perfect method to include a new, slightly different design or some new features. Apart from replacing the existing template files, you can add new ones that are not present in the parent (including custom page templates).

In the end, the whole topic of child themes is quite an easy one to grasp once you spend a little while trying out different things and checking how your site reacts to the things you include in the child theme.

Learning more

The WordPress codex has a page devoted to learning about child themes at `https://codex.wordpress.org/Child_Themes`.

Sharing your theme

If you want to turn your template into a package that other people can use, you just have to take the following steps:

1. Make sure you have the rights to redistribute images, icons, photos, and so on, that you included in your theme.

2. Remove all unnecessary files from your theme's folder. Be sure you don't have backup versions or old copies of any of your files. If you do delete any file, be sure to retest your theme to ensure you didn't accidentally delete something important.

3. Make sure the comment at the top of the `style.css` file is complete and accurate.

4. Create a `Readme.txt` file. This is a good place to let future users know with what version of WordPress your theme is compatible and if it has any special features or requirements.

5. Zip the folder and post your theme's ZIP file on your own website for people to download, or post it directly in the WordPress Theme Directory at `https://wordpress.org/themes/`.

Even though the preceding looks like a standard step-by-step process, it's actually nothing like it. To be honest, your theme has to be a really quality one if it's to be allowed into the directory. For example, every theme undergoes a human review, which often results in your theme not passing it. In this case, you just have to make the requested changes, resubmit your work, and keep trying until you get in.

Then, there's also the issue of licensing. By default, WordPress is available under the GNU **General Public License (GPL)**. In plain English, this means that WordPress (the platform) is free and every derivative work that is built upon it has to be filed under GPL too—this includes themes. In short, every piece of PHP code you find inside WordPress, various themes, or plugins is GPL (that includes premium themes and plugins). When it comes to artwork and CSS, GPL might not apply. If you want to learn more about the GPL licensing, it's best if you go straight to the official legal opinion at `https://wordpress.org/news/2009/07/themes-are-gpl-too/`.

Now, apart from the official directory, you can share your theme through other channels. First of all, you have to decide whether you want your theme to be available for free or not. In the case of the former, you can reach out to some popular blogs on WordPress and WordPress design and simply let them know that you have a theme you'd like to share. Most of the time (if the theme looks attractive), they will have no problem notifying their community that there's a cool new free theme.

If you want to make your theme a premium one, you can go to ThemeForest (`http://themeforest.net/`) and try submitting it there. The only challenge is that your theme must really be a quality one if you don't want to get a lot of refunds.

I'm not forcing you to share your theme with the community right away, but once you build some expertise and build your themes to be really cool and useful, you really should reach out to the community and share your work.

Finally, if you're interested in creating an impact with your new theme in the community, consider launching a website dedicated to your theme. This website will be a place where you can publish a demo version, deliver some documentation, and provide support forums and other things to deliver a great user experience.

 The final versions of all the theme files (including the child theme) are available in the code bundle for this chapter—inside a subfolder labeled `final`.

Summary

You have now crossed to the other side of the WordPress *themes world* — you have learned how to make your own theme. With just the most basic HTML and CSS abilities, you can create a design and turn it into a fully functional WordPress theme.

In this chapter, we saw how to turn your HTML build into a basic theme, create WordPress templates to influence the display of a variety of views on your site, create custom templates to be applied to pages within your site, make your new theme widget-ready, create a child theme, and share your theme with everyone else in the WordPress community.

In the next chapter, we'll discuss the topic of feeds, podcasting, and social media integration. This information will allow you to expand your blogging habits and make your work more diverse and more noticeable on the web.

8
Feeds, Podcasting, and Social Media Integration

Let's start this chapter with a definition. For those of you who don't know, this is what a **feed** is (when it comes to websites):

"A web feed is a data format used for providing users with frequently updated content."

Wikipedia

Let's take a closer look at this concept. The key idea here is "frequently updated content". A website that features a blog, updated news, or any type of content that changes regularly will want to offer users a feed. This is because most users do not want to have to visit such websites every day(nor do they remember). Users will lose track of which websites have new content today, which ones don't, which ones they've already seen, and so on.

If you think about it, feeds are one of the few sensible ways of consuming content on the Internet (irrespective of whether it's written content, audio, or videos). With information overload being one of the most common problems that people experience online in the 21st century, manually visiting every website that we like is becoming quite unmanageable.

Instead, we can use a **feed aggregator** (or **feed reader**). The idea is simple. You can tell the feed reader about all of the regularly updated websites you are interested in, and the feed reader will grab the updated content and display it all in one place. I, for example, used to enjoy one of the most popular feed readers of all time—Google Reader. The only problem was that it ceased to exist on July 1, 2013.

Currently, there are a number of alternatives, which grew strong after Google's moves. I'm a Feedly user right now (`http://www.feedly.com/`), but you are free to choose your own favorite. Also, let me just tell you that, for me, life without a feed reader would really be very difficult. I know that it may sound very strange, or like a big exaggeration, but I mean it. Just to give you some stats, currently, I'm subscribed to over 500 different feeds, but the best thing is that I only need few minutes a day to catch the most important news and articles. How's that for time efficiency? Actually, I don't even need to visit all these sites directly; I can read every article in a feed reader. This also adds up to savings in terms of page load time, as feeds contain fewer advertisements and contain only the textual content in which you are interested. So you don't have to wait for website design elements or ads to render.

What it all boils down to is this: if you are going to create a website with frequently updated content, you'll want to offer your users a feed so that they can add it to their reader. Also, you'll want to make sure you are familiar with feeds and feed readers so that you can understand what your users are seeing and offer them everything they are likely to want.

In this chapter, you will learn about feeds, how to provide feeds for your website's content, and some useful plugins to make all this happen.

But wait, there's more! We're also going to cover podcasting (which for some site owners is an important element of their online presence) and social media integration, which the blogs of today can't function without.

Getting started with feeds

Feeds are pure content (or just summaries of content) presented in a structured way via XML. They are usually organized with the most recent information on top. You can always stay up-to-date using feed aggregators (software that can read feeds). Using them, you can also have the content you want delivered or collected for you how and where you want it. This applies not only to written content from blogs or new websites, but also audio and video content (that is, podcasts).

Typically, web feeds are either in the **Really Simple Syndication (RSS)** or **Atom** format. RSS has changed over the past decade, and thus, is often referred to by a version number. The most up-to-date version of RSS is RSS 2.0.1. The older versions are 0.91 and 1.0. However, to be honest, in my some years' experience with blogging and WordPress, I can't recall a moment when I had to worry about, or even be aware of, the version I'm currently using. It is just one of those things that go unnoticed.

Apart from that, however, RSS is kind of a dying technology these days. The once-popular RSS readers have now either ceased development or have been discontinued completely (just like the earlier mentioned Google Reader). Right now, we have other solutions for consuming content, and the growing popularity of social media makes it even easier to share the posts and pages that we find interesting. People are slowly transitioning from feed readers (solutions where they get to choose the content to read), to apps and social media (solutions that do the choosing for them, either through the followers' efforts or the app's algorithm).

That being said, WordPress is 100 percent ready to handle any content distribution and delivery mechanism imaginable. So you don't have to worry about your site getting lost in the zeitgeist. By default, WordPress automatically helps you format your posts so that they come in nicely through today's feed readers as well as any new content-related apps that tomorrow might bring.

Let me say this again; the functionality of content delivery and content feeds' compatibility is built into WordPress by default. This means you don't have to do anything at all to make it available.

However, you may want to take a look at your blog in a few feed readers to see what your content looks like. The following is a screenshot of **Feedly** (http://feedly.com), a content reader / feed reader that has become the main player in the market:

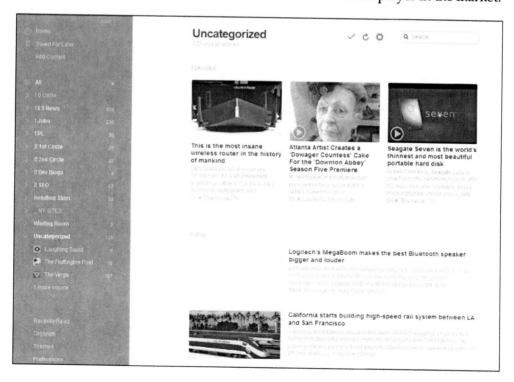

As long as your WordPress is configured correctly, you will have no difficulty displaying your content in Feedly and delivering it to thousands of readers around the globe.

Learning more

You can find an extensive comparison of various feed readers on Wikipedia (in case Feedly isn't your pair of shoes) at `http://en.wikipedia.org/wiki/Comparison_of_feed_aggregators`.

Working with built-in WordPress feeds

Just like I mentioned earlier, luckily for you, feed generation is automated in WordPress. The WordPress installation has a feed generator included. The feed generator creates feeds from posts, comments, and even categories. It also generates all versions of RSS and Atom feeds.

You can find the feed generator for your WordPress blog if you point your browser to any of the following URLs (replace `yoursite.com` with the URL of your WordPress installation), and if you have **pretty permalinks** turned on for your site:

- **RSS 2.0 feed** (`http://yoursite.com/feed/`)
- **RDF/RSS 1.0 feed** (`http://yoursite.com/feed/rdf/`)
- **Atom feed** (`http://yoursite.com/feed/atom/`)
- **Comments RSS 2.0 feed** (`http://yoursite.com/comments/feed/`)

This is what I see in my web browser when I navigate to the RSS 2.0 URL:

Daily Cooking

Just another WordPress site

Some Spanish Dishes
5 listopada 2014 10:31

Let's get this going! Starting with... Now one by one: Bacalao Frito - Fried Cod Calamaritos – Squids SECRET CONTENT

Some Paleo Wisdom with Robb Wolf
16 października 2014 16:34

Check out this great podcast episode by Robb Wolf: http://traffic.libsyn.com/robbwolf/PaleoSolution-240.mp3

> Pliki mediów
> PaleoSolution-240.mp3 (Winamp media file, 0 bajtów)

Great Baby Back Ribs Recipe
16 października 2014 16:09

There's a great video recipe I've found on YouTube. It teaches us how to prepare killer baby back ribs! (by Laura Vitale)

My Top 3 Favorite Dishes
15 października 2014 21:16

Wow, so many dishes to choose from, but I would have to say: Chili con carne. Medium-rare steak. Pizza.

Adding feed links

WordPress automatically generates the feed links that you have seen in the preceding paragraphs, so you don't have to type them in or remember what they are for. If you're using an existing theme, there's a good chance it's already got the feed links in it, in which case you can skip this section.

You can use handy built-in WordPress functions to add feeds to your theme. Actually, this is something we have partially done in the previous chapter. Just to remind you of what I'm talking about, we used a code to enable feed links in the `<head>` section of our custom theme. The following code was placed in the `functions.php` file of the theme:

```
//Adds RSS feed links to <head> for posts and comments.
add_theme_support('automatic-feed-links');
```

This instruction is what makes sure that the automatic feed links will be included in the right place. The presence of these links in the <head> section allows various feed readers to pick up your feeds just by using the main URL of your site. In other words, visitors don't have to know the exact addresses of your feeds' URLs. Instead, they can subscribe through the main site's URL.

The only additional thing that we can do at this point, to make our theme even more usable, is to include some custom feed links in the footer, so that every visitor can click on them directly. This is exactly what I'm going to describe next.

Feeds for the entire website

First, let's start by going back to the footer.php file we created in the previous chapter. If you don't have it at your disposal at the moment, then simply download the code bundle for *Chapter 7, Developing Your Own Theme*, and install it on your site.

Using your FTP software or the built-in WordPress theme editor (available from the wp-admin by navigating to **Appearance | Editor**), edit the footer.php file that's in your theme folder. Just before the Proudly powered by WordPress message, add this:

```
<a href="<?= esc_url(get_bloginfo('rss2_url')) ?>"
  class="rss">Posts</a>
<span class="sep"> | </span>
<a href="<?= esc_url(get_bloginfo('comments_rss2_url')) ?>"
  class="rss">Comments</a>
<span class="sep"> | </span>
```

I've also added an RSS icon in the PNG format to the theme's images folder along with the following CSS to the stylesheet:

```
.rss {
  background: url(images/rss.png) no-repeat;
  background-position: left center;
  padding: 0 0 0 18px;
}
```

Now, when you reload your site, you'll see links for those two feeds in the footer, as shown in the following screenshot:

WordPress will generate the feeds' URLs for you based on your site settings, so that you don't have to hardcode them into your theme. If you want to add links for other kinds of feeds, replace `rss2_url` in the earlier mentioned link with the following:

- For RSS 1.0, use `rdf_url`
- For Atom, use `atom_url`

Feeds for comments

On the individual posts page, we can add a feed to allow users to subscribe to the comments on a particular post. Sometimes, a single post on a blog can draw a lot of attention, with dozens or hundreds of people adding comments. People who comment, and even those who don't, may be interested in following the thread or subscribing to it.

Using your FTP software or the built-in WordPress theme editor, edit the `single.php` file in your theme folder. If you're using the theme we built in *Chapter 7, Developing Your Own Theme,* find the code that we added in it. Scroll to the `comments_template();` function call and add the following code just before it:

```
?>
<p class="rss">
<?php post_comments_feed_link(__( 'Subscribe to these comments',
   'daily-cooking-custom' )); ?>
</p>
<?php
```

 If you are not using the theme we built in *Chapter 7, Developing Your Own Theme,* you can add the preceding text anywhere in `single.php`, so long as it's inside the `if` and `while` loops of the loop.

Now, when you look at the single post page, you'll see the subscription link just above the comments form:

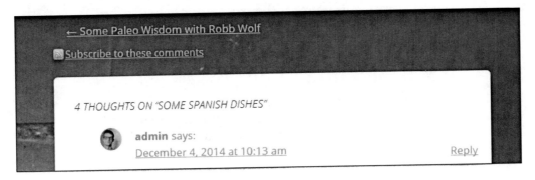

 More built-in feeds are available in WordPress. Learn about them at `https://codex.wordpress.org/WordPress_Feeds`.

Podcasting

A **podcast** is a special feed that includes a reference to an audio or video file instead of just text. People use a podcasting client (such as iTunes or Juice) to collect and listen to the episodes.

 Fun fact
The word "podcast" is a combination of iPod and broadcasting.

Have you ever considered creating your own podcast? It's like having your own radio or TV show. Your subscribers, instead of reading your posts on their computers, can listen to your content through their headphones at any time.

Adding a podcast to your WordPress blog is outrageously easy. While generating your blog's RSS feeds, WordPress automatically adds all the required tags if a music file is linked within that post. These tags are read by podcast clients. Therefore, all you have to do is make a post, and WordPress will do the rest for you.

Creating a podcast

For basic podcasting, there are just two steps you need to take:

1. Record
2. Post

Let's look at these steps in detail.

Recording yourself

Using any commercial or free software, you can record your voice, a conversation, music, or any other sound you'd like to podcast, and then save it as an MP3 file. You may also find that you need to do some editing afterwards.

Some good software to consider for use are as follows:

- I recommend using **Audacity**, which is a free, cross-platform sound recorder and editor. You can download Audacity from `http://audacity.sourceforge.net/`. You may have to do a bit of extra fiddling around to get the MP3 part working, so pay attention to the additional instructions at that point. If you don't want to learn the basics of audio compression and equalization, then you may also want to use a leveling tool such as the **Levelator**, which can be found at `http://www.conversationsnetwork.org/levelator/`. Although it's no longer updated as of the end of 2012, it still works well if you want to level the volume in a simple audio file.

- If you are working on a Mac and want some free software, take a look at **Garage Band**. It comes with the OS, so it will already be installed on your computer.

- If you want to examine some advanced pieces of audio software, called **digital audio workstation (DAW)**, used by professional podcast producers and musicians, then look into **Sonar X2**, **Studio One**, **Logic**, or **ProTools**.

To learn more about the basics of audio recording and production for podcasters, which will make your podcasts sound professional, feel free to check this in-depth tutorial at `http://www.hongkiat.com/blog/audio-production-for-podcasters/`.

Making a post

Now that you've created an MP3 file and it's sitting on your computer, you're ready to make a WordPress post that will be the home for the first episode of your podcast:

1. In the wp-admin, click on **New Post** in the top menu. Enter some initial text into your post if you want to provide a description for the episode. Also, at this point, add a new category called **Podcast** to your blog.

2. Just so we learn the basics of including media files, let's upload your media file via the Media Manager. Later on in this chapter, I will explain why this is not always the most effective approach. However, for now we're here to learn. Start by clicking on the **Add Media** button, and drag and drop your MP3. If all goes well, your file will be on the server shortly (remember that audio files are bigger than images, so uploading will always take a little longer).

3. Next, insert the MP3 file into your post. This is the options screen:

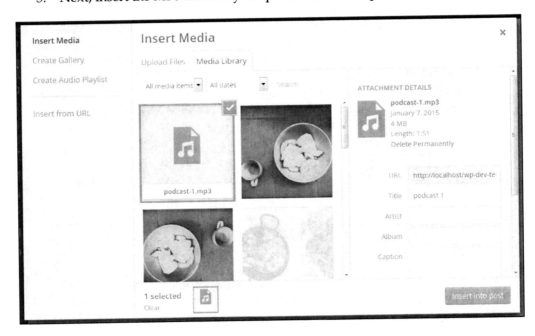

4. WordPress gives you three main possibilities under the **Embed or Link** section. The default one is **Embed Media Player**. If you select it, WordPress will display your audio file inside an interactive player (as shown in the following screenshot). However, here we're going to select the second option, namely **Link to Media File**.

5. Click on **Insert into Post**.

6. Make any other changes or additions you want, and publish the post; you're done! The final result is visible in the following screenshot (it's just a standard link):

That's it. Your website's RSS 2.0 feed and Atom feed can now be used by podcast clients to pick up your podcast.

You can use your own podcast client (in my case, iTunes) to subscribe right away. If you are using iTunes, navigate to **Advanced | Subscribe to podcast** and paste the RSS URL of the new podcast category you just created (for example, `http://yoursite.com/category/podcast/feed/`). At this point, you (and your visitors) can enjoy the new podcast you've just created.

Dedicated podcasting

Setting up a dedicated podcast is easy; we already did it here! You just need to use a separate category for all of your podcast posts. Whenever you post a podcast episode, be sure to assign it only to this category. Also, you would want to make this link available in the sidebar of your site.

First, go to the archive page for your podcast category and copy its URL (for example, `http://yoursite.com/category/podcast/feed/`). Also, to make things easier for iTunes users, you can add an iTunes-specific link. It is the same as your other link, but replace `http://` with `itpc://`.

Now, create a new text widget for your sidebar (refer to *Chapter 5, Plugins and Widgets*), and add this HTML to it (replace `yoursite.com` with your actual domain):

```
<ul>
<li><a href="http://yoursite.com/category/podcast/feed">The
    Podcast</a></li>
<li><a href="itpc://yoursite.com/category/podcast/feed">iTunes
    Podcast Feed</a></li>
</ul>
```

That's it. These simple lines of code will display two neat links pointing to your podcast.

 The WordPress codex has a section on getting started with podcasting. Take a look at `https://codex.wordpress.org/Podcasting`.

Podcasting plugins

We just learned that it's quite easy to add a podcast to your WordPress website. However, if you want additional features, you may want to use a podcasting plugin. Some additional features could be as follows:

- Automatic feed generation
- A preview of what your podcast will look like in iTunes
- Download statistics
- Automatic inclusion of a player within your post on your website
- Support for separate category podcasts

There are quite a number of podcast-related plugins available in the WordPress plugin repository. The three most popular ones are as follows:

- **PowerPress** (`https://wordpress.org/plugins/powerpress/`)
- **Podlove Podcast Publisher** (`https://wordpress.org/plugins/podlove-podcasting-plugin-for-wordpress/`)
- **Podcasting Plugin by TSG** (`https://wordpress.org/plugins/podcasting/`)

For an in-depth guide on how to use the PowerPress plugin (which is my favorite one from the preceding list) and how to configure it correctly, please watch this 30-minute video tutorial by Pat Flynn at `https://www.youtube.com/watch?v=Ei67QMWD4MA#!`.

Through this tutorial, you'll learn how to optimize your podcast and set it up properly so that it can be picked up by iTunes and then shared across the community.

Also, there are hundreds more such plugins that you can find by looking at all the plugins tagged **podcasting** (`https://wordpress.org/plugins/tags/podcasting`). You'll have to read the plugin descriptions and user reviews to decide which of these might be the best match for you.

Using a service to host audio files for free

As I mentioned a while ago, the old-school approach of uploading your podcast straight to your blog has its flaws, which doesn't make it the most effective way to handle things these days. First of all, if you want to host the media file on your main server (the one where your website is hosted), you can quickly encounter serious bandwidth problems, especially if your podcast becomes popular. Also, there's a problem with the maximum upload size in WordPress. Depending on your webhost, you might not be able to upload files larger than 2 MB, 8 MB, or 16 MB (you can contact your webhost's support to clarify this for you). This is what the problem looks like in the uploader:

> **Error** 3. H.I.M - T...nterlude.mp3
>
> 3. H.I.M - The interlude.mp3 exceeds the maximum upload size for this site.

Therefore, if you anticipate having a large number of subscribers, or if you plan to produce such a large volume that you'll run out of space on your own server, you can use an external hosting service that will host your audio files, either for a fee or free of cost. Some options to consider are as follows:

- **Libsyn**: This provides effective and affordable podcast hosting (`http://www.libsyn.com/`)
- **Archive.org**: Once you sign up for an account, you can contribute your audio files to be placed in the podcast directory (`http://archive.org/details/audio`)

- **PodBean**: This provides free podcast hosting (http://www.podbean.com/)

If you choose to do this, first upload your file to the service you've selected and then make a copy of the URL it gives you for the file. Now you need to insert this URL into your WordPress post by using one of the earlier mentioned plugins. After doing so, your podcast episode will be recognized by podcast directories.

Integrating social media

We've briefly mentioned the topic of social media integration in *Chapter 5, Plugins and Widgets*, when discussing the plugins that are worth having on your WordPress site. So right now, let's take a moment to expand upon it and list some more ways in which you can make your site social media friendly, and also see why you'd want to do that in the first place.

Let's start with the *why*. In this day and age, social media is one of the main drivers of traffic for many sites. Even if you just want to share your content with friends and family, or you have some serious business plans regarding your site, you need to have at least some level of social media integration.

Even if you install just simple social media share buttons, you will effectively encourage your visitors to pass on your content to their followers, thus expanding your reach and making your content more popular.

Making your blog social media friendly

There are a handful of ways to make your site social media friendly. The most common approaches are as follows:

- Social media share buttons, which allow your visitors to share your content with their friends and followers
- Social media APIs integration, which make your content look better on social media (design wise)
- Automatic content distribution to social media
- Social media metrics tracking

Let's discuss these one by one.

Setting up social media share buttons

This is something we talked about in *Chapter 5, Plugins and Widgets,* when discussing plugins. There are hundreds of social media plugins available out there that allow you to display a basic set of social media buttons on your site. The one I advise you to use is called **Social Share Starter** (`http://bit.ly/sss-plugin`). Its main advantage is that it's optimized to work on new and low-traffic sites, and doesn't show any negative social proof when displaying the buttons and their share numbers.

You can find the full description, plus a tutorial on how to set everything up, in *Chapter 5, Plugins and Widgets.*

Setting up social media APIs' integration

The next step worth taking to make your content appear more attractive on social media is to integrate it with some social media APIs; particularly that of Twitter.

What exactly their API is and how it works isn't very relevant for the WordPress discussion we're having here. So instead, let's just focus on what the outcome of integrating your site with this API is.

Here's what a standard tweet mentioning a website usually looks like (please notice the overall design, not the text contents):

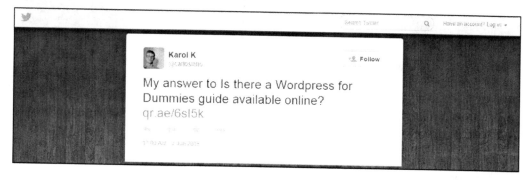

Here's a different tweet, mentioning an article from a site that has Twitter's (Twitter Cards) API enabled:

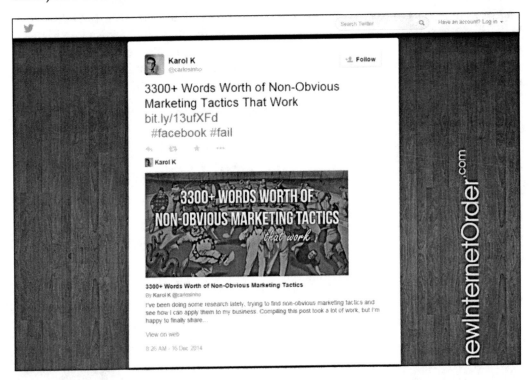

This looks much better. Luckily, having this level of Twitter integration is quite easy. All you need is a plugin called **JM Twitter Cards** (available at `https://wordpress.org/plugins/jm-twitter-cards/`). After installing and activating it, you will be guided through the process of setting everything up and approving your site with Twitter (mandatory step).

Setting up automatic content distribution to social media

The idea behind automatic social media distribution of your content is that you don't have to remember to do so manually whenever you publish a new post. Instead of copying and pasting the URL address of your new post by hand to each individual social media platform, you can have this done automatically.

This can be done in many ways, but let's discuss the two most usable ones, the Jetpack and Revive Old Post plugins.

The Jetpack plugin

The Jetpack plugin is available at `https://wordpress.org/plugins/jetpack/`. We talked about the Jetpack plugin and its many modules in *Chapter 5, Plugins and Widgets*. One of those modules is called **Publicize**. You can activate it by navigating to the **Jetpack | Settings** section of the wp-admin.

After doing so, you will be able to go to **Settings | Sharing** and integrate your site with one of the six available social media platforms:

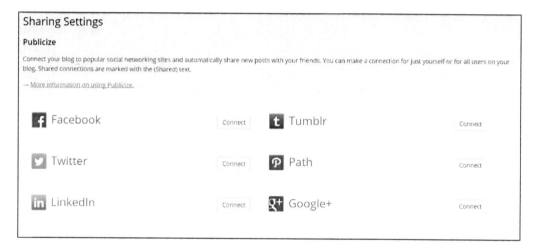

After going through the process of authorizing the plugin with each service, your site will be fully capable of posting each of your new posts to social media automatically.

The Revive Old Post plugin

The Revive Old Post plugin is available at `https://wordpress.org/plugins/tweet-old-post/`. While the Jetpack plugin takes the newest posts on your site and distributes them to your various social media accounts, the Revive Old Post plugin does the same with your archived posts, ultimately giving them a new life. Hence the name Revive Old Post.

After downloading and activating this plugin, go to its section in the wp-admin **Revive Old Post**. Then, switch to the **Accounts** tab. There, you can enable the plugin to work with your social media accounts by clicking on the authorization buttons:

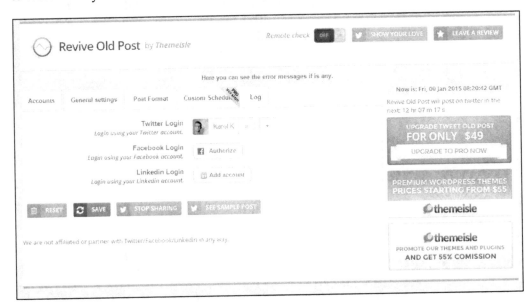

Then, go to the **General settings** tab and handle the time intervals and other details of how you want the plugin to work with your social media accounts. When you're done, just click on the **SAVE** button.

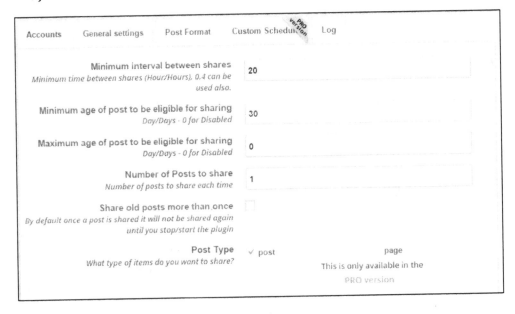

At this point, the plugin will start operating automatically and distribute your random archived posts to your social media accounts.

Note that it's probably a good idea not to share things too often if you don't want to anger your followers and make them unfollow you. For that reason, I wouldn't advise posting more than once a day.

Setting up social media metrics tracking

The final element in our social media integration puzzle is setting up some kind of tracking mechanism that would tell us how popular our content is on social media (in terms of shares).

Granted, you can do this manually by going to each of your posts and checking their share numbers individually (provided you have the Social Share Starter plugin installed). However, there's a quicker method, and it involves another plugin. This one is called **Social Metrics Tracker** and you can get it at `https://wordpress.org/plugins/social-metrics-tracker/`.

In short, this plugin collects social share data from a number of platforms and then displays them to you in a single readable dashboard view. After you install and activate the plugin, you'll need to give it a couple of minutes for it to crawl through your social media accounts and get the data. Soon after that, you will be able to visit the plugin's dashboard by going to the **Social Metrics** section in the wp-admin:

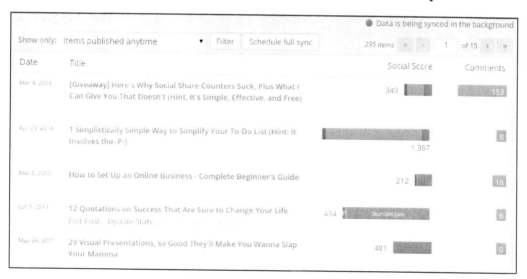

> For some webhosts and setups, this plugin might end up consuming too much of the server's resources. If this happens, consider activating it only occasionally to check your results and then deactivate it again. Doing this even once a week will still give you a great overview of how well your content is performing on social media.

This closes our short guide on how to integrate your WordPress site with social media. I'll admit that we're just scratching the surface here and that there's a lot more that can be done. There are new social media plugins being released literally every week, and describing every single one of them would fill a book on its own. That being said, the methods described here are more than enough to make your WordPress site social media friendly and enable you to share your content effectively with your friends, family, and audience.

Summary

There was a lot going on in this chapter. First, we focused on feeds (RSS) and their importance for every website that aims at being reader friendly. Next, there was the topic of podcasting and a brief getting-started guide to it (how to configure your feeds, what plugins to use, and so on). Finally, we talked about social media integration, tools, and plugins that can make your life a lot easier as an online content publisher.

In the next chapter, we'll discuss the topic of developing your own plugins and widgets, what the basics are and how to get your head around them.

9
Developing Plugins and Widgets

In *Chapter 5, Plugins and Widgets*, you learned how to install **plugins**. Plugins are essentially a way to add to or extend WordPress' built-in functionalities. There are thousands of useful plugins (at the time of writing, the official counter at https://wordpress.org/plugins/ shows over 37,000 plugins) available from the online WordPress community, and they perform all different kinds of functions. In the earlier chapters, we installed plugins that catch spam, back up your site, give you basic SEO features, and more. You can also get plugins that manage your podcasts, track your stats, translate your content into other languages, and much more.

Sometimes, however, you'll find yourself in a situation where the plugin you need just doesn't exist. Luckily, it's quite easy to write a plugin for WordPress that you can use on your own site and share with the larger community if you want to. All you need is some basic PHP knowledge, and you can write any plugin you want.

This chapter is divided into three major parts:

- In the first part, we'll create two plugins by using an easy-to-follow step-by-step process.
- In the second part, we'll create a widget by using the built-in WordPress Widget class.
- In the third part, you will learn what shortcodes are and how to use them.

Plugins

In this section, we'll create a plugin via a simple step-by-step process. We'll first see what the essential requirements are, then try out and test the plugin, and then briefly discuss the PHP code.

Building plugins from scratch

First of all, we're here to learn about WordPress, so in this particular case, we will indeed build things from scratch. This is always the best approach to get an in-depth look into how a particular technology works.

However, later on, once you're working with WordPress on a regular basis managing your own or other people's websites, I actually advise you to always look for an already existing plugin before deciding to write a new one yourself. As I mentioned earlier, there are around 37,000 plugins in the official directory alone, not to mention all the premium plugins available all over the web. In short, if you need some functionality, most likely, *there's a plugin for it*, so you can just go out and get it.

Why is this the recommended approach? If I'm correct, you've chosen to use WordPress because you wanted to make your site as functional as possible with the least amount of effort possible. Following this line of thought, using an existing plugin simply requires much less effort than building one. Also, many existing plugins are already used by thousands of other people and have large communities supporting them. Choosing a quality plugin is therefore a lot safer path to take.

I feel that I should emphasize this clearly because experience tells me that many young WordPress developers tend to press their peers to create things from scratch just for the heck of it despite the fact that there are other and better solutions available.

Moreover, please remember that everything that's a derivative work based on WordPress is available under GPL. So, there's nothing standing in your way to take an existing plugin, build upon it, make it better, and then re-share your version with the world. That way, we all win and there's no redundant work.

But before we can do that, we indeed must learn the craft by constructing something of our own from start to finish. Onward then!

Plugin code requirements

Just as there were requirements for a theme, there are requirements for a plugin. At the very least, your plugin must satisfy the following:

- It must be placed in the `wp-content/plugins` folder (inside the root folder of WordPress).

- It must have a PHP file with a unique name (not used by any other plugin in the main `wp-content/plugins` folder).

- It must have a specially structured comment at the top of the file (see `https://codex.wordpress.org/File_Header`).

That's it. Then, of course, you must have some functions or processing code, but WordPress will recognize any file that meets these requirements as a plugin.

If your plugin is a simple one, then you can just place a unique PHP file straight in your `wp-content/plugins` folder, so it can sit next to the default **Hello Dolly** plugin that WordPress comes with. However, a much better practice is to create a subfolder (again, unique) and place your PHP file there. It makes the `wp-content/plugins` folder seem much more organized. Plus, you never know when your plugin is going to need some additional files (it's always easier to simply add new files to a previously existing plugin folder than to restructure the plugin from scratch).

Basic plugin - adding link icons

As a demonstration, we will create a simple plugin that adds icons to document links within WordPress. For example, in *Chapter 8, Feeds, Podcasting, and Social Media Integration*, we added a link to an MP3 file. It looks like the following now:

Once this plugin is complete, the link will look like the following instead:

> ## NEW PODCAST EPISODE
>
> POSTED ON JANUARY 7, 2015
>
> This is a test post to showcase how to publish a podcast episode.
>
> Here it is: 🎙 podcast 1
>
> POSTED IN PODCAST

To accomplish this, we have to do the following:

1. Provide images of the icons that will be used.
2. Have a PHP function that identifies the links to documents and adds a special CSS class to them.
3. Have a stylesheet that creates the CSS classes for displaying the icons.
4. Tell WordPress that whenever it prints the content of a post (that is, using the `the_content()` function), it has to run the PHP function first.
5. Tell WordPress to include the new styles in the `<head>` tag.

Keep this list in mind as we move forward. Once all these five requirements are met, the plugin will be done. So, let's get started!

Naming and organizing the plugin files

Every plugin should have a unique name so that it does not come into conflict with any other plugin in the WordPress universe. When choosing a name for your plugin and the PHP file, be sure to choose something unique. You may even want to do a Google search for the name you choose in order to be sure that someone else isn't already using it.

Apart from the main plugin file itself, your plugin can contain any number of other files and subfolders. If the situation calls for it, you can even use media files like audio and videos to go along with your plugin. Of course, additional CSS or JS files (or even full libraries) are allowed as well.

In this case, as my plugin will be composed of multiple files (a PHP file, a stylesheet, and some image files), I'm going to create a folder to house my plugin. I'll name the plugin **Add Document Type Styles New** and place it in a folder called `add_doctype_styles_new`. The PHP file, `doctype_styles_new.php`, will live in this folder. I've also collected a number of document type icons (provided by `http://www.freepik.com/` via `http://www.flaticon.com/`).

The folder I created for my plugin now looks like this:

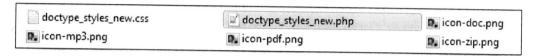

 It is best practice to also create folders like `images`, `css`, and `js` inside your plugin's folder if what you're building will consist of more files.

Now that I've got the images in my folder, I've taken care of the *first* requirement in the list of requirements my plugin has to meet.

 If your plugin has any unusual installation or configuration options, you may also want to include a `readme.txt` file in this folder that explains this. This readme file will be useful both as a reminder to you and as an instructional document to others who may use your plugin in the future. If you plan to submit your plugin to the WordPress plugin directory, you will be required to create a readme file. To get the template for such a file, please visit `https://wordpress.org/extend/plugins/about/readme.txt`.

As mentioned earlier, your plugin has to start with a special comment that tells WordPress how to describe the plugin to users on the plugins page. Now that I've got my folder and a blank PHP file created, I'll insert the special comment. It has to be structured like the following. This really is fundamental (explained at `https://codex.wordpress.org/File_Header`).

```php
<?php
/*
Plugin Name: Add Document Type Styles New
Plugin URI: http://newinternetorder.com/plugins
Description: Detects URLs in your posts and pages and displays nice
document type icons next to them. Includes support for PDF, DOC, MP3,
and ZIP.
Version: 1.0
```

```
Author: Karol K
Author URI: http://karol.cc/
Text Domain: add_doctype_styles_new
License: GNU General Public License v2 or later
*/
```

> Another good piece of information to have in your plugin is about licensing. Most plugins use the **GNU General Public License (GPL)**. This license essentially means that anyone can use, copy, and enhance your code, and that they are not allowed to prevent anyone else from redistributing it. I've also added a note about the GPL to my plugin's PHP file. Remember that all PHP code you encounter in any WordPress plugin is GPL by default. However, graphic files, CSS, JavaScript, and other elements might have a different license, so be careful when copying other people's work and making it part of your own.
>
> You can read more about the license at `https://www.gnu.org/copyleft/gpl.html`.

That's all about the introductory code. Now, we can add the meat.

Writing the plugin's core functions

The core of any plugin is the unique PHP code that you bring to the table. This is the part of the plugin that makes it what it is. Since this plugin is so simple, it only has a few lines of code in the middle.

The *second* requirement the plugin has to meet is *have a PHP function that identifies links to documents and adds a special class to them.* The following function does just that. Note that in keeping with my efforts to ensure that my code is unique, I've prefixed both of my functions with `doctype_styles_new`:

```
function doctype_styles_new_regex($text) {
    $text = preg_replace('/href=([\'|"][[:alnum:]|
    [:punct:]]*)\.(pdf|doc|mp3|zip)([\'|"])/', 'href=\\1.\\2\\3
    class="link \\2"', $text);
    return $text;
}
```

When the function is given some `$text`, it will perform a search for any HTML anchor tag linking to a PDF, DOC, MP3, or ZIP file, and replace it with a class to that anchor. Then, the function returns the altered `$text`.

The *third* requirement the plugin has to meet is *have a stylesheet that creates classes for displaying the icons*. The following function fetches our stylesheet:

```
function doctype_styles_new_styles() {
  wp_register_style('doctypes_styles', plugins_url
    ('doctype_styles_new.css', __FILE__));
  wp_enqueue_style('doctypes_styles');
}
```

As you can see, this function uses the same enqueue mechanism that we used in *Chapter 7, Developing Your Own Theme*, when registering the stylesheets for our custom theme. Here's the CSS file the preceding function fetches (inside doctype_styles_new.css):

```
.link {
  background-repeat: no-repeat;
  background-position: left center;
  padding: 0 0 0 18px;
}
.pdf { background-image: url(icon-pdf.png); }
.doc { background-image: url(icon-doc.png); }
.mp3 { background-image: url(icon-mp3.png); }
.zip { background-image: url(icon-zip.png); }
```

Indeed a very simple file, containing just a handful of styles and icons to distinguish our document links!

Adding hooks to the plugin

We get our code to actually run when it is supposed to by making use of WordPress **hooks**. The way in which plugin hooks work is as follows: at various times while WordPress is running, they check to see whether any plugins have registered functions to run at that time. If there are, the functions are executed. These functions modify the default behavior of WordPress. The WordPress Codex says it best:

[...] There are two kinds of hooks:

1. Actions: Actions are the hooks that the WordPress core launches at specific points during execution, or when specific events occur. Your plugin can specify that one or more of its PHP functions are executed at these points, using the Action API.

2. Filters: Filters are the hooks that WordPress launches to modify text of various types before adding it to the database or sending it to the browser screen. Your plugin can specify that one or more of its PHP functions is executed to modify specific types of text at these times, using the Filter API.

This means that you can tell WordPress to run your plugin's functions at the same time when it runs any of its built-in functions. In our case, we want our plugin's first function, `doctype_styles_new_regex()`, to be run as a filter along with WordPress' `the_content()`. (This is the *fourth* requirement a plugin has to meet.)

Now, add the following code to the bottom of the plugin:

```
add_filter('the_content', 'doctype_styles_new_regex');
```

This uses the `add_filter` hook that tells WordPress to register a function named `doctype_styles_new_regex()` when it is running the function called `the_content()`. By the way, if you have more than one function that you want added as a filter to the content, you can add a third argument to the `add_filter()` function. This third argument would be a number representing the load priority (the default value is 10, highest priority is 1, and there are no particular limits for the lowest priority—you can even assign values such as 100 or 999), and WordPress would run your functions in the ascending order.

All that's left in our list of requirements that a plugin has to meet is the *fifth* requirement: tell WordPress to include the new styles in the `<head>` tag. This is actually done the same way it's been done for themes, which is through the following hook using `add_action()` with the `wp_enqueue_scripts` handle:

```
add_action('wp_enqueue_scripts', 'doctype_styles_new_styles');
```

Here is the complete plugin PHP file:

```php
<?php
/*
Plugin Name: Add Document Type Styles New
Plugin URI: http://newinternetorder.com/plugins
Description: Detects URLs in your posts and pages and displays nice
document type icons next to them. Includes support for PDF, DOC, MP3
and ZIP.
Version: 1.0
Author: Karol K
Author URI: http://karol.cc/
Text Domain: add_doctype_styles_new
License: GNU General Public License v2 or later

This program is distributed in the hope that it will be useful,
but WITHOUT ANY WARRANTY; without even the implied warranty of
MERCHANTABILITY or FITNESS FOR A PARTICULAR PURPOSE. See the GNU
General Public License for more details. | This is a fork of a plugin
called "Add Document Type Styles" created by Aaron Hodge Silver
(http://springthistle.com) | Icons made by http://www.freepik.com from
http://www.flaticon.com - licensed under CC BY 3.0.
```

```
*/

// this function does the magic
function doctype_styles_new_regex($text) {
  $text = preg_replace('/href=([\'|"][[:alnum:]|
    [:punct:]]*)\.(pdf|doc|mp3|zip)([\'|"])/', 'href=\\1.\\2\\3
    class="link \\2"', $text);
  return $text;
}

// this functions adds the stylesheet to the head
function doctype_styles_new_styles() {
    wp_register_style('doctypes_styles', plugins_url('doctype_styles_
new.css', __FILE__));
    wp_enqueue_style('doctypes_styles');
}

// HOOKS =============

add_filter('the_content', 'doctype_styles_new_regex', 9);
add_action('wp_enqueue_scripts', 'doctype_styles_new_styles');
```

Please make sure that there are no blank spaces before < ?php. If there are any spaces, the PHP code will break, complaining that headers have already been sent. This is quite a common mistake developers stumble into during their initial attempts with WordPress plugins.

It's also a generally good idea to not use the PHP closing tags (? >) at the end of your PHP files. It saves you from some of the most unfortunate execution errors.

Make sure you save and close this PHP file. You can now do one of two things:

- Using your FTP client, upload add_doctype_styles_new/ to your wp-content/plugins/ folder

- Zip up your folder into add_doctype_styles_new.zip and use the plugin uploader in wp-admin to add this plugin to your WordPress installation

This version of the plugin is available in the code bundle for this chapter — inside a subfolder labeled phase 1. Our plugin files will go through a couple of phases before we have the final version.

Once the plugin is installed, it will show up on the plugins page:

	Plugin	Description
	Add Document Type Styles New	Detects URLs in your posts and pages and displays nice document type
	Activate Edit Delete	icons next to them. Includes support for: PDF, DOC, MP3 and ZIP.
		Version 1.0	By Karol K	Visit plugin site

Now, you can activate it and test it out.

 If you need more in-depth advice on installing and working with plugins, then feel free to review *Chapter 5, Plugins and Widgets,* where we discussed plugins and widgets in detail.

Trying out the plugin

If you look at the podcast post we created in an earlier chapter, you'll notice that an MP3 icon has been added to it.

NEW PODCAST EPISODE

POSTED ON JANUARY 7, 2015

This is a test post to showcase how to publish a podcast episode.

Here it is: 📄 podcast 1

POSTED IN PODCAST

You can also try adding a new post with links to PDF, ZIP, or DOC files. This can be done by uploading the files through the media manager and clicking on **Insert into Post**. Then, when you view the post, you'll see that even more icons have been added to it by the plugin.

Now that you've learned about a basic plugin that uses hooks to piggyback on the existing WordPress functionality, let's enhance this plugin by giving the user some controls.

Adding an admin page

Some plugins add a page to wp-admin where you or the user can edit plugin options. We've seen this with **W3 Total Cache**, **WordPress SEO**, and others. Now, let's modify our plugin to give the user some control over which document types are supported. The following is what the new management page will look like when we are done:

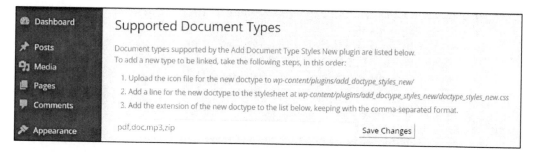

First, deactivate the plugin we just wrote. We'll make changes to it and then reactivate it. Following are the steps we'll carry out to modify the plugin in order to make this new page possible:

- Add functions that create an admin page and save the user's input in a new option.
- Modify the `doctype_styles_new_regex()` function so that it retrieves the user's input.
- Add hooks for the admin page functions.

Let's get started!

Adding management page functions

The management page that we will create is going to add an option to wp-admin. This uses the existing space in the WordPress `options` table in the database, so no database modifications are required. The name of the new option has to be unique. I'm going to call the new option `doctype_styles_new_supportedtypes`.

There are six functions we need to add to the plugin so that an admin page can be added to wp-admin. Let's take a look at the first two:

1. The *first* function adds the new option `doctype_styles_new_supportedtypes` when the plugin is activated, and sets the default value:

    ```
    function set_supportedtypes_options() {
        add_option("doctype_styles_new_supportedtypes",
          "pdf,doc,mp3,zip");
    }
    ```

2. The *second* function removes the new option when the plugin is deactivated:

```
function unset_supportedtypes_options () {
  delete_option("doctype_styles_new_supportedtypes");
}
```

3. Let's look at the new *third* function:

```
function modify_menu_for_supportedtypes() {
  add_submenu_page(
   'options-general.php',        //The new options page will
      be added as a submenu to the Settings menu.
   'Document Type Styles',     //Page <title>
   'Document Type Styles',     //Menu title
   'manage_options',           //Capability
   'add_doctype_styles_new',   //Slug
   'supportedtypes_options'    //Function to call
  );
}
```

This function adds a new item to the **Settings** menu in wp-admin by using the add_submenu_page() function call. This takes six arguments, namely, where the options page should be placed, page title, menu link text, the user at the maximum level who can access the link, what file to open (none, in this case), and the function to call, supportedtypes_options().

4. The supportedtypes_options() function is, in fact, the *fourth* new function we are adding.

```
function supportedtypes_options() {
  echo '<div class="wrap"><h2>Supported Document
    Types</h2>';
  if (isset($_POST['submit'])) {
    update_supportedtypes_options();
  }
  print_supportedtypes_form();
  echo '</div>';
}
```

This function actually displays our new page. It prints a title, checks to see if someone has clicked on the submit button; if the submit button has been clicked, the supportedtypes_options() function updates the options, and then prints the form.

5. The new *fifth* function we have to add is responsible for updating options if the submit button has been clicked:

```
function update_supportedtypes_options() {
  $updated = false;
  if ($_POST['doctype_styles_new_supportedtypes']) {
    $safe_val = addslashes(strip_tags($_POST
      ['doctype_styles_new_supportedtypes']));
    update_option('doctype_styles_new_supportedtypes',
      $safe_val);
    $updated = true;
  }

  if ($updated) {
    echo '<div id="message" class="updated fade">';
    echo '<p>Supported types successfully updated!</p>';
    echo '</div>';
  } else {
    echo '<div id="message" class="error fade">';
    echo '<p>Unable to update supported types!</p>';
    echo '</div>';
  }
}
```

6. The last function we need to add, the new *sixth* function, prints the form that the users will see. Please make sure to have no spaces before or after the closing tag (EOF;):

```
function print_supportedtypes_form() {
  $val_doctype_styles_new_supportedtypes =
    stripslashes(get_option('
    doctype_styles_new_supportedtypes'));
  echo <<<EOF
<p>Document types supported by the Add Document Type Styles New
plugin are listed below.<br />To add a new type to be linked, take
the following steps, in this order:
<ol>
  <li>Upload the icon file for the new doctype to <i>wp-
    content/plugins/add_doctype_styles_new/</i></li>
  <li>Add a line for the new doctype to the stylesheet at
    <i>wp-content/plugins/add_doctype_styles_new/
    doctype_styles_new.css</i></li>
  <li>Add the extension of the new doctype to the list
    below, keeping with the comma-separated format.</li>
</ol>
</p>
```

```
<form method="post">
  <input type="text" name=
    "doctype_styles_new_supportedtypes" size="50" value="$val_
doctype_styles_new_supportedtypes" />
  <input type="submit" name="submit" value="Save Changes"
    />
</form>
EOF;
}
```

These six functions together take care of adding a link in the menu, adding the management page for this link, and updating the new option.

Modifying the doctype_styles_new_regex() function

Now that the users are able to edit the list of supported document types by appending the document types they want, we should have a way of telling the `doctype_styles_new_regex()` function to use the user's list instead of the built-in list. To do so, we need to use `get_option('doctype_styles_new_supportedtypes')` in our `doctype_styles_new_regex()` function. The `get_option()` function will retrieve the value that the user has saved in the new option we just created. Modify your `doctype_styles_new_regex()` function so that it looks like this:

```
function ahs_doctypes_regex($text) {
    $types = get_option('doctype_styles_new_supportedtypes');
    $types = preg_replace('/,\s*/', '|', $types);

    $text = preg_replace('/href=([\'|"][[:alnum:]|
        [:punct:]]*)\.('.$types.')([\'|"])/i', 'href=\\1.\\2\\3
        class="link \\2"', $text);

    return $text;
}
```

Adding hooks

We have added our management page functions, but now we have to tell WordPress to use them. To do so, we just need to add the following three new hooks:

```
add_action('admin_menu', 'modify_menu_for_supportedtypes');
register_activation_hook(__FILE__, "set_supportedtypes_options");
register_deactivation_hook(__FILE__,
    "unset_supportedtypes_options");
```

The first hook tells WordPress to add our link to the menu when it creates the menu with `admin_menu()`. The next two hooks tell WordPress to call the activation and deactivation functions when the plugin is activated or deactivated.

 This version of the plugin is available in the code bundle for this chapter—inside a subfolder labeled `final`. It is the final version of our plugin.

Trying out the plugin

We have added all of the new functions. Now it's time to save the file and see what happens. You can go ahead and reactivate the plugin. Now, when you look at the **Settings** menu, you will see that the new link has been added:

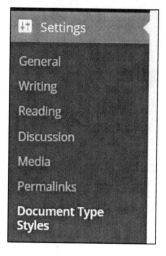

Click on it to see the management page:

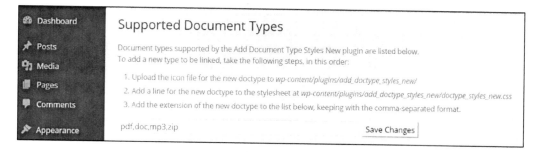

If you follow the three steps here on the management page (upload the file icon, add a new style to the stylesheet, and add the extension to the option), then that new document type will be supported.

There are already a number of ways in which this plugin could be improved. Some of them are as follows:

- Instead of making the user upload his or her new icon using FTP, the plugin could allow the user to upload the new icon directly via the new management page.
- The plugin could display the icons for the supported document types on the management page so that the users see what they look like.
- The plugin could check to make sure that for every document type in the option field there is an existing icon, else it displays an error to the user.

Perhaps, you'd like to try to make these changes yourself!

Testing your plugins

Just a minute ago, we've tried out our new plugin, so it's probably a good moment to say a word or two about testing your plugins and making sure that they don't cause any problems for regular users in general.

Our particular plugin is a very simple one; the only thing it does is process each link it finds inside any post's or page's content and add a custom icon next to it. However, even such a simple plugin can be a possible security breach point. For example, the only place where the user can input anything is the plugins section in wp-admin (the field handling the supported file types). Now, there is a possibility that someone might use this field to input a piece of specific PHP code instead of a standard file type, for instance, code that is meant to perform a specific action on the server side, which could result in a serious security breach. That is why our `update_supportedtypes_options()` function has these two lines:

```
$safe_val = addslashes(strip_tags($_POST
    ['doctype_styles_new_supportedtypes']));
update_option('doctype_styles_new_supportedtypes', $safe_val);
```

Thanks to them, everything that the user inputs will have all PHP and HTML tags stripped by `strip_tags()`, and then every character that needs to be quoted in database queries will be handled by `addslashes()`. Using such functions is a just-in-case practice, but it tends to be something that eventually pays off.

Apart from testing our work against some of the common hacking practices such as code injection and SQL injection, we also need to handle all kinds of unconventional uses we can think of. For instance, would anything bad happen if someone put a value that's not a standard file type? Or what if the CSS file goes missing all of a sudden? These are just some of the questions a good testing session should answer.

One more good way of testing plugins is to hand them over to a handful of trusted users and ask for feedback. Someone who's entirely new to your plugin will usually do a way better job at testing it than you — the author.

Of course, this short section here only scratches the surface of plugin testing and code testing in general, so I encourage you to give it a closer look on your own. There are many great resources on the Internet and in the nearest bookstore.

A plugin with DB access – capturing searched words

We're going to leave the **doctypes** plugin behind now, and create a new plugin, featuring active use of the database. Let's create a simple plugin that stores all the words that visitors search for (when using the blog's search function).

The database table structure for this plugin will be as follows:

The table name is `wp_searchedwords`:

Field	Type	Null	Key	Default	Extra
Id	INT	NOT NULL	PRI		auto_ increment
Word	VARCHAR(255)			NULL	
created	DATETIME	NOT NULL		Today 00:00:01	

Now, let's write the plugin code.

 Even though I say that the table is named `wp_searchedwords`, it won't always be the case. It's all based on the table prefix that's set on your site (the default one is indeed `wp_`). Here, I'm going to refer to the table as `wp_searchedwords` anyway, out of convenience.

Getting the plugin to talk to the database

The first part of this plugin has to be run only when the plugin is activated. This will be the initialization function. One of its tasks is to create or update the database table (the table will be created only if it hasn't been created before):

```
function searchedwords_init($content) {
  global $wpdb;
  $sw_table_name = $wpdb->prefix.'searchedwords';

  //creating the table (if it doesn't exist) or updating it if
    necessary
  if(isset($_GET['activate']) && 'true' == $_GET['activate']) {
    $sql = 'CREATE TABLE `'.$sw_table_name.'` (
      id INT NOT NULL AUTO_INCREMENT,
      word VARCHAR(255),
      created DATETIME NOT NULL DEFAULT \''.date('Y-m-d').'
        00:00:01\',
      PRIMARY KEY  (id)
    )';

    require_once(ABSPATH.'wp-admin/includes/upgrade.php');
    dbDelta($sql);
  }

  // in case a search has just been performed, store the searched
    word
  if (!empty($_GET['s'])) {
    $current_searched_words = explode(" ",urldecode($_GET['s']));
    foreach ($current_searched_words as $word) {
      $wpdb->query($wpdb->prepare("INSERT into `$sw_table_name`
        VALUES (null,'%s','".date('Y-m-d H:i:s')."')", $word));
    }
  }
}
```

This function connects to the database by using various function calls like `dbDelta()`, `$wpdb->query()`, and `$wpdb->prepare()`. The `dbDelta()` function takes care of creating the table or updating it (whatever is needed at the time; find out more at `https://codex.wordpress.org/Creating_Tables_with_Plugins`). Apart from this, when dealing with the WordPress database, you can utilize any database-related PHP function in existence. Or, you can use the WordPress' class member function `$wpdb->get_results()`. The function we're using here also stores the searched word in the database table if a search has just been performed. This is done through the `$wpdb->query()` and `$wpdb->prepare()` functions.

Adding management page functions

We now need a familiar-looking function that adds a management page to the admin menu. In this case, we use `add_management_page()` instead of `add_submenu_page()` because this plugin is more of a tool than something that needs settings:

```
function modify_menu_for_searchedwords() {
  $page = add_management_page(
    "Capture Searched Words",
    "Capture Searched Words",
    'manage_options',
    'capture_searches_new',
    'searchedwords_page'
  );
}
```

For this plugin, we're not going to load any custom styling or CSS files. The topic here is to just showcase how database connection can be done, so we're going to keep everything else ultra-simple and minimal. Therefore, the only thing we have to do at this point is write a function that retrieves the information from the database and displays it on the new management page (again, everything is done through the `$wpdb` object).

```
function searchedwords_page() {
  global $wpdb;
  $sw_table_name = $wpdb->prefix.'searchedwords';


  $searched_words = $wpdb->get_results("SELECT COUNT(word) AS
    occurrence, word FROM `$sw_table_name` GROUP BY word ORDER BY
    occurrence DESC");
  ?>
<div class="wrap" style="max-width: 600px;">
<h2>Searched Words</h2>
<table class="wp-list-table widefat">
<thead>
  <tr>
    <th scope="col">Search Words</th>
    <th scope="col"># of Searches</th>
  </tr>
</thead>
<tbody>
  <?php
  if($searched_words !== NULL) {
    foreach($searched_words as $searched_word) {
```

```
        echo '<tr valign="top"><td>'.$searched_word-
            >word.'</td><td>'.$searched_word->occurrence.'</td></tr>';
    }
    $searched_perfomed = true;
  }
  else {
    echo '<tr valign="top"><td colspan="2"><strong>No searches
        have been performed yet</strong></td></tr>';
  }
  ?>
</tbody>
</table>
</div>
  <?php
}
```

That's it. The previous plugin had more functions because data was being captured from the user and being saved. Here, that's not necessary.

Lastly, we just need to add two hooks:

```
add_filter('init', 'searchedwords_init');
add_action('admin_menu', 'modify_menu_for_searchedwords');
```

The first hook tells WordPress to run the initialization function when the plugin is activated, or when a search is performed. The second hook modifies the admin menu to add a link to the new management page.

 This version of the plugin is available in the code bundle for this chapter—inside a subfolder labeled `final`. It is the first and final version of our plugin.

Trying out the plugin

As with the last plugin, you can now either upload your plugin using FTP to `wp-content/plugins` or turn it into a ZIP file and add it using the uploader to wp-admin.

Once you've installed it, activate it. Then, look at the menu under **Tools** and you'll see a link to the new management page:

When you click on **Capture Searched Words**, you'll see a new page that the plugin created:

Searched Words

Search Words	# of Searches
spanish	2
podcast	1
chili	1

As you can see, I did perform some searches beforehand just to have something to show on this new page. You can do the same by placing a search field widget in your sidebar (the next screenshot), and then experimenting with different search words and phrases. The plugin will pick them all up and display the most searched ones in its section in wp-admin:

Learning more

There are hundreds of hooks available in WordPress—way too many to cover in this book. You can learn more about them by going online. Start out at these online reference sites:

- The *Plugin API* article contains very thorough information about writing plugins and using hooks (`https://codex.wordpress.org/Plugin_API`).

- For a complete list of action hooks, visit `https://codex.wordpress.org/Plugin_API/Action_Reference`.

- For a complete list of filter hooks, visit `https://codex.wordpress.org/Plugin_API/Filter_Reference`.

- You may also want to take a step back and look at the general Plugin Resources page in the WordPress Codex at `https://codex.wordpress.org/Plugin_Resources`.

- If you want to submit your plugin to the WordPress plugin repository, you'll have to take steps similar to those you took when preparing a theme, and you'll also have to get hooked up to the WordPress SVN repository. Learn more about how to submit a plugin to the WordPress plugin repository at `https://codex.wordpress.org/Plugin_Submission_and_Promotion`.

Widgets

Writing a widget bears some similarities to writing a plugin, but in some ways it's easier because there is a widget class that you can leverage for some of the functionalities. In other ways, it's also a bit more time-consuming as there's a lot of mandatory code that every widget has to feature.

Custom tag cloud widget

In this section, we'll see how to write a widget that displays a custom tag cloud that we can then place in the sidebar. There will also be the possibility to change the title of the widget, and although this is a tag cloud widget, we'll be able to switch tags to categories and display them using a tag-cloud-like style as well. In its final form, the widget will look like this:

Just as a comparison, here's what the standard tag cloud widget (the native one in WordPress) looks like:

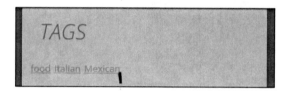

Let's get started!

Naming our widget

In this case, we're going to create the widget as a standalone plugin. So, just like any other plugin, it needs a unique name and a unique appearance in the `wp-content/plugins` folder.

 I encourage you to search the Web whenever you're creating a new widget or plugin just to make sure that there's nothing out there going by the same name. On top of that, use "namespace" as a prefix with every file name (and function name) that you're creating. For example, mine is "kk_".

I'll name the new plugin file (which holds the widget) `kk_tag_cloud_widget.php` and put it in its own `kk_tag_cloud_widget` folder inside `wp-content/plugins`.

This main PHP file starts just like any other plugin, with this declaration:

```php
<?php
/*
Plugin Name: Karol K's Tag Cloud Widget
Description: Displays a nice tag cloud.
Plugin URI: http://newinternetorder.com/plugins
Version: 1.0
Author: Karol K
Author URI: http://karol.cc/
License: GNU General Public License v2 or later
*/
```

The widget structure

When you are building a widget by using the widget class, your widget needs to have the following structure:

```php
class UNIQUE_WIDGET_NAME extends WP_Widget {

  public function __construct() {
    $widget_ops = array();
    $control_ops = array();
    parent::__construct('base id', 'name', $widget_ops,
      $control_ops);
  }

  public function widget($args, $instance) {
    // used when the sidebar calls the widget
  }

  public function form($instance) {
    // prints the form on the widgets page
  }

  public function update($new_instance, $old_instance) {
    // used when the user saves his/her widget options
  }
}

// initiate the widget

// register the widget
```

My unique widget name for this project is KK_Widget_Tag_Cloud. Now, let's go over each of the preceding functions one by one and understand what's going on.

The widget initiation function

Let's start with the widget initiation function. Blank, it looks like this:

```
public function __construct() {
  $widget_ops = array();
  $control_ops = array();
  parent::__construct('base-id', 'name', $widget_ops,
    $control_ops);
}
```

In this function, which is the constructor of the class, we initialize various things that the WP_Widget class is expecting. The first two variables, to which you can give any name you want, are just a handy way to set the two array variables expected by the third line of code.

Let's take a look at these three lines of code:

- The $widget_ops variable is where you can set the class name, which is given to the div widget itself, and the description, which is shown in wp-admin on the widgets page.

- The $control_ops variable is where you can set options for the control box in wp-admin on the widget page, like the width and height of the widget and the ID prefix used for the names and IDs of the items inside. For my basic widget, I'm not going to use this variable (it's optional).

- When you call the parent class's constructor, WP_Widget(), you'll tell it the widget's unique ID, the widget's display title, and pass along the two arrays you created.

For this widget, my code now looks like this:

```
public function __construct() {
  parent::__construct(
    'kk-tag-cloud',
    'KK Tag Cloud',
    array(
      'description' => 'Your most used tags in cloud format; same
        height; custom background'
    )
  );
}
```

The widget form function

The widget form function has to be named `form()`. You may not rename it if you want the widget class to know what its purpose is. You also need to have an argument in there, which I'm calling `$instance`, which the class also expects. This is where the current widget settings are stored.

This function needs to have all of the functionalities to create the form that users will see when adding the widget to a sidebar. Let's look at some abbreviated code and then explore what it's doing:

```php
public function form($instance) {
    $instance = wp_parse_args((array) $instance, array('template' =>
        ''));
    $current_taxonomy = $this->_get_current_taxonomy($instance);
    ?>
    <p>
        <label for="<?php echo $this->get_field_id('title');
            ?>">Title</label>
        <input type="text" class="widefat" id="<?php echo $this-
            >get_field_id('title'); ?>" name="<?php echo $this-
            >get_field_name('title'); ?>" value="<?php if
(isset($instance['title'])) {echo esc_attr($instance['title']);}
        ?>" />
    </p>
    <p>
        <label for="<?php echo $this->get_field_id('taxonomy');
            ?>">Taxonomy</label>
        <select class="widefat" id="<?php echo $this-
            >get_field_id('taxonomy'); ?>" name="<?php echo $this-
            >get_field_name('taxonomy'); ?>">
        <?php foreach(get_object_taxonomies('post') as $taxonomy)  :
        $tax = get_taxonomy($taxonomy);
        if(!$tax->show_tagcloud || empty($tax->labels->name))
            continue;
        ?>
        <option value="<?php echo esc_attr($taxonomy) ?>" <?php
            selected($taxonomy, $current_taxonomy); ?>><?php echo $tax-
            >labels->name; ?></option>
        <?php endforeach; ?>
        </select>
    </p>
    <?php
}
```

First, you use a WordPress function named `wp_parse_args()`, which creates an `$instance` array that your form will use. What's in it depends on what defaults you've set and what settings the user has already saved.

Then, you create form fields. Note that for each form field, I make use of the built-in functions that will create unique names and IDs and input the existing values.

- `$this->get-field_id()` creates a unique ID based on the widget instance (remember, you can create more than one instance of this widget).

- `$this->get_field_name()` creates a unique name based on the widget instance.

- The `$instance` array is where you will find the current values for the widget, whether they are defaults or user-saved data.

All the other code in there is just regular PHP and HTML. Note that if you give the user the ability to set a title, name that field `title`, WordPress will show it on the widget form when it's minimized. The widget form this will create will look like this:

The widget save function

When a user clicks the **Save** button on the widget form, WordPress uses AJAX to run your save function. You need to be sure to save whatever the user types in, which is all we're doing in this case, but you can put other functionalities here if it's appropriate for your widget (for example, database interactions, conversions, calculations, and so on). The final code for this function is as follows:

```php
public function update($new_instance, $old_instance) {
    $instance['title'] = $new_instance['title'];
    $instance['taxonomy'] = stripslashes($new_instance['taxonomy']);
    return $instance;
}
```

Be sure this function is named update() and is prepared to accept two instances, one with the old data and one with the just-submitted data. You can write your code to check $new_instance for problems, and thus, return $old_instance if the new one isn't valid. The $instance data you return will be what's shown in the update widget form.

The widget print function

The third main function in your widget class is the one that is called by the sidebar when it's time to actually show the widget to people visiting the website. It needs to retrieve any relevant saved user data and print out information for the website visitor. In this case, our final print function looks like this:

```php
public function widget($args, $instance) {
    extract($args);
    $current_taxonomy = $this->_get_current_taxonomy($instance);
    if(!empty($instance['title'])) {
        $title = $instance['title'];
    }
    else {
        if('post_tag' == $current_taxonomy) {
            $title = 'Tags';
        }
        else {
            $tax = get_taxonomy($current_taxonomy);
            $title = $tax->labels->name;
        }
    }
    $title = apply_filters('widget_title', $title, $instance, $this-
        >id_base);

    $before_widget = '<div class="widget-container
        kk_widget_tag_cloud">';
    $after_widget = '</div>';
    $before_title = '<h1 class="widget-title">';
    $after_title = '</h1>';

    echo $before_widget;
    if ( $title ) { echo $before_title . $title . $after_title; }
    echo '<div class="kk_tagcloud">';
    wp_tag_cloud(apply_filters('widget_tag_cloud_args',
        array('taxonomy' => $current_taxonomy)));
    echo "</div>\n";
    echo $after_widget;
}
```

The preceding function calls one more helper function responsible for fetching the current taxonomy. A very simple one, though:

```
function _get_current_taxonomy($instance) {
  if ( !empty($instance['taxonomy']) &&
    taxonomy_exists($instance['taxonomy']) )
    return $instance['taxonomy'];
  return 'post_tag';
}
```

The first thing I do in the main function is extract the data in the instance, which has the information the website administrator had saved when filling out the widget form. Then, the widget takes a look into the selected taxonomy (tags or categories) and displays all individual items as a simple one-line list.

Custom widget styles

Our small widget has its own stylesheet that needs to be included in the current theme's head section, like any other stylesheet.

The file is named kk_tag_cloud_widget.css and contains the following:

```
.kk_widget_tag_cloud .kk_tagcloud {
    line-height: 1.5em;
}

.kk_widget_tag_cloud .kk_tagcloud a {
    display: inline-block;
    margin: 3px 2px;
    padding: 0 11px;
    border-radius: 3px;
    -webkit-border-radius: 3px;
    background: #eee;
    color: #279090;
    font-size: 12px !important;
    line-height: 30px;
    text-transform: uppercase;
}

.kk_widget_tag_cloud .kk_tagcloud a:hover {
    color: #f2f2f2;
    background: #404040;
}
```

Nothing fancy, just a set of classes that will make sure that the widget looks great. The only thing we have to do with this stylesheet is enqueue it through a standard WordPress hook. Place this in your plugin's main file:

```
function kk_tag_cloud_widget_styles_load() {
  wp_register_style('kk_tag_cloud_widget_styles',
    plugins_url('kk_tag_cloud_widget.css', __FILE__ ));
  wp_enqueue_style('kk_tag_cloud_widget_styles');
}
add_action('wp_enqueue_scripts',
  'kk_tag_cloud_widget_styles_load');
```

Initiating and hooking up the widget

That's it for widget functionality! Now, you just need to add a little piece of code that will hook the widget up to the rest of WordPress:

```
function KK_Widget_Tag_Cloud_Reg() {
  register_widget('KK_Widget_Tag_Cloud');
}
add_action('widgets_init', 'KK_Widget_Tag_Cloud_Reg');
```

This tells WordPress that when it initiates widgets, it should be sure to register our new widget.

 This version of the widget is available in the code bundle for this chapter—inside a subfolder labeled phase 1. We'll still be adding one more feature before we can call it the final version.

Trying out the widget

Your widget is ready to go! Save all your changes, and upload your widget to the wp-content/plugins folder. Go to the **Installed Plugins** page, and you'll see your widget waiting to be activated, as usual. After you click on the **Activate** button, you can navigate to **Appearance | Widgets**. You'll see the widget waiting to be added to a sidebar:

KK Tag Cloud

Your most used tags in cloud
format; same height; custom
background

Drag the widget to a sidebar, and then click on the little down arrow to edit it. You'll see the options slide down, as shown in the following screenshot:

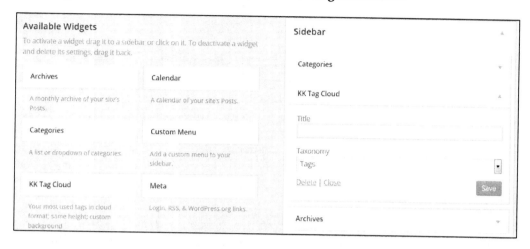

You can enter a **Title** or leave it blank for the default, and choose **Taxonomy** to use. Then, click on **Save** as you would with any widget. When you return to the frontend of the site and reload, the new tag cloud will be right there:

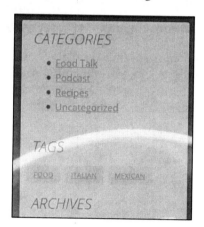

Learning more

You can browse the following online reference sites to learn more about widgets:

- The WordPress Widgets API is located at
  `https://codex.wordpress.org/Widgets_API`

- WordPress lists a number of widgets at
  `https://codex.wordpress.org/WordPress_Widgets`

- If you want to find more widgets to install on your website, visit the widgets section of the plugin repository at `https://wordpress.org/plugins/tags/widget`

Bundling a widget with an existing plugin

If you're writing a plugin and you'd like to make a widget available with it, you don't have to create a separate widget plugin. Just include all of the widget code—like what we created in the preceding section—in with your plugin's PHP file. When the user activates the plugin, the widget you created will automatically show up on the widgets page in wp-admin. No need for a separate file!

Shortcodes

Shortcodes are a handy way to let a nontechnical person, such as an editor of a website, include dynamic functionality within pages and posts, without having to actually use any PHP, complex HTML structures, or custom JavaScript. In other words, shortcodes are handy reusable pieces of code, yet they don't require any actual coding experience or knowledge on the end user's part.

Shortcodes and the way they work

The way a shortcode works is that you tell WordPress to look at the text within square brackets (`[]`) and evaluate it by running a PHP function. That PHP function can live in the `functions.php` file of your theme, or in a plugin file, or in a widget file. Let's create a simple shortcode and include it with our most recent widget.

Types of shortcodes

Shortcodes are a pretty simple concept by definition, but we can still distinguish three main types:

- **Single-tag shortcodes**: These shortcodes are executed with just a single tag, for example, `[my_first_shortcode/]`.

- **Double-tag shortcodes**: These shortcodes are executed with opening and closing tags, for example, `[my_2nd_shortcode]some text here[/my_2nd_shortcode]` (please notice that the closing tag has an additional `/`). As you can see, there's also some content within the tags. This content can be processed by the shortcode function.

- **Shortcodes with attributes**: These shortcodes can have one or two tags and also a number of attributes we can use to customize the output, for example, `[my_3rd_shortcode name="Karol" twitter="carlosinho"]`some text here`[/my_3rd_shortcode]`.

Creating a simple shortcode

Let's create a simple shortcode that will make it possible to use our widget's output inside any given post or page.

This is going to be a double-tag shortcode with one additional attribute, which we'll use to indicate whether the output should be formatted using our custom CSS or WordPress' native styling.

Let's start by creating a new function at the bottom of our `kk_tag_cloud_widget.php` file, and then, we'll go through each individual line:

```
function kk_tag_cloud_handler($atts, $content=null) {
  extract(shortcode_atts(array(
    'use_css' => '1',
    'taxonomy' => 'post_tag'
  ), $atts));

  $tax = 'post_tag';
  if(taxonomy_exists($taxonomy)) $tax = $taxonomy;

  $result = '';

  if ('0' != $use_css) {
    $result .= '<div class="kk_widget_tag_cloud"><div
      class="kk_tagcloud">';
  }
  if (null != $content) {
    $result .= addslashes(strip_tags($content)).' ';
  }
  $result .= wp_tag_cloud(apply_filters(
    'widget_tag_cloud_args',
    array('taxonomy' => $tax, 'echo' => false)
  ));
  if ('0' != $use_css) {
    $result .= '</div></div>';
  }

  return $result;
}
```

First of all, note that this function does not *echo* or *print* anything. It just returns a string. If you let your function print, it won't look correct on the website.

Inside our function, the first line handles the custom attributes that the shortcode receives (in this case, just the `use_css` parameter for indicating whether the styles should be used or not, and the `taxonomy` parameter to indicate the taxonomy that should be shown in the shortcode). WordPress will hand off the `$atts` argument automatically, and we only have to use the `extract()` function to turn the attributes the user submits into variables available in the function. The values in the array passed to `extract()` set the defaults, in case the user chooses no options. In general, there is no limit to the number of options that you can make available to the shortcode users.

The next line extracts the taxonomy identifier and tries to turn it into a valid taxonomy. In case the user's input is not valid, the default `post_tag` taxonomy will be used. The final part of the function handles the display based on the state of the `use_css` attribute. Pretty basic at this point! There's also a possibility to include custom text as the main content of the shortcode. This can be useful in some situations.

What we have to do now is tell WordPress that this function is a shortcode, and we do so by using a hook. Be sure to choose something unique. I've chosen `kk_tag_cloud` as the name for this shortcode, so the hook looks like this:

```
add_shortcode('kk_tag_cloud', 'kk_tag_cloud_handler');
```

To use this shortcode in our content, all we have to do is edit any given post or page and put a line like this in it:

```
[kk_tag_cloud taxonomy="category"]Select the category you'd like
    to read next:[/kk_tag_cloud]
```

Such usage will have the following effect:

We can also use the shortcode like this:

```
[kk_tag_cloud use_css="0" taxonomy="category"]Select the category
    you'd like to read next:[/kk_tag_cloud]
```

This will disable the custom styles and produce this effect:

To display the tag cloud in its default form (showing the tags and using the custom stylesheet), all we have to do is execute the shortcode like this:

```
[kk_tag_cloud][/kk_tag_cloud]
```

The effect is shown in the following screenshot:

FOOD   ITALIAN   MEXICAN

There are very few limitations regarding what you can and cannot do with shortcodes. However, the most common uses are for embedding online videos from sites such as YouTube (using the [youtube] shortcode, for example), or for showing various social media boxes and activity streams.

 This version of the widget is available in the code bundle for this chapter—inside a subfolder labeled final. It is the final version of our widget.

Enabling shortcodes in widgets

By default, shortcodes are ignored inside widgets. So, assume that you add a text widget with your shortcode in it, as shown in the following screenshot:

Then, all that would show is the shortcode itself:

This can be fixed by adding the following line just after our shortcode definition:

```
add_filter('widget_text', 'do_shortcode', 11);
```

The third parameter in this function (11) specifies the order in which the functions associated with the `widget_text` action are executed. Using 11 means that our shortcode functions will be executed later on in the queue. You can learn more about this parameter and the whole `add_filter()` function at `https://codex.wordpress.org/Function_Reference/add_filter`.

Now, all shortcodes on the site will be evaluated in widgets. In other words, you can place any shortcode inside a text widget.

In this particular case, however, you can see that enabling our shortcode inside a text widget has very little sense, as we can clearly just use our tag cloud widget normally instead. But for other implementations (other shortcodes), it can indeed be useful.

Summary

In this chapter, you learned everything you need to know about creating basic plugins and widgets. Now, you know how to structure the PHP file, where to put your functions, and how to use hooks. You also learned about adding management pages and enabling plugins and widgets to have database access. On top of all this, you learned how to create shortcodes, a powerful tool that lets you make dynamic functionalities available to all WordPress users. With your existing knowledge of PHP and HTML, you now have the tools to get started with writing every plugin and widget your heart may desire.

The next chapter will be all about community blogging—running multi-user blogs, and other aspects of turning your site into a serious online magazine.

10
Community Blogging

So far in this book, we've focused on working with a personal website: one that belongs to, and is used by just one person. However, many blogs are used in a different way - there may be a single blog or website with a variety of writers, editors, and administrators. This makes the site more like a community project or even an online magazine.

Furthermore, it's by no means uncommon for bigger online publishers to use WordPress as the base of their websites. In which case, the site has a number of authors, editors, reviewers, and overall contributors with varying responsibilities. Not to mention the technical staff or designers.

In this chapter, we'll discuss allowing a blog to have multiple authors with differing levels of control over the blog's administration and content. We'll explore user management for multiple users on one blog, as well as other aspects of blogging as a member of a community. We'll also take a look at using a non-blog website with multiple users.

Concerns for a multi-author blog

A multi-author blog is useful when a group of people with similar interests want to collaborate and share space to publish their writing, or if an organization or company wants to have an online magazine. If that group wants to publish news on a particular topic, or on many topics in a broad sense, then they'll each need to be able to log in and post their content, update their profile, and so on. For example, I can decide that I want every member of my family to be able to contribute to my Daily Cooking blog. Each of my sisters, brothers, cousins, aunts, and uncles can add their recipes and discoveries regarding food, which has the potential to make my food blog a richer and more exciting place for visitors.

However, content moderation is also essential to a multi-author blog. The best way to keep a blog clean and relevant to the topic is by using a moderation flow that restricts the display of content until it travels through an approval process. Such practice is usually called workflow. A workflow makes working in large groups much easier and more manageable.

User roles and abilities

WordPress includes the ability to have an unlimited number of users. Each user can be assigned one of five different roles. Let's look at these roles one at a time, starting with the most powerful one.

Administrator

When you installed WordPress, it created a user with administrative powers for you. This role is called administrator, and every WordPress site must have at least one admin (you will not be allowed to delete them all). As you have already seen in the earlier chapters, administrators can do everything.

 The administrator's primary purpose is to manage everything about a website.

In general, you're not going to want to have a lot of administrators on a single blog or website. It is best to keep just one administrator for a blog with 10 to 20 authors and editors or perhaps up to three administrators for a blog with dozens of users.

Some examples of the actions that only a user with the administrator role can take are as follows:

- Switch blog theme
- Add, edit, activate, or deactivate plugins
- Add, edit, or delete users
- Manage general blog options and settings

When creating more administrator accounts (or managing the main one), make sure to use only complex passwords that are hard to break using any sort of brute-force methods. In a nutshell, use as many numbers, special characters, combinations of uppercase and lowercase letters as you can. A lot of hacking attempts revolve around password guessing, so the more complex your password is, the tougher it will be to break.

Editor

After the administrator, the editor has the most powerful role. This role is for the users who need to manage everything about the content of a website, but don't need to be able to change the basic structure, design or functionality of the blog itself (that's for administrators).

 The editor's primary purpose is to manage the content of a blog.

To get an idea of what the screen looks when a user logs in as an editor, let's take a look at the editor's menu (to the right) in comparison with the administrator's menu (to the left):

As you can see, the top section is unchanged (apart from the **Updates** link). However, nearly the entire bottom menu, with **Appearance**, **Plugins**, **Users** (which is replaced with **Profile**), and **Settings**, has disappeared. We can see that the editor is left with only the ability to edit his or her own profile, and to access the **Tools** section, which includes any plugin pages that allow editor-level users.

The examples of actions that a user with the editor role can take are as follows:

- Manage all posts
- Create and edit pages
- Moderate comments
- Manage categories, tags, and links
- Edit other users' content

There's one very useful aspect of the editor's role. If you take a closer look, you'll see that it has all the credentials that one would need to publish any piece of content on a given WordPress site. This makes it perfect for everyday use, even for single-author blogs/sites. Therefore, what I actually encourage you to do is set a separate editor account for yourself, and then use it for posting and editing content, instead of working with the default administrator account. This setup is a lot safer, particularly if someone tries to hijack your password or in case of any other mishap to your account. The site itself won't get harmed (considering the fact that editors can't install new plugins or delete any existing ones).

For multi-author blogs/sites, the editor role is meant to be assigned to users who are in charge of the content published on the site. Essentially, like the name itself indicates, the "editor" role is perfect for editors.

Author

Authors have much less access than editors. Authors can add and edit their own posts, and manage the posts made by their subordinates. However, they can neither edit posts made by other authors, nor manage comments on posts that don't belong to them.

 The author's primary purpose is to manage his or her own content.

To get an idea of the experience of a user with the author role, let's take a look at the author's menu (to the right) in comparison with the editor's menu (to the left):

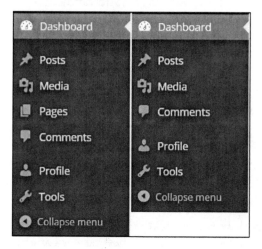

As you can see in the preceding screenshot, the **Pages** section has disappeared. Additionally, if the author looks at the complete list of posts, they will only have the ability to view, and not edit, quick edit, or delete posts that he or she did not author (highlighted):

As you would imagine, the author role is perfect for, well…authors – users who are actively involved in creating content for your site. Authors can, for example, do the following:

- Submit and publish their posts
- Manage their posts after the publication
- Moderate the comments under their posts

Contributor

Contributors are only able to write posts and submit them for review. These posts will be in **Pending Review** status until an editor, or administrator agrees to publish them. Contributors cannot upload images or other files, view the media library, add categories, edit comments, or any of the other tasks available to more advanced users.

 The contributor's primary purpose is to submit content for consideration.

One important thing worth mentioning is that although contributors can create and submit their work for review, once the article is published, they no longer have the ability to edit it in any way. However, they do get access to the comments section (for moderation).

When it comes to the real-world applications of this role, it's most commonly used when working with guest bloggers or any other regular contributors who are not part of your in-house team. Guest blogging is really popular nowadays, and handling it through contributor accounts is much less labor-intensive than receiving articles via e-mail and then having to copy-and-paste them to WordPress.

Subscriber

Subscribers have no ability to do anything at all. They can only log in and edit their profile (adjust their first name, last name, password, biographical information, and so on), and that's it. Depending on the permissions set in **Settings | Discussion**, blog visitors may have to sign up as subscribers in order to be able to post comments. Also, there are some plugins that handle sending informational updates to subscribers, such as newsletters or e-mail notifications of new posts.

 A subscriber has no editorial power over the website. It's a placeholder role.

Most of the time, this role is used as a placeholder. Take, for example, a specific author who had been contributing to your site regularly in the past, but hasn't submitted anything in months. Instead of deleting their account completely, you can simply change their role to that of a subscriber.

Managing users

To manage users, log in (as an administrator, of course) and navigate to **Users**. You'll see a list of your existing users, as seen in the following screenshot:

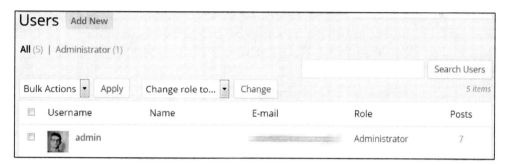

When we installed WordPress, it created only our first user (which is how we've been logging in all this time). So let's create a new user, and assign that user the next most powerful role - editor. To do this, navigate to **Users | Add New**. You'll see the **Add New User** form as shown in the next screenshot:

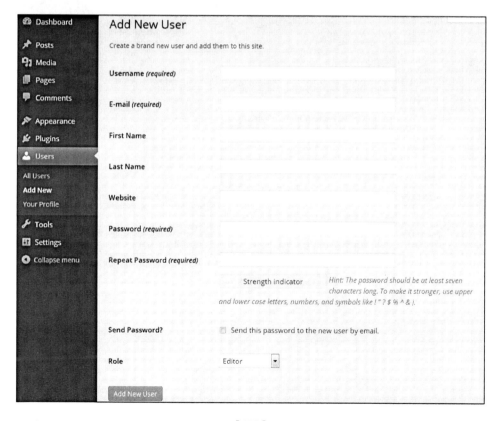

On this form, only the **Username**, **E-mail**, and **Password** fields are required. You can also change the **Role** from the default (**Subscriber**) to one of the other roles. In this case, I've selected **Editor**. Then, I click on the **Add New User** button. Apart from the required fields, it's also a good practice to fill in **First Name** and **Last Name**. This can make the task of further managing the user accounts much clearer.

I can repeat this process to add an author, a contributor and a subscriber. When I'm done, the **Users** page (where the users can be managed) will look like the next screenshot:

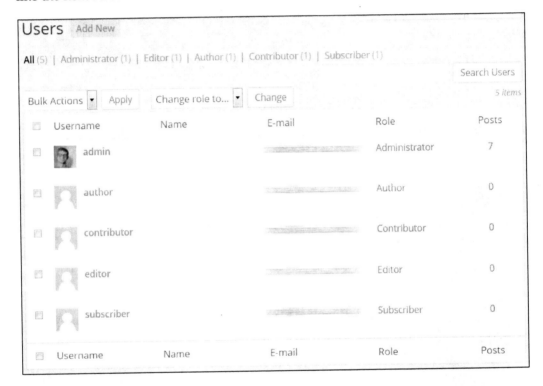

As with any other management list in wp-admin, you can roll over a row to see the management links. In this case, you can edit or delete users. You can use the checkboxes and the **Bulk Actions** menu, or use the filter links to view only users with particular roles. You can change the role of one or more users on this page by checking the box (or boxes) and using the **Change role to...** drop-down menu.

Enabling users to self-register

Adding users by yourself is not the only way to add users to your WordPress website. You can also give your users the ability to register themselves. First, navigate to **Settings | General** and make sure you've checked **Anyone can register** next to **Membership**.

I strongly recommend leaving **New User Default Role** as **Subscriber**, though **Contributor** would also be fine if the purpose of your blog requires it. However, allowing new users to automatically be assigned a role with more power than that is just asking for trouble.

Next, add a link somewhere on your blog that links the users to the login and registration pages. The easiest way to do this is to use the widget named **Meta**, which comes with your WordPress installation. It will add a box to your sidebar with a few useful links, including **Log in** and **Register**.

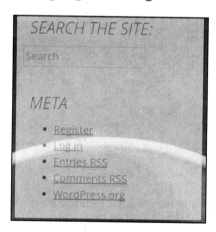

Of course, if this is not exactly the collection of links that you want, you can create your own widget (we talked about widgets in *Chapter 5, Plugins and Widgets*). Users clicking on **Register** will be taken to the following basic registration page that asks for only **Username** and **E-mail, as seen in the following screenshot:**

After submitting this form, the user will be e-mailed a password, and the main site administrator will be sent an e-mail notification of the new registration. The user can now log in and edit his/her profile, or do more if an administrator changes their role.

Learning more

You can learn more about the built-in WordPress roles and capabilities at `https://codex.wordpress.org/Roles_and_Capabilities`.

User management plugins

At the time of writing, there are over 350 plugins tagged as "users" in the WordPress plugin directory (`https://wordpress.org/plugins/tags/users`). We can actually divide those plugins into many groups as the functionality offered is exceptionally wide. For example, there are plugins for the following:

- Dealing with various author accounts, co-authoring posts, and multi-author sites

- Constructing membership sites around WordPress where members can get access to premium packages of content based on their subscription model

- Building a classic e-commerce store where everybody can make a purchase from the available directory of "things"

- Building an online forum based on WordPress

- Building an e-mail newsletter sent to a given site's users directly from within WordPress, instead of using external services

- Launching a social network on WordPress

- Managing user profiles for registered users

As you can see, the number of possibilities is really striking. If we want to, we can do essentially anything with a WordPress site and its users. Only our imagination is the limit.

Finally, let's not forget about one of the more popular areas in modern website launch – social networks (like Facebook). As it turns out, you don't need a huge budget at your disposal in order to launch such a network. A plugin like **BuddyPress** (`https://buddypress.org/`) has all the functionality you'd need and, best of all, it's free. We'll actually give BuddyPress a closer look in the next chapter where we'll focus on building non-blog websites, but I just wanted to mention it here to keep the message complete.

Summary

In this chapter, we learned how to manage a group of users working with a single blog, which is a community of users. Community blogging can play an important role in a user group, or a news website. We also learned how to manage the different levels of privileges for users in a community.

In the next chapter, we'll walk through the process of creating a complete non-blog website from scratch.

11
Creating a Non-blog Website
Part 1 – The Basics

As you have seen while reading this book, WordPress comes fully equipped to power a blog with all its particular requirements of post handling, categorization, chronological display, and so on. However, powering blogs is not WordPress' only purpose. In fact, there are millions of websites out there right now running WordPress, where blogging is not the primary focus of the website. I myself have built a number of such sites.

Just to give you a general idea of what's possible, here's a list of some popular non-blog type websites that you can build and launch using WordPress (we will cover some of them in more detail later in this and the next chapter):

- **Static websites**: Featuring just a handful of static subpages that are not meant to be updated very often; also, the main content is not organized chronologically like blog posts.

- **Corporate or business websites**: Similar to the previous type, but usually a bit bigger in size and in the number of subpages; additionally, for most business sites, their design appears very official and toned down.

- **One-page websites**: Websites that only have a single page of content; used mostly as a business card type site, or used by businesses that don't have a lot of content to showcase on their site. Even though the whole site is comprised of just one page, the designs are usually attractive with a lot of dynamic transition effects and parallax scrolling backgrounds.

- **E-commerce stores**: Websites where anyone can browse through a number of products and then use a shopping cart to make a purchase. Apart from the shopping cart functionality, there's also online payment integration and often a backend inventory management system.

- **Membership websites**: A kind of site where some of the content is available only to those users who have signed up for a membership and (often) paid a small fee for the privilege; such members-only areas can contain any type of content that the site owner finds suitable – WordPress doesn't limit this in any way.

- **Video blogs**: Just like a standard blog; only instead of text-based posts, the blogger publishes video-posts.

- **Photo blogs**: Just like video blogs, only revolving around photos; a very common type of blog for photographers, graphic designers and other people of similar professions.

- **Product websites**: In short, it's a type of site very similar to an e-commerce store, only this time, we're usually dealing with just a single product on sale. It's a very popular type of website for all kinds of web apps, iOS or Android apps.

- **Social networks**: Just like Facebook, only run on WordPress.

- **Niche business websites**: Some examples of such sites are local restaurant websites, hotel websites, coffee shop websites, personal portfolio websites, art gallery websites, and so on.

Again, if I were to explain, in brief, what a general non-blog website is, I'd say that it's any kind of website where the blog is not the main functionality used by the website owner. And of course, non-blog websites make up the majority of the Internet as a whole. However, since we're discussing WordPress here, which many still believe to be a blog system only, I just want to assure you that it's no longer the case. These days, WordPress can be used for virtually anything.

In this chapter and the next, we will go through some of the types of websites just mentioned and present an effective way of building them with WordPress. We'll also use the knowledge which we've acquired in the previous chapters, so it's best that you get familiar with everything that's been going on so far before consuming the information in the following pages.

Also, there are a number of new pieces of functionality that we have not explored in previous chapters, and this is what we will be focusing on. These include the following:

- Designating a standard page to be the front page of the website

- Creating a custom post type with a custom taxonomy

- Altering custom post type display in the wp-admin

Let's get started!

The must-do tasks

Even though there are many different types of sites that one can build with WordPress, there are some steps that are mandatory for all of them.

For instance, no matter what type of website you want to launch, you always have to start by installing WordPress properly. This is exactly what we talked about in *Chapter 2, Getting Started with WordPress*. Virtually, nothing is different at this point. The installation process is the same, all the steps are the same, and the final result is the same too – you end up with a clean, blank WordPress installation. Also, whenever installing specific themes and plugins, make sure to follow the same guidelines which we discussed in *Chapter 5, Plugins and Widgets*, and *Chapter 6, Choosing and Installing Themes*.

Last but not the least, to ensure that your site is secure and has a good user management structure, you have to keep in mind all the best practices revolving around user accounts, and editorial workflow (publishing new content).

Basically, the only element that's different when building a non-blog website is the process of picking the theme and selecting the exact plugins for the site. Additionally, if you want to take it to the next level, you'll have to look into implementing various functionalities by hand or getting a custom solution made for you by a professional.

Luckily though, the process itself is not much more difficult than working with a standard blog. So once you have some experience with WordPress under your belt, you'll be able to get it done just as quickly.

Static websites

Let's start with static websites, as they are the simplest type of non-blog websites and, also, the easiest ones to create (which shouldn't be surprising).

The best part about static websites is that building them doesn't require any specific themes or plugins. The secret is your mindset as the developer. In essence, to pull this off effectively, the only things you need to do are the following:

1. Utilize the WordPress' pages functionality
2. Tune up the default home page to create a more static experience

The process

Firstly, let's tackle one common misconception. The point of a static website isn't to make the content hardcoded into the HTML or PHP files at all. The actual point is to abandon the standard chronological organization of content (to abandon the blog functionality) and to focus on building a site where pages exist on their own, independently of one another. So, in the end, we can still edit everything pretty easily through the wp-admin, and the only difference is that we're not using the standard WordPress' posts for anything. Instead, we're focusing on the WordPress' pages.

During the setup process of a good static page you'll have to do the following:

1. Pick a WordPress theme that fits your goals and one that looks attractive for your particular project (something we talked about in *Chapter 6, Choosing and Installing Themes*); this is actually a mandatory step for any type of non-blog website. Quite simply, not every theme will fit every type of website. So whenever picking a specific one, keep in mind what you want to use the website for—this is going to make your work easier as a developer, and make the website better for future visitors once the site is launched.

2. Create a list of all static pages that you want to make a part of your website. For instance, for a local pet grooming service, the pages could be: gallery, offer and pricing, testimonials, contact, and map.

3. Create each page in the wp-admin (through **Pages** | **Add New**).

4. Create one more page, call it HOME and tweak it to provide a good home page experience. For instance, start by focusing on the elements that a first-time visitor would consider useful on your home page. A good home page should answer the question of "what is this site about?"

5. Create easy-to-grasp menus to make navigation a breeze.

Steps 1 to 3 are pretty straightforward, so let's just focus on the last two.

Building your home page

By default, WordPress takes the main blog listing (the chronological list of posts) and uses it as the home page. This is not a desired situation in our case since there will be no posts. What we'll do instead is create a custom page and then use it as a static front page (home page).

We'll start by doing something very familiar to us by this point – go to **Pages** | **Add New** and create a new page titled HOME. What you'll place on this page is up to you. Essentially, a home page should be a great starting page for anyone who visits a given site for the first time. For instance, I've decided to go with a short introductory message, a list of some popular articles on the site, a contact form provided by the **Contact Form 7** plugin, and an interactive map by Google Maps.

Once you have your page ready, the only thing you have to do is assign it as the front page. Go to **Settings** | **Reading**, click on the radio button next to **A static page** and select your new page as the **Front page**, like this:

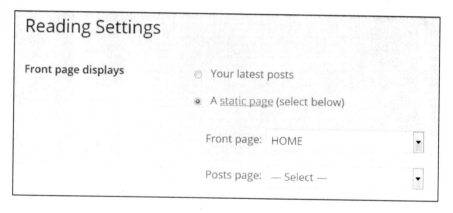

The other setting – **Posts page** is not important at this stage, as posts are not the focus of this particular project. When I go to my main website now, the home page no longer presents the standard listing. Now I can see this:

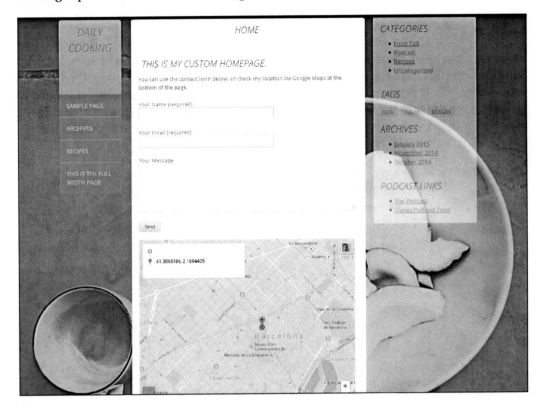

I have to admit, the word **HOME** doesn't look that pretty, so I will probably change it to something like "Welcome" to make it more visitor-friendly, but this is only an example.

If you want to make your home page more fancy, you can create a custom page template (described in *Chapter 7, Developing Your Own Theme*), which will allow you to include any design elements you might need along with a wealth of custom functionality. Again, it all depends on the project.

Creating easy-to-grasp menus

The last element of this static-website puzzle is a proper menu (or proper menus). Because our home page is just like any other page one can create in WordPress, it will appear in the default pages menu (pages widget), which isn't the most optimized situation.

Therefore, whenever working with static websites, make sure to use only custom menus created in **Appearance | Menus**. This gives you full control over what gets displayed either in the header, the sidebar, or anywhere else on the site. For example, you can see that I've added a new link pointing to the home page in the main menu on my site:

Just like I said, nothing difficult here.

Corporate or business websites

When we look at the main purpose of corporate or business websites, it becomes apparent that their construction is very similar to static websites. The only difference is that they are much bigger (more pages and more content), and their design seems much more official. Also, most businesses like to publish some occasional announcements, so a blog-like functionality is required too (but it still won't be the main element on the site).

In essence, creating a quality corporate site with WordPress is all about picking (or building) the right theme. If you do a quick bit of research on the web, you'll see that most corporate sites (at least the good ones) feature hardly any design. The thing that makes them stand out is their very subtle branding (through a certain color scheme or clever use of logos) and stellar navigation layout.

What this means is that the easiest way to build a great corporate site with WordPress is to do the following:

- Pick a clean theme with good content organization and featuring almost none of the design bells and whistles
- Include specific branding elements and pick the right color scheme
- Build a nice user-friendly navigation structure through custom menus
- Construct a custom home page
- Add one visual element in the form of a home page slider – to make the site seem more alive (optional)

Let's go through this list one by one.

Picking a clean theme

This is something we talked about in the previous chapters, so let me just point you towards some of the top places where you can get WordPress themes real quick. They are: the official directory (https://wordpress.org/themes/), ThemeIsle (https://themeisle.com/), ThemeFuse (http://themefuse.com/), StudioPress (http://www.studiopress.com/), and ThemeForest (http://themeforest.net/category/wordpress). The thing to keep in mind is to go straight to the business-related part of the theme directory you're browsing. For example, at Theme Forest, go straight to http://themeforest.net/category/wordpress/corporate. This will make the selection process a lot quicker.

 Keep in mind that if it's a free theme you're after, you should always get it from the official directory (we discussed this in *Chapter 6, Choosing and Installing Themes*). Also, if you want to build a theme on your own, look into some of the free theme frameworks like Gantry (http://www.gantry-framework.org/), or Thematic (http://thematictheme.com/).

The features to look for in a quality corporate theme are as follows:

- Minimal design that lets you include your branding elements
- Easy way of adding a logo and other graphics
- Custom header functionality
- Favicon support
- Responsive layout (meaning that it'll be equally as attractive on a desktop computer as on a mobile phone)
- Widget areas
- Breadcrumbs
- Customizable sidebars
- Customizable layouts (for example, full-width, 1-sidebar, 2-sidebar, and so on)
- Multi-author support (there's usually a number of people taking care of a corporate site simultaneously)
- Built-in color schemes to choose from
- SEO-compatible
- Custom page templates for home page, contact page, FAQ, offer, gallery, team, testimonials, 404 error, portfolio, and so on
- Cross-browser compatible

Your theme doesn't have to do all of these mentioned things, but this list should be a good benchmark in determining how suitable the theme you're about to pick is when it comes to running a corporate site.

Branding elements

From a business point of view, branding is the most important parameter of a recognizable site. Therefore, make sure that the logo and the corporate identity of the company both match the color scheme of the theme. Also, as I mentioned in the previous section, a good theme should allow you to pick the color scheme from one of the predefined ones.

Finally, turn the logo into a favicon and upload it to the site too (this can be done through your theme's built-in favicon functionality or via a plugin like **All In One Favicon** available at `https://wordpress.org/plugins/all-in-one-favicon/`). This will give the site some additional visibility in the bookmarks menu (should the visitor bookmark it).

Good navigation

This is probably the toughest part of the job when building a corporate site, mainly because we can never be sure how much content the site is eventually going to feature. There's always the danger that our navigation will either be too much for the handful of pages of content, or too little for hundreds of pages. There are, however, some good practices that you can follow:

- Focus on providing an extensive menu in the footer. This will make sure that every visitor will be able to find what they're looking for once they scroll down to the bottom of the page. This is easily doable with footer widget areas, which every good corporate theme should provide you with. Here's an example by Samsung:

- Create a top menu with only a couple of the most essential pages. Sometimes, News and About will be enough:

- Create a sidebar menu linking to the important areas of the site, like specific categories, products, announcements, or other things the average visitor might find interesting.

- Use breadcrumbs. Breadcrumbs are small links that present the path of the visitor in relation to the home page. Most themes provide this functionality by default. It's best to place them just below the header. Here's an example (highlighted):

- Display a visible search field. A big number of visitors coming to a corporate site are after a specific piece of information, so they naturally start looking for a search field right away. Therefore, making their life easier is a very good idea. A good placement for a search field is in the header and in the main sidebar (sidebar menu) for good visibility.

Custom home page

Just as with static websites, the default blog listing rarely makes a good home page for a corporate site either. Going with a custom home page is always a better strategy and gives us a more optimized way of presenting the company, its goals, and its field of expertise. To create such a home page, you can safely follow the instructions given earlier in this chapter, when we were discussing static websites.

Now, like I said, showing the default blog listing as the home page is not a good approach here. We should provide at least some integration with the blog-part of the website. The two most sensible solutions are to either link to a blog listing page in a visible place on the home page, or include a simplified listing as a widget in one of the available widget areas on the home page itself.

The latter can be done by the **Recent Posts** widget that's available in WordPress by default (we covered widgets and how to use them in *Chapter 5, Plugins and Widgets*). The former can be done as follows:

1. Create a new page (**Pages | Add New**) and call it "NEWS". The page doesn't have to feature any content. It only needs to exist with a unique name. I'm suggesting "NEWS" because it gives a clear indication of what's going on.

2. Go to **Settings | Reading** and set your new page as the default **Posts page**, like this:

3. As you can see, there's also the old HOME page that's currently set as the **Front page**; we're going to leave it like that.

4. Place the link to the new blog section (NEWS) in the top menu (preferably). You can do it in **Appearance | Menus**.

5. Now, if you navigate to your new NEWS page (something like `http://yoursite.com/news`), you will see the default blog listing, which the company—the owner of the website—can use to publish various announcements or whatever else they see fit.

Optional slider

The last element worth discussing here is a home page slider. Although most corporate websites are not about the graphics, this single visual element is often added. Animated sliders make any website seem more alive and attractive to the visitor. For a corporate site, the slider can present photos from events, individual announcements, product offers, contact details, and a number of other things.

Some themes will come with a slider functionality built in right from the get-go. If they don't, you can always get a plugin to handle the job. The only downside is that most slider plugins are not free. Among those that are free, I can point out two.

Meteor Slides

Meteor Slides is available at https://wordpress.org/plugins/meteor-slides/. It allows you to pick specific images from the media library (or upload new ones), set them as slides, and then display them wherever you wish. You can display images either through a widget or by using a shortcode (`[meteor_slideshow]`). The slides themselves are actually organized as a new separate content type – **Slides** – right next to the default content types like **Posts** and **Pages** (more on custom content types in the next chapter):

This means that you can manage them just like you would manage your standard posts and pages. The only downside is that the plugin in its current form doesn't allow you to display custom text content as a slide. You're basically limited to images only.

It's kind of difficult to show you what the slider looks like through a static screenshot, but anyway, just so you get the general idea, here's my current home page after using the [meteor_slideshow] shortcode at the top of the content block (please notice the navigation arrows on either side of the image):

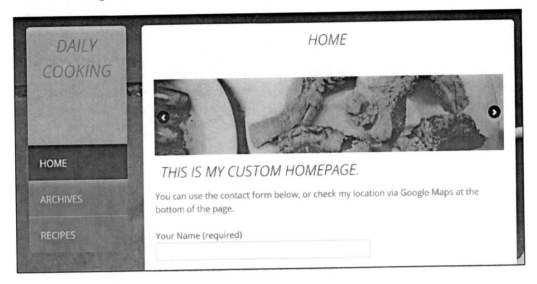

Master Slider

Master Slider is available at https://wordpress.org/plugins/master-slider/. This is the second free slider plugin I can recommend. Even though it's the lite version, it still offers an impressive range of features and a lot of possible ways to create a slideshow.

Right after installing the plugin and going to its section in the wp-admin (right below **Settings**), you'll see this interface:

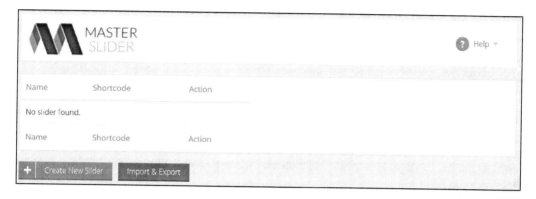

Once you click on the **Create New Slider** button, you'll get to choose from a number of pre-defined styles, or build a fully customized one:

Select the one labeled **Slider with Slide Info** and proceed forward. The screens that follow offer a lot of possible customizations and extra options. It's best if you try experimenting with this for a while to get a grasp on what's possible with this plugin. To get started, you get a set of sample data to work with. Gradually swapping it to your own content is a good way to begin using this plugin. For instance, with this plugin, you can adjust things like the slides' transitions, the navigation from slide to slide, the appearance of each slide, or editing each slide individually, and much more. Describing everything here would probably take a chapter of its own. Anyway, here's what I was able to get after some tuning up (the slider itself can be placed anywhere you wish with a simple shortcode, in my case, `[masterslider id="1"]`):

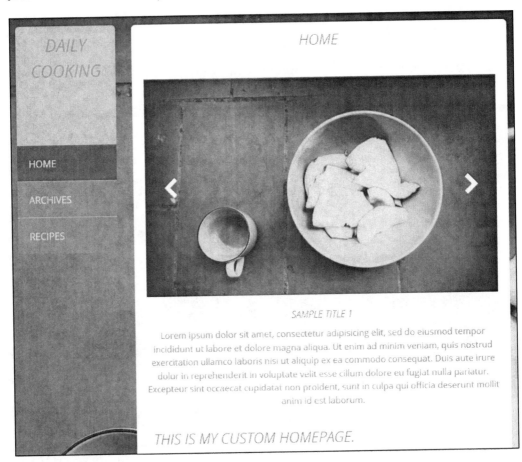

In the preceding screenshot, please notice the custom slide description below the image.

In general, sliders are not a mandatory thing for corporate sites, but they might improve the user experience, so they're probably worth a try.

One-page websites

One-page websites are a relatively new invention in the online world. A couple of years ago, webmasters were not that keen on having just a single page to make up their entire website. It simply seemed like not working hard enough on your website's presence. These days, however, things have changed. It's no longer looked down upon. In fact, single-page websites are the new trend.

In some way, a one-page or a single-page website is similar to a static website. You mostly get to work with WordPress pages rather than its blog functionality and after you set that page in place, it will likely stay that way for a longer period of time - it will remain static. Now, the difference between static websites and one-page websites is obvious (by definition). On one-page websites, you simply get to work with only one page as opposed to having a number of them.

Just to give you a general overview of what a one-page site looks like, please visit `http://karol.cc/`. It's my personal website, which I use to market my freelance writing services:

As you can see, the website is built up of just a single page - the home page. However, each block on that page is visually separated from the previous and the next one. This visual separation is one of the most important aspects of single-page websites. So as with many types of websites, creating a truly great-looking one-page site is about picking the right theme - something that your target audience will enjoy and appreciate. The easiest way to build a great one-page site with WordPress is to do the following:

- Pick a theme that's marketed explicitly as a one-page theme and has a clean design, with good-looking content blocks on the main page
- Include specific branding elements and pick the right color scheme
- Make sure to prepare a number of high quality images, which you can use in the background

Let's go through this list one by one.

Picking a one-page theme

Just as with most other categories, one-page themes are now highly popular in most theme stores on the web. The best places to go include: again, the official directory (https://wordpress.org/themes/), ThemeIsle (https://themeisle.com/), and ThemeForest (http://themeforest.net/category/wordpress). Not all of them, however, feature specialized categories for one-page themes, so you might have to use the search option to find something interesting. Searching for terms like single page or one page should give you great results.

The features to look for in a quality one-page theme are as follows:

- Minimal design that lets you include your branding elements
- Easy way of adding a logo and other graphics
- Custom header functionality
- Parallax scrolling option (where the background images move by the camera slower than the foreground)
- Responsive layout (meaning that it'll be equally as attractive on a desktop computer as on a mobile phone)
- Widget areas
- Built-in color schemes to choose from
- SEO-compatible
- Cross-browser compatible

The more of the preceding features your theme includes, the better. If anything is missing, you can always find a plugin that will fill the void. After all, there's a plugin for everything, remember?

Branding elements

Branding elements are particularly important with one-page sites because, by definition, you don't get much online real estate to work with, so to speak. If there's just one page on the site, you need to make sure that it's as in tune with your brand and its identity as possible. Therefore, a good theme should allow you to place elements like your own logo, social media links, and custom graphics in places like the header, footer, and the background. Luckily, those sorts of features are considered the standard among modern WordPress themes, so you probably won't have to worry about this part at all.

High-quality images

One of the main flaws with one-page themes is that they often rely heavily on good visuals and high quality images. The designs are often simple and very minimalist, and their attractive appearance is based on the images used in the background of the site. Unfortunately, finding such images is entirely up to you. Themes rarely come with unique images that you would be able to use on your site.

How to get those images? You can buy them in places like `http://www.istockphoto.com/--` that's one solution. But you can also get a lot of great images for free in places like `https://unsplash.com/` or `http://jaymantri.com/`. The last solution is, of course, to take your own photos and use them on your site.

As an example, I will get one of the most popular one-page themes in the WordPress directory right now - **Zerif Lite** (available at `https://wordpress.org/themes/zerif-lite`) and do some basic tuning up around it to show you how one-page themes work.

Right after downloading and activating the theme (standard procedure; please see *Chapter 6, Choosing and Installing Themes,* for the how-to), you can go straight to the WordPress Customizer at **Appearance | Customize**. You'll see a large customization panel there. With it, I can change the main headline on the site, the buttons below, the appearance of individual blocks, and also the background image of the whole site:

After a handful of tweaks, I end up with a great-looking one-page site. You can see what my final header looks like in the next screenshot:

That's pretty much it when it comes to launching a nice one-page site with WordPress. The most remarkable thing here is how easy it is to actually do. Just imagine how much time it would take to create something like this (considering the nice transitions and background-foreground interactions) from the ground-up. Or, the cost required to set it up. The possibilities that WordPress delivers these days are really incredible.

Summary

We covered a lot of excellent material in this chapter. We started by listing some of the popular types of non-blog websites that you can build successfully with WordPress. Then, we went through some of those types individually and discussed the specific elements to focus on, in order to guarantee a quality final product.

The next chapter is part two of our guide to creating a non-blog website. In that, we'll go through some of the more user-centered types of websites, like membership sites, photo and video blogs, and finally, building your own social network.

12

Creating a Non-blog Website Part 2 – Community Websites and Custom Content Elements

Let's get straight down to business here. In the previous chapter, you saw different types of non-blog websites. This chapter is a continuation of that topic, so let's do two things. First, let's go through some of the more trendy uses of WordPress and focus on a step-by-step process of reaching a great final result. Then, let's discuss some of the custom content elements you can create in WordPress, such as custom post types, custom taxonomies, and the process of customizing the admin display slightly.

Membership websites

When talking of WordPress, from a technical point of view, a membership site is not very different from a standard blog site. The only thing that sets it apart is the fact that some of the content is protected by a level of access rights. In other words, the content is premium, and if anyone wants to get access to it, they usually have to take out their wallets and pay a small fee.

Even though membership sites might sound like a very niche thing to build with WordPress, there are actually more and more such sites being launched every year. Many online businesses, especially in the educational niches, have realized that the membership model is the one that provides very predictable profits and can be promoted in a variety of different ways.

But let's stick with WordPress as our main topic and leave the marketing issues aside. Starting with some technical aspects of building a membership site, these are the functionalities a membership site can/should offer:

- The possibility to feature various types of content, including text (standard articles), audio, video, PDF files, presentations, and photos
- An easy method of user registration and subscription
- Different levels of subscriptions (with different access rights)
- Integrated online payments (for premium subscriptions)
- Free trials
- Easy user account management and subscription management
- E-mail newsletter integration
- Teaser content (when you're showing part of the premium content to persuade visitors into subscribing)
- Internal stats

The list of functionality is quite extensive, and some of it might not be that clear at first, but we're going to explain everything in just a while. Just like with our previous examples, we're going to build a functional membership site here and discuss some of the more important aspects of the process along the way.

For this purpose, let's use the theme from *Chapter 7, Developing Your Own Theme*, again. Like I said, membership sites are very similar in construction to standard blogs. And although you can look for specialized themes, often, the default theme you're using right now will do the job well enough. The only requirement is that from a user's/visitor's point of view, your membership site theme should provide good content presentation and should be able to handle various types of content. That is all.

Taking the simple approach

Even though the recommended approach of building a membership site is based on using specialized plugins, there's also an alternative path you can take. But it's neither functional nor professional, so I'm mentioning it just to keep the message complete. I'm talking about using the simple password protection feature that's built into WordPress by default.

Basically, if you want to limit access to a given piece of content, all you have to do is go to the wp-admin and then to **Posts** or **Pages** and click the **Quick Edit** link beneath a given piece of content. There's a **Password** field at the bottom. After filling it out and clicking **Update**, your content will no longer publicly visible from that point onwards. Anyone who wants to view it has to enter the password.

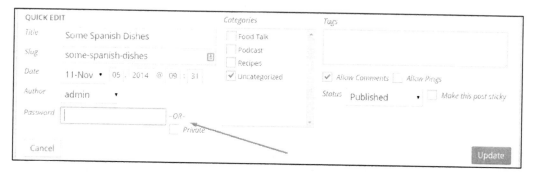

Although this simple method works and does the job of limiting access to specific pieces of content, it's not the prettiest one, at least not for serious membership sites. Besides, it doesn't handle the subscription process itself and forces you to find a way to deliver the passwords to your subscribers manually.

As it turns out, the simplest solutions are not always the best.

Using membership plugins

The only sensible method of building a membership site on WordPress is using the help of some of the specialized membership plugins. Of course, just like with any other type of site, you can still devote your time and effort to building everything from the ground up by hand. But similarly to e-commerce stores, it would take way too long before you could show any true quality effects. So membership plugins it is!

As usual, there are many plugins available on the market, and finding the perfect one for your particular project might take a while, especially if you want to test every feature before making the site available to the world and your customers.

Now, the only downside is that most of those membership plugins come at a premium. Seriously premium, so to speak. Some price tags go as high as $ 297 (I'm going to point you toward a free solution in just a minute).

Therefore, if you do have some money to invest in your membership site, I would advise you to look into the following two plugins:

- **WishList Member** (available at `http://member.wishlistproducts.com/`): This is used by hundreds of sites worldwide, and it's probably the most popular membership plugin available. The single site license is $ 97, and it provides a number of side services apart from the platform itself (training videos, unlimited updates, unlimited support, and so on). The multisite license is $ 297. Although that's not cheap it may be a great idea for professional web designers and developers.

- **WP-Member** (available at `http://wp-member.com/`): This is slightly cheaper than WishList Member, currently priced at $ 47 (single site) and $ 97 (multisite). There's also an additional developer license for $ 147.

When it comes to functionality, both plugins offer an extraordinary amount of stuff. Also, both cover all of the items I mentioned on the list a couple of pages ago with some additional bells and whistles (for example, secure RSS feeds and data encryption).

Now, I'm not actually advising you to spend any money at this point, but you're here to learn, so I'm only mentioning these plugins because they are at the top of the game in their field (that is, membership plugins for WordPress).

Taking the free approach

This is probably a good point at which to talk about a solution that's way cheaper to apply. Actually, the plugin I'm about to describe is free. It's simply called **Membership** and you can get it at `https://wordpress.org/plugins/membership/`.

The sole fact that it is free doesn't mean that it offers a poor range of features or it isn't built with quality in mind. This is still one of the top membership site plugins available. Why is it free? It's based on a **freemium** model. This means that if you want to get more functionality or unlock some of the extra features, you'll have to get the Pro version, which is $ 39.60 per month.

Installing the plugin

This is a standard installation process. All you have to do is either go to `https://wordpress.org/plugins/membership/` to get the plugin and then upload it to your plugins folder. Or you can fetch it straight from the **Plugins | Add New** section in the wp-admin.

When you activate the plugin, you will be prompted to enable the plugin's functionality. This can be done from the admin bar in your wp-admin:

After doing so, you'll see a completely new section in the main sidebar, right below **Settings**. It's called **Membership**.

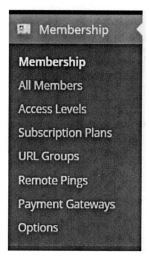

At this point, I advise you to go through the short user guide that will begin displaying automatically when you try to visit the **Membership** section. This will give you a basic overview of the plugin:

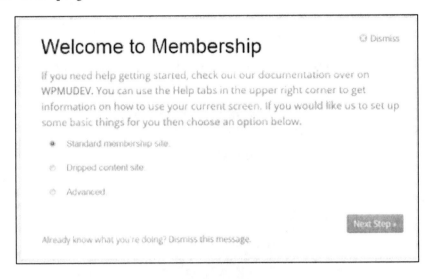

The main block that's displayed right in the middle lets you get started quickly by creating your first membership site. We'll just select **Standard membership site** and proceed to the next step.

The free version of the plugin allows you to create two levels of access. Let's call ours "Free" and "Premium". (I'm also selecting PayPal as the gateway for handling payments.)

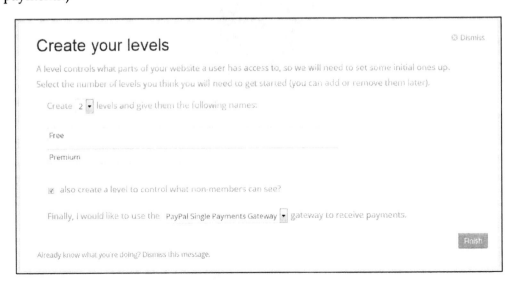

When I click **Finish**, I'm basically done with the setup process. That wasn't hard, was it?

Using the plugin

Right after the setup process is complete, you will be presented with another on-screen user guide on how to use the plugin for doing everyday work. This guide is quite a long one (with 34 steps), but it does present all of the most crucial functionalities of Membership. So, in fact, I do advise you to go through it from start to finish.

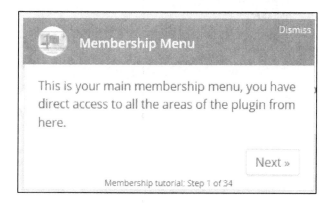

In short, the individual sections of the plugin allow you to do the following tasks:

- Manage subscribers through **Membership | All Members**
- Manage subscription levels through **Membership | Access Levels**
- Manage subscription plans through **Membership | Subscription Plans**
- Manage payment gateways through **Membership | Payment Gateways**
- Other options through **Membership | Options**. This is where you can control other areas of the site that haven't been covered elsewhere.

Now, let's talk about how managing your content actually works and what you can do to prevent some users from accessing its premium parts. Don't be afraid by the fact that the way this plugin handles content management is quite advanced. First, we have the access level settings available in **Membership | Access Levels**. Once you go there, you will be able to set each access level to utilize a collection of **Positive Rules**, **Negative Rules**, or **Advanced** rules. Basically, positive rules are where we can assign the content that a given access level can view, while negative rules do the opposite thing. For example, if you add all of your posts to the set of negative rules, you will effectively prevent every free member from viewing any of them:

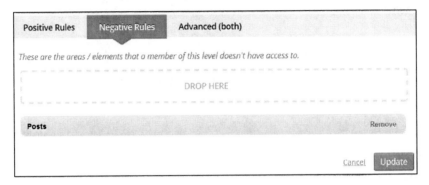

Bear in mind that this is just an example, and that setting everything up properly so it actually makes sense in a real-world application will take a significant amount of time.

There are a lot more features waiting for you inside Membership, and I do encourage you to test them yourself if you're ever building a full-blown membership site. But for now, it's about time we switch to the next type of site on the list – multimedia blogs.

Video blogs and photo blogs

Let's cover these two types of WordPress sites together because the individual goals for each are often very similar (although their designs may still be a bit different). In short, a video blog is one where the author mainly publishes videos, instead of traditional text-based posts. A photo blog, on the other hand, is essentially the same thing, the only difference being it revolves around photos.

Now, why would you even bother with a customized setup for a video blog or a photo blog in the first place when you can just use a standard WordPress installation with a traditional blogging-optimized theme? Well, to be honest here, you can go with a standard setup indeed, and your video/photo blog will be just about fine. But with some additional work (but not much) put into building something that's tailor-made for multimedia blogs, your site can get a big advantage over your competition, mostly in terms of usability and content presentation.

For instance, let's focus on some of the interesting features you can add to a video blog:

- Main blog listing built as a grid layout with big thumbnails, so every visitor can see the snapshots of the videos right away
- Videos on the main listing presented as concise blocks containing the thumbnail and a small amount of text to convince people to click on the video
- Wide main blog listing with just a narrow sidebar on the left (or right)
- Integrated social media features (including the YouTube subscription buttons)
- Social media comments fetched from the platform where the video is originally hosted
- Custom backend to host the videos on the blog (or on an external server)
- Shareable embed code, so your visitors can embed the videos easily
- Custom player to replace the native YouTube or Vimeo players

And for a photo blog, some interesting features are:

- Custom home page featuring one main photo ("photo of the day")
- Automatic photo slider on the home page
- Lightbox functionality for viewing the photos in full size
- Wide main blog listing
- Integrated social media features
- Social media comments
- Custom backend to host photos
- Shareable embed code
- Custom photo controls (such as save, view full size, share, and so on)

As you can see, most of these features can work equally well on both video blogs and photo blogs. As usual with WordPress, you can get most of them either by obtaining a quality theme or by using some third-party plugins. Let's cover both of these approaches.

Exploring themes for video and photo sites

Being quite popular kinds of blogs, both video and photo blogs have a very wide range of themes available on the Internet. But be careful!. Searching for a theme on Google can get you in trouble. Well, maybe not in trouble per se, but if you end up downloading a theme from a random site, you have no guarantee that it's a secure solution and that there's no malicious or encrypted code inside. A much better method is to either go to the official directory or to some of the recognized theme stores.

For starters, let's check what's available out there:

- **Metro CreativeX** available at
  `https://wordpress.org/themes/metro-creativex`
- **Portfolio Press** available at
  `https://wordpress.org/themes/portfolio-press`
- **Foliogine PRO** available at
  `https://themeisle.com/themes/foliogine-pro/`
- **PhotoArtist** available at `http://themefuse.com/wp-themes-shop/`
  `wordpress-photography-theme/`

Getting any of the premium themes will require an investment, so do it only if you're devoted to creating a really high-quality multimedia blog.

Getting plugins for video and photo sites

As I said, apart from video and photo optimized themes, you can also get a number of plugins that will make your site more functional. The good news is that we're only going to focus on free plugins.

Let's start with two plugins that I already mentioned in *Chapter 11, Creating a Non-blog Website Part 1 – The Basics*:

- **Meteor Slides** available at
  `https://wordpress.org/plugins/meteor-slides/`
- **Master Slider** available at
  `https://wordpress.org/plugins/master-slider/`

These are both great plugins for getting a nice slider functionality. This sort of thing does a good job at improving the overall user experience, especially when dealing with a multimedia-driven site. For a detailed description of these plugins, please review the previous chapter's section about building a static site.

Now, these are the other plugins that can come handy:

- **WP Smush** (https://wordpress.org/plugins/wp-smushit/):
  This plugin doesn't present any particular output on the frontend of your
  site because what it actually does is automatically optimize your images in
  the background. This is a great plugin for saving your bandwidth, especially
  if you're publishing a lot of images. The installation process is quite standard.
  Once the plugin is activated, it starts working in the background with no
  supervision required.

- **Lightbox** (https://wordpress.org/plugins/lightbox/): This plugin
  delivers a really good looking lightbox functionality. The best thing about
  this plugin is that it's ultra easy to use. All you have to do is activate it and
  it will immediately start taking care of the images you're displaying on your
  blog. The plugin will intercept image clicks and show the image file in a nice
  lightbox instead of loading them individually (on a blank page).

Lastly, I have one more social media plugin which I'd like to show you. It's simply
called **Facebook** and it's the official Facebook plugin for WordPress (available at
https://wordpress.org/plugins/facebook/).

This plugin can give a good level of integration between your main site and your
Facebook page or profile. With it, you can publish new posts to Facebook almost
automatically and also allow Facebook users to comment on your content using their
accounts. This is just a small part of the full functionality. I'd advise you to give this
plugin a closer look yourself. As it's an official plugin, every new functionality that
Facebook makes available for WordPress blogs is sure to be introduced as quickly
as possible.

Just to sum up the topic of multimedia blogs, I have to point out that this is a very
crowded area among both theme and plugin developers. The plugins mentioned
here will give you a good start, but having your finger on the pulse and paying
attention to what's new on the market (cool new plugins and themes) is the actual
best way to keep your photo or video blog on top of its game. That being said,
getting and testing every new plugin out there is not the recommended approach.
However, from time to time, you can find a true gem that's going to help you take
your blog to the next level.

Social networks

Finally, it's time to discuss one of the most surprising topics in relation to building various types of websites with WordPress. As it turns out, the platform can be very well used to run a fully functional social network. In other words, you can have your own Facebook if you'd like to… at least when it comes to functionality.

And speaking of functionality, in short, a social network built with WordPress can offer the following features:

- Support to any number of user accounts
- Facebook-like publishing method for users (a "Wall" or an activity stream)
- Forums
- Blogs and micro blogs
- Friends
- Groups
- Private messages
- Comments
- Photo and video content
- Much much more

That being said, building and then running a well-constructed social network utilizing all of the available features will require some serious work. This is way beyond the scope of this book. So here we're only going to focus on the basic setup process and getting started. If you're planning to launch an actual social network and make it available to the world, you should probably get more info, either by going to the official online documentation or obtaining some more publications on the topic.

Essentially, social networking on WordPress works through one specific plugin – **BuddyPress**. Although calling it just a plugin is a massive understatement. BuddyPress is actually a whole online publishing environment on its own that integrates with WordPress. Unlike other plugins, it doesn't just display some custom content here and there. It actually changes the whole appearance (structure) of your WordPress site to make it look and operate like a social network.

Let's take the topic step by step, starting with installation.

Installing a social network

There's nothing fancy here, but all you have to do is either go to
`https://buddypress.org/`, download the main plugin and then upload
it to your WordPress site, or search for the plugin from within the wp-admin
(**Plugins | Add New**) using the name `BuddyPress`. The installation process of
the plugin itself is quite standard, meaning that after getting it on your server,
you only have to click the **Activate** button. Right after doing so, you will see
the following welcome screen:

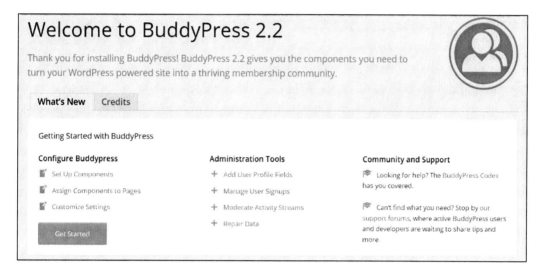

It's actually advisable to go through the information in this to get a basic
understanding of the platform and the things it has to offer.

Next, visit the settings section under **Settings | BuddyPress**. First, pick the components you'd like to use on your new social network. For testing purposes, I just enabled all of them:

Component	Description
🖼 Extended Profiles	Customize your community with fully editable profile fields that allow your users to describe themselves.
🎛 Account Settings	Allow your users to modify their account and notification settings directly from within their profiles.
⋕ Friend Connections	Let your users make connections so they can track the activity of others and focus on the people they care about the most.
🗨 Private Messaging	Allow your users to talk to each other directly and in private. Not just limited to one-on-one discussions, messages can be sent between any number of members.
📢 Activity Streams	Global, personal, and group activity streams with threaded commenting, direct posting, favoriting, and @mentions, all with full RSS feed and email notification support.
🔔 Notifications	Notify members of relevant activity with a toolbar bubble and/or via email, and allow them to customize their notification settings.
♣ User Groups	Groups allow your users to organize themselves into specific public, private or hidden sections with separate activity streams and member listings.
Ⓦ Site Tracking	Record activity for new posts and comments from your site.
BuddyPress Core	It's what makes time travel BuddyPress possible!
Community Members	Everything in a BuddyPress community revolves around its members.
Component	Description

 To get more information about available components, feel free to visit https://codex.buddypress.org/legacy/getting-started/configure-buddypress-components/.

The second tab on this settings page – titled **Pages** – lets you assign the pages that will house some standard areas of your social network such as the activity stream, user groups, member profiles, and so on. You can create new pages here or use the ones that BuddyPress has already created during installation.

Finally, there's the last tab – **Settings** – where you can adjust some of the other standard settings such as the presence of the top toolbar, various profile settings, and group settings.

That's all about the main settings area. As you can see, the plugin is designed in a way that makes using it as easy as possible.

Designing your social network

In its current form, BuddyPress can work with any WordPress theme. That's right, you don't have to get an optimized social networking design if you don't want to. BuddyPress will manage to display its contents inside either the main content block of your current theme or the widget areas you have available.

However, as usual, if you want to make your social network look more professional, then you should probably look around and get something that's specially optimized for social networks. The best rule of thumb when you're searching for such themes, in my opinion, is to compare them against the biggest social network of them all – Facebook. Although some people don't enjoy the design that Facebook offers, it is still the most successful social network around, so they are clearly doing something right. Treating it as a benchmark of sorts is, therefore, a very good idea.

If you want to find a nice list of BuddyPress-compatible themes, the WordPress directory comes to the rescue yet again. When you go to `https://wordpress.org/themes/search/buddypress/`, you'll find a filtered list of themes that have been tested with BuddyPress and are optimized to work as a social network.

Once you've found yourself a nice-looking theme, you can go straight to working with your new social network without focusing any more on the setup. However, if you really want to get to know the platform and the way it's built, I advise you to go to the official documentation, which is one of the best BuddyPress resources available (`https://codex.buddypress.org/`). It's also where you can learn all the ins and outs of BuddyPress development, creating your own themes or even BuddyPress extension plugins.

Extending the functionality

BuddyPress is constructed in a way that provides the basic social networking functionality and site organization. If you want to extend your social media site and give it some new features, you can install a number of BuddyPress plugins. You can find them at `https://buddypress.org/extend/plugins/`. Basically, they are just like other WordPress plugins (the installation process is the same), but instead of delivering some new functionality to WordPress, they focus more on BuddyPress.

There is a lot more waiting for you inside BuddyPress, and I actually encourage you to do some researching and learning on your own, especially if you're planning to launch a social network at some point. But for now, I think that we've got the topic covered at least when it comes to giving you an introduction to social networking with WordPress, and getting started with the best social networking plugin available — BuddyPress.

Introducing custom post types

While building some of the sites described in the current and the previous chapters, you may stumble upon what's called custom post types. Or you may even decide to create them yourself for the purpose of your individual projects. But let's take it from the top. The custom post type functionality was added to WordPress in version 3.0 because people wanted to be able to specify new objects. The most commonly known objects are posts and pages, but there are actually already three other custom types in the WordPress backend: attachments, revisions, and navigation menus. However, if we feel that the situation/project calls for it, we can create any number of new post types by taking advantage of the custom post type functionality and its wide versatility.

The need for custom post types can appear in many scenarios. For instance, when a writer is building a personal portfolio site, they might need a custom post type named **book** to present their publications in an attractive way instead of just using standard posts. This is exactly what we're about to do in this section of the chapter. So gear up to learn how custom post types work by building a new one.

For this purpose, we'll go back to our main cooking blog theme – Daily Cooking Custom. In its default form, it doesn't feature any custom post types, and that's a good thing as we've got a blank canvas to work on.

To specify that you'd like to have a custom post type in your theme, you can add some code to your theme's `functions.php` file. This is what we'll be doing. However, keep in mind that you can also attach the custom post type to a plugin or a widget if you don't want it to be tied to a particular theme.

Registering a new post type

To register a new post type, all you have to do is add some simple code to your `functions.php` file. It's good practice to tie the creation of the new type to the `init` function of the theme, so that it gets called at the right moment in the booting process. The initial - blank - custom post type code looks like this:

```
function book_init() {
    register_post_type('book');
}
add_action('init', 'book_init');
```

The `register_post_type()` function takes an array as its second parameter, and in that array you can specify whether the object is public or should be involved in rewriting the URL, what elements it supports on its editing page, and so on. Let's set up an array of all the arguments and then pass it to the function. Now our code looks like this:

```
function book_init() {
  $args = array(
    'description' => 'A custom post type that holds my books',
    'public' => true,
    'rewrite' => array('slug' => 'books'),
    'has_archive' => true,
    'supports' => array('title', 'editor', 'author', 'excerpt',
      'custom-fields', 'thumbnail')
  );
  register_post_type('book', $args);
  flush_rewrite_rules();
}
add_action('init', 'book_init');
```

I've chosen each of these parameters because they make sense for the book custom post type. Let's take a look at them:

- `description`: This one's pretty self-explanatory.
- `public`: This means that the post type is available publicly, like how posts and pages in fact are, rather than hidden behind the scenes. It'll get a user interface and can be shown in navigation menus, and so on.
- `rewrite`: This specifies that the post type can be used in the rewrite rules for pretty permalinks.
- `has_archive`: This enables post type archives (a classic index page like we can see for our standard posts).
- `supports`: This is an array of the capabilities which users see when they're creating or editing an item. For books, we're including six items.

The final function call – `flush_rewrite_rules()` – will allow us to show a standard archive listing of the books later on (just like a standard post listing but for our custom post type).

 These are just some of the arguments you can pass. Read about the others in the codex at https://codex.wordpress.org/ Function_Reference/register_post_type.

Now that we've got the basic post type set up, let's add some labels.

Adding labels

You can add labels to your custom post type so that WordPress knows what to say while talking about it. First, let's simply create an array of all the labels. Put this as the first thing inside the `book_init()` function:

```
$labels = array(
    'name' => 'Books',
    'singular_name' => 'Book',
    'add_new' => 'Add New',
    'add_new_item' => 'Add New Book',
    'edit_item' => 'Edit Book',
    'new_item' => 'New Book',
    'view_item' => 'View Book',
    'search_items' => 'Search Books',
    'not_found' =>  'No books found',
    'not_found_in_trash' => 'No books found in Trash'
);
```

Then, add a single line of code to the `$args` array telling it to use the labels, as shown in the following snippet (highlighted):

```
$args = array(
    'labels' => $labels,
    'description' => 'A custom post type that holds my books',
/* the rest of the function remains the same */
```

The next step is to add messages, which is what WordPress tells the user when they are doing stuff with books.

Adding messages

Whenever a user updates, previews, or does anything with a book, you'll want them to see an accurate message. All we need to do is create an array of messages and then hook them to WordPress. Here's the code for doing that:

```
function book_updated_messages( $messages ) {
    $messages['book'] = array(
        '', /* Unused. Messages start at index 1. */
        sprintf('Book updated. <a href="%s">View book</a>', esc_url
            (get_permalink($post_ID))),
        'Custom field updated.',
        'Custom field deleted.',
        'Book updated.',
        (isset($_GET['revision']) ? sprintf('Book restored to revision
            from %s', wp_post_revision_title((int)$_GET['revision'],
            false)) : false),
```

```
   print('Book published. <a href="%s">View book</a>', esc_url
     (get_permalink($post_ID))),
   'Book saved.',
   sprintf('Book submitted. <a target="_blank" href="%s">Preview
     book</a>', esc_url(add_query_arg('preview', 'true',
     get_permalink($post_ID)))),
   sprintf('Book scheduled for: <strong>1$s</strong>. <a
     target="_blank" href="%2$s">Preview book</a>', date_i18n('M
     j, Y @ G:i', strtotime($post->post_date)),
     esc_url(get_permalink($post_ID))),
   sprintf('Book draft updated. <a target="_blank"
     href="%s">Preview book</a>', esc_url(add_query_arg
     ('preview', 'true', get_permalink($post_ID))))
 );
 return $messages;
}
add_filter('post_updated_messages', 'book_updated_messages');
```

This code creates a function named `book_updated_messages()` that sets up an array of messages and returns it. We call this using the filter for `post_updated_messages`.

Now, our custom post type is ready to use! Go to your wp-admin and reload it. You'll see that a new menu has appeared under **Comments**. It's called **Books**. Let's add a book:

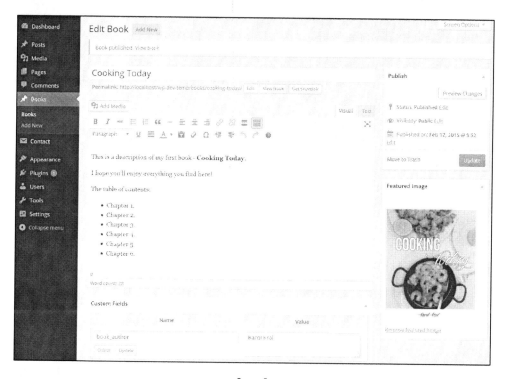

Note that I gave it a custom field named `book_author`, I also uploaded a featured image for the book cover. Now, when you go to the main **Books** page, you'll see the book listed:

If you click on the **View** link under the book's title, you'll see the book displayed using the `single.php` theme template, which won't be the most reader-friendly experience. Therefore, let's make some new template files to display our books.

Creating book template files

WordPress needs to know how to display your new post type. You have to create a template for a single book and one for the listing of books.

First, we'll make a book version of `single.php`. It must be named `single-POST_ TYPE_NAME.php`, which in our case is `single-book.php`. Using `page.php` as our starting point (as it's already the closest to what we'd like our book page to look like), we're going to add the display of the custom field `book_author` and the featured image. So, let's start by taking our `page.php` file, making a copy of it and renaming it to `single-book.php`. Also, let's make a copy of `content-page.php` and call it `content-book.php`. Next, it's time to include all the elements.

Here's what the two files look like. First, `single-book.php` looks like this:

```php
<?php
/**
 * The template for displaying a single book.
 *
 * @package Daily Cooking Custom
 */
?><?php get_header(); ?>

<div id="primary" class="content-area">
```

```
<main id="main" class="site-main" role="main">
  <?php while (have_posts()) : the_post(); ?>

    <?php get_template_part('content', 'book'); ?>

  <?php endwhile; // end of the loop. ?>

  </main><!-- #main -->
</div><!-- #primary -->

<?php get_sidebar(); ?>
<?php get_footer(); ?>
```

The only change that's been made to this file is highlighted in the preceding listing (the `get_template_part()` function call). Next, the `content-book.php` file looks like this:

```
<?php
/**
 * The template used for displaying book content
 *
 * @package Daily Cooking Custom
 */
?>

<article id="post-<?php the_ID(); ?>" <?php post_class(); ?>>
  <header class="entry-header">
    <?php the_title('<h1 class="entry-title">', '</h1>'); ?>
  </header>

  <div class="entry-content">
    <?php if(has_post_thumbnail()) : ?>
      <div class="post-image alignleft"><?php echo
        get_the_post_thumbnail($post->ID, 'medium', array('style'
        => 'border: 1px solid black;')); ?></div>
    <?php endif; ?>
    <?php echo '<p><em>by '.get_post_meta($post->ID,
      'book_author', true).'</em></p>'; ?>
    <?php the_content(); ?>
  </div>

  <footer class="entry-footer">
  </footer>
</article><!-- #post-## -->
```

Now let's take our custom field – book_author – and display it right below the featured image. We can do this by adding one new line of code (highlighted) in between the featured image code and the main content code, as shown in the following code snippet:

```php
<?php if(has_post_thumbnail()) : ?>
  <div class="post-image alignleft"><?php echo
    get_the_post_thumbnail($post->ID, 'medium', array('style' =>
    'border: 1px solid black;')); ?></div>
<?php endif; ?>
<?php echo '<p><em>by '.get_post_meta($post->ID, 'book_author',
  true).'</em></p>'; ?>
<?php the_content(); ?>
```

At this point, when you visit a single book page, the author's name is displayed and the book cover shows up automatically:

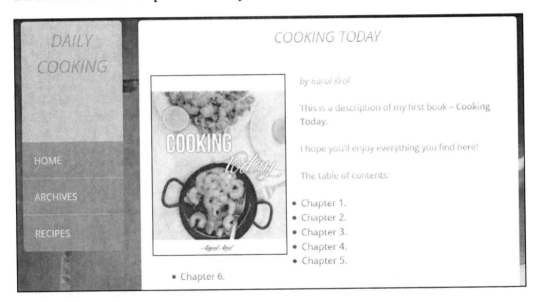

Our next task is a page that will show a listing of the books like what `index.php` does. If you go to `http://YOURSITE.com/books/` now, you'll see something like this:

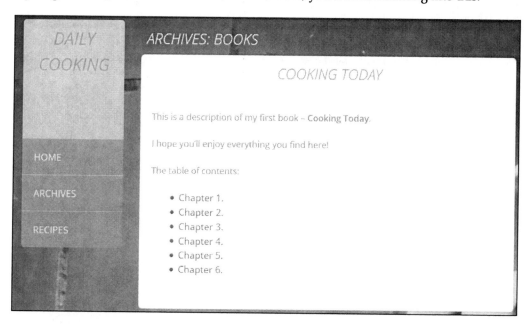

This is basically a standard archive listing. In fact, WordPress uses the default `archive.php` file to show the listing of every new custom post type. We can customize this by creating a new template file and calling it `archive-book.php`. To be more exact, every template file controlling the archive for any new custom post type has to be named `archive-POST_TYPE.php`. The easiest way to create such file is by making a copy of the standard `archive.php` file or the `index.php` file and renaming it to `archive-book.php`. Then we can take it from there and modify the file to fit our requirements. So what I'm going to do here is use my `index.php` as the template and do some tuning up around it.

Right now, my new `archive-book.php` file doesn't offer any custom way of displaying my books. Here's what it looks like (please notice the highlighted part - the main loop):

```php
<?php
/**
 * The listing of books.
 *
 * @package Daily Cooking Custom
 */
?><?php get_header(); ?>
```

```php
<div id="primary" class="content-area">
  <main id="main" class="site-main" role="main">

 ?php if (have_posts()) : ?>

    <?php /* Start the Loop */ ?>
    <?php while (have_posts()) : the_post(); ?>
    <?php get_template_part('listing', 'book'); ?>
    <?php endwhile; ?>

    <?php daily_cooking_custom_paging_nav(); ?>

  <?php else : ?>

    <?php get_template_part('content', 'none'); ?>

  <?php endif; ?>

  </main><!-- #main -->
</div><!-- #primary -->

<?php get_sidebar(); ?>
<?php get_footer(); ?>
```

As you can see, the actual display is done by the `get_template_part('listing', 'book')` function call. In order to make this line work, we have to create the listing file itself. The simplest way of doing this is by making a copy of `content.php` and modifying it slightly. First, rename it to `listing-book.php`.

Right away, I'm going to erase some of the unneeded sections and leave only those that can be used to make our books' listing look great. Next, I will also include a thumbnail display. Quite frankly, I don't have to do this, but I believe that the book listing will look better with smaller thumbnails. Finally, I will also display the author of each book. The finished file will look like this:

```php
<?php
/**
 * @package Daily Cooking Custom
 */
?>
<article id="post-<?php the_ID(); ?>" <?php post_class(); ?>>
  <header class="entry-header">
    <?php the_title(sprintf('<h1 class="entry-title"><a href="%s"
      rel="bookmark">', esc_url(get_permalink())), '</a>"</h1>');
      ?>
```

```
    </header>

    <div class="entry-content">
      <?php if(has_post_thumbnail()) : ?>
        <div class="post-image alignleft">
          <?php echo '<a href="'.esc_url(get_permalink()).'"
            >'.get_the_post_thumbnail($post->ID, 'thumbnail')
            .'</a>'; ?>
        </div>
      <?php endif; ?>

      <div class="entry clearfix">
        <p><em>by <?php echo get_post_meta($post->ID, 'book_author',
          true); ?></em></p>
        <?php the_content(sprintf(__('Continue reading %s <span
          class="meta-nav">&rarr;</span>', 'daily-cooking-custom'),
          the_title('<span class="screen-reader-text">"',
          '"</span>', false))); ?>
      </div>
    </div>

    <footer class="entry-footer">
    </footer>
  </article><!-- #post-## -->
```

And here's the final effect (I've added one more book just for demonstration purposes):

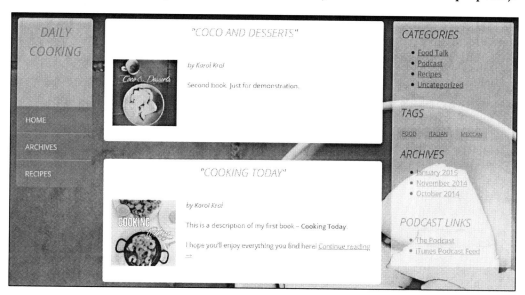

Registering and using a custom taxonomy

Just to follow the example given a while ago with our custom post type for books, let's now create a custom taxonomy. Essentially, you might not want to mix book categories and post categories, so we are going to create a custom taxonomy named **Book Categories**.

Add the following code to your `functions.php` file:

```
function build_taxonomies() {
  register_taxonomy(
    'book_category',
    'book',
    array(
      'hierarchical' => true,
      'label' => 'Book Category',
      'query_var' => true,
      'rewrite' => array('slug' => 'available-books')
    )
  );
}
add_action('init', 'build_taxonomies', 0);
```

Like the `register_post_type()` function, the `register_taxonomy()` function allows you to register a new taxonomy within WordPress. You can read up on the details of all of the parameters you can add in the codex (`https://codex.wordpress.org/Function_Reference/register_taxonomy`). For now, you can see that we're calling it `book_category`; it belongs to the object type `book` and is hierarchical, and you can query it too. It needs to be included in the rewrite of URLs with a custom slug `available-books`.

Next, we need to make this taxonomy available to books. Simply find the `$args` array we used while registering the book post type (the `book_init()` function) and add this item to the array (highlighted):

```
$args = array(
  'labels' => $labels,
  'description' => 'A custom post type that holds my books',
  'public' => true,
  'rewrite' => array('slug' => 'books'),
  'has_archive' => true,
  'taxonomies' => array('book_category'),
  'supports' => array('title', 'editor', 'author', 'excerpt',
    'custom-fields', 'thumbnail')
);
```

When you return to the wp-admin and edit a book, you'll see that the book categories have appeared on the right, and they are also in the main navigation on the left:

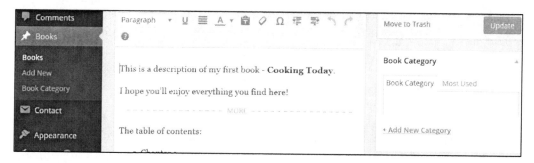

After you've added some categories and assigned them to the books, let's take a look at displaying those categories on the front of the website. First, we'll add them to the single book display. Open content-book.php and add this code in an appropriate place within the loop ;for example, you can add it right after the the_content() function call (highlighted):

```
<div class="entry-content">
  <?php if(has_post_thumbnail()) : ?>
    <div class="post-image alignleft"><?php echo
      get_the_post_thumbnail($post->ID, 'medium', array('style' =>
      'border: 1px solid black;')); ?></div>
  <?php endif; ?>
  <?php echo '<p><em>by '.get_post_meta($post->ID, 'book_author',
    true).'</em></p>'; ?>
  <?php the_content(); ?>
  <?php echo get_the_term_list($post->ID, 'book_category',
    '<em>Categories: ', ', ', '</em>'); ?>
</div>
```

You're using the function get_the_term_list(), which takes the following arguments:

- ID of the post ($post->ID)
- Name of the taxonomy (book_category)
- Print before the list (Categories:)
- Separate items in the list with (,)
- Print after the list ()

Also, now that you have categories, you can visit **Appearance** | **Menus** and add links to those categories to your header menu, and you can also create a custom menu with all the categories and add it to one of the sidebars.

Note that if you get a 404 error from WordPress at any point during the creation of your custom post type and custom taxonomy when you don't think you should, then visit **Settings** | **Permalinks**. Sometimes WordPress needs to refresh the permalinks to make the new links work correctly.

Customizing the admin display

The final thing you can do to realize your new book custom post type fully is to change its display in the wp-admin. You don't need to know the WordPress user who created a given book, but you do want to see the book categories and the thumbnail. Let's go back to `functions.php`. First, we'll change the columns that are displayed:

```
function ahskk_custom_columns($defaults) {
  global $wp_query, $pagenow;
  if ($pagenow == 'edit.php') {
    unset($defaults['author']);
    unset($defaults['categories']);
    unset($defaults['date']);
    $defaults['book_category'] = 'Categories';
    $defaults['thumbnail'] = 'Image';
  }
  return $defaults;
}
add_filter('manage_book_posts_columns', 'ahskk_custom_columns');
function ahskk_show_columns($name) {
  global $post;
  switch ($name) {
    case 'book_category':
      echo get_the_term_list($post->ID, 'book_category', '', ', ',
        '');
      break;
    case 'thumbnail':
      if (has_post_thumbnail($post->ID)) echo
        get_the_post_thumbnail($post->ID, array('40', '40'));
      break;
  }
}
Add_action('manage_book_posts_custom_column',
  'ahskk_show_columns');
```

The first function says "don't show author, date, and categories, but do show book categories and thumbnail," and the second function says "for the book categories column, print the list of categories, and for the thumbnail column, print the `get_post_thumbnail()` function."

Revisit the **Books** page in the wp-admin, and it now looks like the following screenshot:

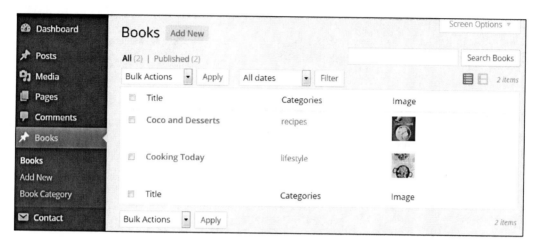

Summary

This chapter was part two of our non-blog website journey with WordPress. I hope you enjoyed the material. Here, you went through the process of setting up video blogs, photo blogs, membership sites, and social networks. Along the way, you took a closer look at some interesting plugins and their functionalities, just to make your lives easier as WordPress developers. Finally, you created a custom post type and a corresponding custom taxonomy.

The next and final chapter of this book will cover some general maintenance and troubleshooting techniques for WordPress administrators as well as provide a list of useful functions, CSS styles, and template files.

I believe that at this point, you are well-equipped to work with WordPress and use it to build your next great site! WordPress is a top-notch CMS, which has matured tremendously over the years. The WordPress admin panel is designed to be user-friendly and is being continuously improved. The code that underlies WordPress is robust and is the creation of a large community of dedicated developers. Additionally, WordPress' functionality can be extended through the use of plugins and themes.

I hope you enjoyed this book and got off on the right footing by learning the process of administering and using WordPress for your own site, whatever that may be. Be sure to stay connected to the WordPress open source community! Thank you for reading; you rock!

13

Administrating WordPress

This chapter will provide information to help you with the WordPress administrative tasks. A few topics that have been covered elsewhere in the book are explained in greater detail here.

I'll review the essentials, and then give you some important links that you can visit for more details. This chapter is a kind of **cheat sheet** that you can refer to for quick answers to common administrative issues.

System requirements

The minimum system requirement for WordPress is a web server with the following software installed:

- PHP version 5.2.4 or greater (recommended PHP 5.4 or greater)
- MySQL version 5.0 or greater (recommended MySQL 5.5 or greater)

Although Apache and Nginx are highly recommended by the WordPress developers, any server running PHP and MySQL will do.

 Learn more about system requirements at
https://wordpress.org/about/requirements/.

Your system will also need to be set up in a particular way if you want to use pretty permalinks, which give you nice-looking URLs throughout your site.

Enabling permalinks

We talked about permalinks in *Chapter 2, Getting Started with WordPress,* so please start by giving it a quick glance to refresh your memory.

Permalinks are a great functionality in WordPress. They allow you to take advantage of great looking URLs but, in order to use them, you must have a web server with mod_rewrite enabled.

Most commercial web hosts have this module turned on by default, so there's no need to do any additional tuning up. However—for a local installation, if you are using Windows IIS, for example—then some tweaks might be required. There are ways to implement permalinks on IIS; the most straightforward being to buy Helicon's ISAPI_Rewrite (`http://www.helicontech.com/isapi_rewrite/`). There are other ways as well; start at the following codex link. This topic is too extensive to be explored in depth in this book, but I encourage you to search the Internet for other people's solutions.

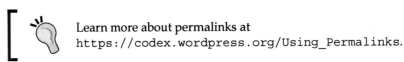

Learn more about permalinks at
`https://codex.wordpress.org/Using_Permalinks`.

The importance of backing up

I promise you, if you ever lose any data stored either on your local computer or on your website, you'll instantly understand the importance of backing up. The fact is that a hard disk failing is not a matter of *if*, it's a matter of *when*. All it actually takes is a glitch in your server or a hacker's infection. And although most web hosts offer some kind of backup services, it's good to have your own additional system setup (just in case). There are a couple of approaches to dealing with backups, which I will outline in the following sections.

Easy, quick, and frequent content backups

The most important part of your website, and also the part that you will never be able to re-create, is the content contained in the database. You should back up your database frequently. Exactly how often will depend on the number of times you change your content.

If you're running a blog, take a backup whenever you've posted two or three new posts. If you're running a non-blog website, back up every time you make significant changes to your content or add new pages.

The question you should ask yourself is, "If my server or host completely fizzles out today, how much time would it take me to re-create what's not already backed up?"

Luckily, your website content is pretty easy to back up. You can directly export the content of your database using phpMyAdmin or any other database tool provided by your host.

You can also install the **WordPress Backup to Dropbox** plugin that I described in *Chapter 5, Plugins and Widgets*. It's easy to use and will help you back up not only the database but also the filesystem of your site (all files, uploads, themes, plugins, and other PHP code). The installation process of the plugin is 100 percent standard, so it doesn't require any additional explaining.

Backing up everything

In addition to your database, there are other irreplaceable files that make up your WordPress website. These include the following:

- The theme you are using
- The plugins you've installed and activated
- The files you've uploaded
- The code you've changed by hand

WordPress stores all of these things (except for the last one, since you can modify any file you wish) in the same folder named `wp-content/`. Every time you change your theme and install a new plugin, you should make sure that you have a backup of these things on your home computer. After that, you don't need to back these two things up regularly because they won't change.

However, the files you upload (for example media files, images, audio, icons, and so on) are a collection that change over time as you add more files. If you add a photo with each blog post, then that collection changes as frequently as you post. You should be sure to create a backup of the `wp-content/uploads/` folder pretty regularly.

This you can do manually via FTP or through the WordPress Backup to Dropbox plugin mentioned earlier. When dealing with FTP, it's good to have an FTP program with a synchronize feature so you won't have to constantly re-download older files, or do a lot of hunting and pecking for new ones. In the end, using WordPress Backup to Dropbox is still a lot simpler and more user-friendly than playing with FTP.

Getting a managed solution

There are various ways of getting your site safely backed up, and one of them is to sign up to a managed solution that handles the process for you, with no supervision required. One of the popular services like this is called **CodeGuard** (get it at https://www.codeguard.com/), where there's a free trial available. CodeGuard handles your site backups automatically, based on a schedule. Every day it analyzes your site, and backs up every new entry in the database and every file in your site's filesystem, then notifies you if it finds any changes. This allows you to keep your finger on the pulse and act fast if there's anything suspicious going on. For example, when your files change but you are not the person making the changes, it might mean a hacker attack. CodeGuard also offers a time-machine-like functionality. This feature enables you to restore your site to one of its previous versions in case anything goes wrong and your site stops working.

Upgrading WordPress

In *Chapter 2*, *Getting Started with WordPress*, we briefly discussed upgrading your existing WordPress version to the latest available version. In this section, we will take a closer look at the upgrade process.

So what about the built-in upgrader?

As of WordPress 2.6, you can do an upgrade with one click from within WordPress. This is actually an advisable approach and one that's much faster than going the manual way. These days, WordPress is perfectly capable of handling almost all of the steps on its own, and it only needs our input to do a couple of pre- and post-upgrade operations. In the following section, we're going to describe how to work with the WordPress' upgrade feature.

Steps for upgrading

The steps involved in upgrading WordPress are as follows:

1. Back up your database.
2. Back up your WordPress files.
3. Run the WordPress' upgrade feature.
4. Update permalinks and `.htaccess`.
5. Install updated plugins and themes.

Each step has been described in detail in the following sections of the chapter.

Backing up your database

Before upgrading WordPress, you should always back up the database. If anything goes horribly wrong with your upgrade, you won't lose everything. We reviewed how to back up your WordPress website earlier in this chapter, so you can refer back to that for specific instructions.

Backing up your WordPress files

Remember, the complete content of what creates your site is not only contained in the database, but also in certain files on the server. Always back up all your files as well, just in case something goes wrong with the upgrade. Again, refer back to the backup instructions given earlier if you need to review the steps.

Running the WordPress upgrade feature

WordPress takes care of the next step for you: running the upgrade. This script usually takes a look at your database and makes alterations to it so that it is compatible with the new version of WordPress. It also updates the default WordPress core files and other elements of the platform.

To access it, just point your browser to your wp-admin, then go to **Dashboard | Updates**. If the site needs an update, this is what you'll see:

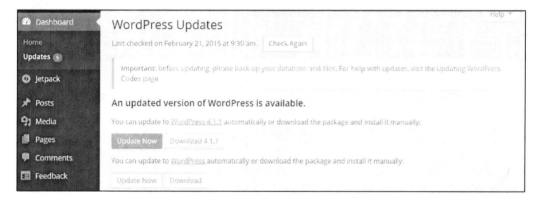

All you have to do now is click the **Update Now** button. After the process is finished, you will be redirected to a new welcome screen:

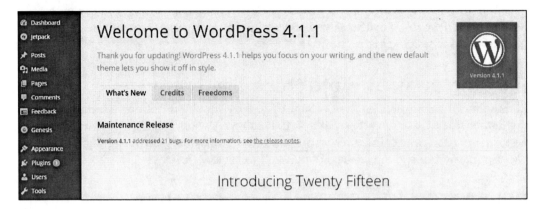

Updating permalinks and .htaccess

You may have to update the permalink settings so that they match the previous installation. Your permalink settings dictate what the `.htaccess` file should look like. If WordPress cannot access your `.htaccess` file because of permissions problems, then the permalinks page will display a message letting you know about it. That message will also tell you what text needs to be in the `.htaccess` file, so that you can create or update it yourself.

Lastly, if you've previously used a plugin like **BulletProof Security** (available at `https://wordpress.org/plugins/bulletproof-security/`) to handle your `.htaccess` file, then enabling the plugin again after the upgrade should give the `.htaccess` file a correct structure again.

Installing updated plugins and themes

In your wp-admin, visit the plugins page again. If there are new versions of any of your installed but now inactive plugins, there'll be a note telling you so. If you have any plugins that are not part of the WordPress Plugin Directory, this is a good time to check the websites for those plugins to see if there's an upgrade available.

 You can also take a look at the *Plugin Compatibility* lists at `https://codex.wordpress.org/Plugins/Plugin_Compatibility`.

Once you're sure that the plugins you want to use are up-to-date, activate them one at a time so that there are no problems. This is also a good time to check for updates for the theme that you are using. You can check for a new version on the developer's website, or in the WordPress Theme Directory. Of course, you have to be sure you haven't made any theme customizations directly to the theme that you're using. If you have, they will be overwritten when you run the theme update. If you want to customize an existing theme, be sure to make a child theme (covered in *Chapter 7, Developing Your Own Theme*).

Migrating or restoring a WordPress website

Sometimes, you may find yourself in a situation where you need to move your WordPress website from one server to another or from one URL to another. Alternatively, if something gets fried on your server and is restored, you need to recreate your damaged WordPress website. Here you'll essentially need to do the same things as you would in a migration.

I highly recommend that you check out the article at `https://codex.wordpress.org/Moving_WordPress` in the WordPress codex, which has detailed step-by-step instructions on how to migrate your WordPress website under a variety of different circumstances.

That page will be kept up-to-date as time moves on. If you need to do a migration and don't have access to the codex right now, you can follow these steps for migration:

1. Download a backup of your database (as described earlier in this chapter, in the *Backing up your database* section). If your URL is going to change, you may want to use a different plugin to download your database. It's called **WP Migrate DB** (`https://wordpress.org/plugins/wp-migrate-db/`). This plugin will change the URLs for you.

2. Download all your files (as described earlier in this chapter, in the *Backing up your WordPress files* section).

3. Look in your downloaded files for `wp-config.php`. Find the lines that define the connection to the database. Edit those lines so that they now have the database name, username, password, and the hostname for your new database.

4. Upload all your files to your new server.

5. Implement your SQL file in the new database.

6. Change the permissions of your `wp-content` folder if necessary, so that you'll be able to upload files without any problems.

7. Change the absolute path of your WordPress folder in the database. You can do this by getting a custom script like `https://interconnectit.com/products/search-and-replace-for-wordpress-databases/`; please follow the URL for a step-by-step tutorial.

8. Log in to your new wp-admin, and check the permalinks. You may have to reset them if your `.htaccess` file didn't come over properly.

You're done!

If you're restoring your site on the same server, with no changes to the location or the database, then you can skip steps 3 and 7. Steps 1 and 2 (to back up) should be done before the meltdown!

Acting in case of a site crash

This is quite unfortunate, but it does happen from time to time. One day, you might wake up and find your site not working, just like that. Getting it back on can take a while depending on the cause of the crash. Here are some of the most common reasons for a WordPress site crashing:

- Bad hosting service running the site
- Poor quality themes or plugins with badly structured code
- Weak passwords for admin accounts (prone to hacker attacks)

Here's my routine when dealing with a site that has just crashed:

1. Deactivate or even delete all plugins. Actually, you don't have to delete anything, just rename the main `plugins` directory so WordPress won't be able to find it.

2. Rename the current theme folder, so WordPress goes back to the default theme.

3. Take a working backup copy of the site and restore all contents from it.

4. Overwrite all your WordPress core files with new ones. Proceed as if you want to upgrade WordPress manually (described earlier in this chapter).

It's important to check if your site has started working again after handling each step. Most of the time, you don't have to go through all the steps; your site will probably start working again somewhere in the middle of the process.

If your site has started working again, then you can begin reactivating your theme and your plugins one by one. Check if the site is still working after each activation.

 To get a more detailed guide on how to restore WordPress after a crash, feel free to visit `http://themefuse.com/restoring-wordpress-after-a-crash/`.

Setting file permissions

To install and maintain WordPress properly, you may need to change permissions to different files and folders in the WordPress folder, so that uploads and built-in updates will work from within WordPress. Usually, this affects people on Unix servers, though it affects some Windows servers as well.

Explaining file permissions

File permissions are settings that indicate who is allowed to do what. That is, some users may have permission to alter the contents of a file, some may have permission to only read it, and some may not even have read/write access. In addition to read/write permissions, there are also "execute" permissions. If a file is executable, then this permission indicates who can execute that file.

For Unix file permissions at a glance, look at the following chart:

File/folder	Owner permission	Group permission	User permission	Total	Numerical equivalent
/	rwx	rw	Rw	rwxrw-rw-	766
/.htaccess	rwx	rw	Rw	rwxrw-rw-	766
/wp-admin	rwx	r--	r--	rwxr--r--	744
/wp-includes	rwx	r--	r--	rwxr--r--	744
/wp-content	rwx	rwx	rw-	rwxrwxrw-	776
/wp-content/themes	rwx	rwx	rw-	rwxrwxrw-	776
/wp-content/plugins	rwx	rw-	rw-	rwxrw-rw-	766

Permissions for WordPress

The best permission scheme for a WordPress installation is for all of the files to be owned by your user (your server's user, not your WordPress user), and to be writable by your user. Other than that, any file that WordPress will need to modify (such as, well, just about anything in wp-content) should be group-owned by both your user and the webserver's user (often called dhapache or nobody).

If you've installed your WordPress website yourself, then you shouldn't need to modify any permissions for all WordPress functionalities to work.

If you're having trouble using the built-in upgrader or plugin installer, do not chmod everything to 777 (world-writable). Instead, check with the hosting provider or people who run your server, and ask what they recommend.

How to set permissions

You can change permissions to files and folders using any FTP client. If you have shell access, you can use shell commands to change file permissions. If you're using an FTP client, select the files you want to change permissions for, and look for menus like **Get Info**, **File Attributes**, or **Change Permissions**. There will be a GUI, often with checkboxes, that lets you choose permissions for different files. Some hosting control panels, such as Fantastico, allow you to change permissions through the control panel itself.

If you are using shell, change the file permissions with the chmod command. For example, the wp-admin folder should be set as rwxr--r-- or 744; and to change the permissions for the wp-admin/ folder, run the following command:

```
chmod -R wp-admin 744
```

 Learn more about WordPress and file permissions at https://codex.wordpress.org/Changing_File_Permissions.

Troubleshooting

In this section, we will discuss problems that may arise during the installation and execution of WordPress, and provide solutions for troubleshooting them.

Troubleshooting during installation

Most of the problems discussed here have been taken from the WordPress installation FAQs and troubleshooting FAQs.

Headers already sent

- **Problem**: When you point your browser at your website, you may get an error that displays a "headers already sent" message on your page. The whole page may look scrambled, and it will not function.

- **Cause**: WordPress uses PHP session functions. If anything is sent by the server to the browser before these session functions, even if it's just a blank space, then the session functions will not work properly.

- **Solution**: You have to figure out where the error lies. Usually, it is a file that you have edited manually. If you remember, you edited the wp-config.php file while installing WordPress. Open the file with your text editor, and make sure that there is nothing before <?php in the first line or after ?> in the last line. Another precaution would be to erase the final ?> line altogether.

Page comes with only PHP code

- **Problem**: When you point your browser at your website, it displays the PHP code instead of its contents.

- **Cause**: This happens when your server is not parsing PHP, but is instead treating it the same as any text or HTML file. This is a server configuration problem; either PHP is not installed on your server, or it is not configured to function properly.

- **Solution**: To solve this problem, contact the system administrator for your server or try installing PHP.

Cannot connect to the MySQL database

- **Problem**: WordPress cannot connect to the MySQL database, and is displaying an error.

- **Cause**: This might happen if:
  - The database parameters are incorrect
  - The daemon/service is not running properly
  - Your server is running an outdated version of MySQL

- **Solution**: To solve this problem, you can try the following:

  ○ Open your `wp-config.php` file, and check that the database parameters are correct.

  ○ If you are sure that these settings are correct, check if the MySQL daemon/service is running properly. If MySQL is not running, run this service. If MySQL is already running, try restarting the service. If you are not running your own server, check in with your host company's support people.

  ○ If you are sure that your database parameters are fine, and MySQL is also running, then connect to MySQL using your MySQL command-line tool and run these commands:

  ```
  set password = OLD_PASSWORD('your_current_password');
  flush privileges;
  ```

  This will use the old encryption of passwords so that PHP can connect to MySQL.

Basic troubleshooting

As you have probably already figured out, the best place to look for troubleshooting tips is the WordPress.org website, both the codex and the support forum. The codex even has a page devoted to basic troubleshooting (`https://codex.wordpress.org/Troubleshooting`). There's also an updated Troubleshooting Master List for each new version of WordPress. The newest one at the time of writing is at `https://wordpress.org/support/topic/read-this-first-wordpress-41-master-list` (you can always find the current version by going to `https://wordpress.org/search/wordpress+master+list?forums=1.`).

The following are some of the most common problems that people encounter when setting up WordPress; if you don't see yours here, I encourage you to visit the codex.

Cannot see posts

- **Problem**: Posts are not seen, and the message "search doesn't meet criteria" is displayed.
- **Cause**: This can happen because of caching. For example, you have searched once, and WordPress stored the search result inside its cache; so every time you visit the page, you see the old result.
- **Solution**: You can solve this problem by clearing the cache and cookies from your browser.

I don't receive the e-mailed passwords

- **Problem**: You don't receive the e-mailed passwords.

- **Cause**: This problem may happen if your web server has no **Simple Mail Transfer Protocol (SMTP)** server installed, or if the mail function is explicitly disabled.

- **Solution**: Please contact your system administrator, or try installing **Sendmail** (or any other mail server) properly.

Tips for theme development

In *Chapter 7, Developing Your Own Theme,* we covered theme development pretty thoroughly, though you can get a more in-depth tutorial in theme development from the excellent book *WordPress Theme Design, Tessa Blakeley Silver, Packt Publishing.*

This section lists the top template tags and stylesheet classes that you'll want to have if you're going to be developing themes. These are the most essential ones, with some of my personal favorites thrown in.

Template tags

The following is a list of the most used template tags. For a complete list, visit the codex. The article at `https://codex.wordpress.org/Template_Tags` is a good place to start. You can also have a look into the *Function Reference* sheet at `https://codex.wordpress.org/Function_Reference/`. In the list that follows, I do not cover the parameters that can be passed to these functions. You'll want to visit the codex to find out about the default settings for each tag and how to override them.

The **header and informational tags** are as follows:

The tag	What it does
`wp_title()`	Prints an appropriate title for your blog (the post title, the archives title, the page title, or whatever is appropriate for the current page)
`bloginfo('name')`	Prints out the name of your blog, as specified on the main options page in your wp-admin. You can also use a similar tag – `get_bloginfo()`, which returns the information instead of displaying it
`wp_head()`	An essential part of the `<head></head>` tag, because a variety of things get printed out by this tag, depending on the details of the blog

The tag	What it does
`bloginfo('stylesheet_url')`	Prints out the path to the stylesheet of the current theme.
`bloginfo('rss2_url')`	Prints out the RSS 2.0 feed URL for your blog.
`body_class()`	Prints out a list of appropriate class names in the body tag. It should be used to replace `<body>` like this: `<body <?php body_class(); ?>>`

The following tags can be used **inside the loop**:

The tag	What it does
`the_title()`	Prints out the title of the current post or page.
`the_time()`	Prints out the date and time of the post or page.
`the_content()`	Prints out the formatted post or page content.
`the_category()`	Prints out a list of the categories that belong to this post.
`the_tags()`	Prints out a list of the tags associated with this post.
`the_author()`	Prints out the name of the post or page author.
`edit_post_link()`	If the person viewing the blog is a logged-in blog user, this tag will print out a link for editing the post (very handy!)
`the_permalink()`	Prints out the URL of the post or page itself (must be used within a `<a href=""></a>` tag).
`comments_popup_link()`	If `comments_popup_script` is not used, this displays a normal link to the comments for the post or page.

`post_class()`	If you put this tag inside the `<div>` tag for your posts, it will generate a list of classes for the categories and tags that belong to this post. For example, if you put this in your template as follows:
	
	`<div <?php post_class(); ?>>`
	
	WordPress will print something like this:
	
	`<div class="post category-recipes category-locavore tag-holiday tag-pasta tag-recipe tag-spinach">`

`get_post_meta()`	Use this function to get the value stored in a custom field. Just pass this function the current post ID, the name of the custom field you want, and `true` to get the value of that custom field.
`get_the_post_thumbnail()`	Prints out a complete `img` tag for the featured image.

The following tags can be used for **lists and navigation**:

The tag	What it does
previous_post_ link()	When viewing a single post, this prints a link to the previous post (the one with the preceding newest timestamp)
next_post_link()	When viewing a single post, this prints a link to the next post (the one with the next newer timestamp)
wp_list_pages()	Prints a list of all the pages in your WordPress site
wp_get_archives()	Prints a list of archives (by post, month, and so on)

The following tags can be used to **include PHP files**:

The tag	What it does
get_header()	Includes header.php from the current theme folder
get_footer()	Includes footer.php from the current theme folder
get_sidebar()	Includes sidebar.php from the current theme folder
comments_template()	Prints the standard list of comments and comment-submission forms, unless there is a file in the theme folder named comments.php, in which case that is included instead
get_search_form()	Prints the standard search form
include(TEMPLATEPATH. '/filename.php')	Includes filename.php from the current theme folder

The following are some of the most useful **conditional** tags. Note that some of them can take a parameter, so be sure to look them up in the codex for details.

The tag	What it does
is_front_page()	Returns true if user is viewing the front page of the site, regardless of whether it's the most recent blog post or page
is_home()	Returns true if user is viewing the main page of your blog, which can either be the front page of your site or the page you designated as the **Posts** page in **Settings | Reading**
is_page()	Returns true if user is viewing a page
is_single()	Returns true if user is viewing a single post
is_archive()	Returns true if user is viewing an archive page of blog posts (monthly, yearly, category, tag, and so on)
is_search()	Returns true if user is viewing search results

The tag	What it does
`has_post_thumbnail()`	Returns `true` if the post (the only parameter is a post ID) has a featured image or designated thumbnail assigned to it

Learn more about conditional tags at `https://codex.wordpress.org/Conditional_Tags`.

Class styles generated by WordPress

WordPress helpfully applies classes to just about everything that it generates, thus making it easy for you to style WordPress-generated elements on your page.

Here is a starter list of those styles. If you want to know about the other styles, create a template and view the source of the page it creates.

Class or ID	Where to find it
`.page_item`	On the `<li>` tag of every page in the generated page list.
`.current_page_item`	On the `<li>` tag of the current page in the generated page list.
`.current_page_parent`	On the `<li>` tag of the parent of the current page in the generated page list.
`.page-item-23`	On the `<li>` tag of the page with ID=23 (there is one of these for each page) in the generated page list.
`.menu-item`	On the `<li>` tag of every item in the generated nav list. As with pages, menu-item-parent, current-menu-item, and so on are also generated for appropriate items.
`.widget`	On the `<li>` tag of every widget.
`.cat-item`	On the `<li>` tag of every category in the generated category list.
`.current-cat`	On the `<li>` tag of the current category in the generated category list.
`.cat-item-13`	On the `<li>` tag of the category with ID=13 (there is one of these for each category) in the generated category list.
`#searchform`	On the `<form>` tag for the generated search form.

Learning more

If you want to learn more about how WordPress deals with CSS and various style classes, please visit any of the following resources:

- The official guide on CSS in WordPress (https://codex.wordpress.org/CSS)
- Default WordPress Generated CSS Cheat Sheet for Beginners (http://www.wpbeginner.com/wp-themes/default-wordpress-generated-css-cheat-sheet-for-beginners/)
- Back to Basics With WordPress CSS: Understanding the Native Classes (http://css-tricks.com/back-basics-wordpress-css-understanding-native-classes/)

Summary

In this chapter, we covered many of the common administrative tasks that you might face when you're managing a WordPress-driven website. This includes backing up your database and files, moving your WordPress installation from one server or folder to another, and doing general problem-solving and troubleshooting. We also covered some of the most basic and useful template tags that you'll need when creating your own WordPress themes.

You should now feel well-equipped to address all the usual administrative tasks for your website or blog.

WordPress is a top-notch CMS, which has matured tremendously over the years. The WordPress Admin panel is designed to be user-friendly, and is continually being improved. The code that underlies WordPress is robust, and is the creation of a large community of dedicated developers. Additionally, WordPress' functionality can be extended through the use of plugins.

I hope you have enjoyed this book, and have gotten a strong start for administering and using WordPress for your own site, whatever it may be. Be sure to stay connected to the WordPress open source community!

Index

Symbols

$control_ops variable 279
$widget_ops variable 279
<head> tag 198

A

action hooks
  URL 276
add_filter() function
  URL 290
additional writing options
  about 81
  external blogging tools 82
  mobile apps, for iOS and Android 83, 84
  posting, via e-mail 82
  Press This 81
admin conventions 49
administrator 294
admin page, plugins
  adding 265
  doctype_styles_new_regex() function,
      modifying 268
  hooks, adding 268
  management page functions,
      adding 265-268
advanced post options
  about 71
  author, changing 77
  content, protecting 77, 78
  Custom Fields 74, 75
  custom post format settings 79, 80
  Discussion box 73
  excerpt 71, 72

pingbacks 72
post revisions, working with 75, 76
post slug 78
trackbacks 72
Akismet
  about 93
  activating 95
  API key, obtaining 93, 94
  URL 93
All In One Favicon
  URL 313
Archive.org
  URL 247
archive template
  about 211
  creating 211
Atom feed
  URL 238
Audacity
  URL 243
authors 296, 297
auto-installation, plugin 134-136
automatic content distribution, setting up to
      social media
  about 250
  Jetpack plugin 251
  Revive Old Post plugin 251-253

B

background
  about 109, 110
  Background Attachment option 111
  Background Position option 111
  Background Repeat option 110

backing up
about 137
importance 358
backups
about 358
content backups 358, 359
managed solution, obtaining 360
performing 359
basic content
creating 193
footer 199-201
functions.php file 193-197
header 199-201
sidebar 201
blog 3
blogging, common terms
about 4
categories 4
comments 5
home page 7
menus 6
page 6
plugins 5
post 4
RSS 6
tags 4
themes 5
users 7
widgets 6
blog, posting
additional writing options 81
advanced post options 71
common post options 54
simple post, adding 52-54
body_class() function 216
Book Categories, custom taxonomy
creating 352
book custom post type
description parameter 343
has_archive parameter 343
public parameter 343
rewrite parameter 343
supports parameter 343
BuddyPress plugin
about 338
URL, for components 340
URL 339

built-in feeds
about 238
URL 242

C

caching 142
categories
about 96
adding 96
managing 96
cheat sheet 357
child theme
creating 228, 229
stylesheet, creating 230
theme folder, creating 229
using 230, 231
CodeGuard
about 360
URL 360
Codex. *See* **WordPress Codex**
comments
about 5, 85
adding 85
avatar display settings 89, 90
blacklisting 88, 89
comment spam, eliminating 92
discussion settings 86
moderating 90-92
moderation settings 86-88
notification settings 86, 87
submission settings 86, 87
comment spam elimination
Akismet, activating 95
Akismet API key, obtaining 93, 94
performing 92
Comments RSS 2.0 feed
URL 238
common post options
about 54
audio, adding to blog posts 65, 66
categories 55, 56
default image sizes, controlling 60, 61
drafts 69
featured image, designating 63
image, adding in posts 57-59
lead and body 68

limited editing possibilities 66
media, adding to blog posts 63
pending articles 69, 70
tags 55, 56
Text editor, using 67, 68
timestamps 70
uploaded image, editing 61, 62
videos, adding to blog posts 63-65
Visual editor, using 67
community blogging
about 293
multi-author blog, concerns 293
user management plugins 303
user roles 294
users, managing 299
conditional tags
URL 372
Contact Form 7 plugin 309
content
about 4, 123
exporting 125, 126
importing 124, 125
Content Management System (CMS) 157
contributor 298
corporate or business websites
about 311
clean theme, picking 312
custom home page 315, 316
elements, branding 313
good navigation 314, 315
Master Slider 318-320
Meteor Slides 317
optional slider 316
corporate theme
features 313
Custom Fields 74, 75
Custom Menus 6
custom page template
creating 218
using 218-224
custom post types
about 342
admin display, customizing 354, 355
book template files, creating 346-351
custom taxonomy, registering 352
custom taxonomy, using 352, 353
labels, adding 344

messages, adding 344-346
new post type, registering 342, 343
custom tag cloud widget
about 276
form function 280, 281
hooking up 284
initiating 284
initiation function 279
naming 277
print function 282, 283
save function 281
structure 278
styles 283
using 284, 285

D

dedicated podcast
setting up 245, 246
digital audio workstation (DAW) 243
double-tag shortcodes 286
Dropbox
URL 138

E

editor 295
excerpt 71
external blogging tools 82

F

Facebook plugin
URL 337
features, WordPress
about 7
active in development 8
extendable 8
large community of contributors 8
long time in refining 7
feed aggregator (feed reader) 235
feed generator 238
feed links
adding 239
feeds, for comments 241
feeds, for whole website 240
Feedly
about 6

URL 236
Wikipedia reference link 238
feeds 235-237
Fetch
URL 25
file permissions
explaining 365
permissions, for WordPress 366
setting 365, 366
Filezilla
URL 25
filter hooks
URL 276
filter menu 51
Foliogine PRO
URL 336
freemium model 330
FTP client 25
functions.php file 193-197

G

Gantry
URL 181
Garage Band 243
general blog information, wp-admin panel
creating 41, 42
Genesis
URL 181
GNU General Public License (GPL) 232
Google Analytics
about 140
enabling 140
URL 140
Google Analytics by Yoast plugin
about 140
activating 141
URL 140
GPL licensing 232
Gravatar (Globally Recognized Avatar)
about 47, 48
URL 47

H

header 107, 108
HTML build, converting into theme
about 190

basic WordPress content, creating 193
loop 202-207
theme folder, creating 190-193

I

image gallery
adding 118
images
selecting 119-122
uploading 119-122
index.php file
about 208
footer.php file 209
header.php file 208
sidebar.php file 209
installation, WordPress
environment, preparing 24
files, uploading 25, 26
manual installation 24
ISAPI_Rewrite
URL 358

J

Jetpack
about 131, 151, 251
setting up 151, 152
URL 132
JM Twitter Cards
URL 250

K

Kraken
URL 57

L

Levelator
URL 243
Libsyn
URL 247
Lightbox
about 337
URL 337
Logic 243
loop 202-207

M

manual plugin installation 131-133
MarsEdit
  URL 83
Master Slider
  about 318-320
  URL 318
media library
  about 113-115
  image gallery, adding 118
  images, selecting 119-122
  images, uploading 119-122
  Media Manager 115-118
  page, selecting 118
  post, selecting 118
Membership plugin
  installing 331, 332
  URL 330
  using 333, 334
membership websites
  about 327, 328
  free approach 330
  functionalities 328
  membership plugins, using 329, 330
  simple approach 328, 329
menus
  about 6, 103
  adding 103-106
  displaying 106, 107
Meteor Slides
  about 317
  URL 317
Metro CreativeX
  URL 336
multi-author blog 293, 294
must-have plugins
  about 137
  Google Analytics by Yoast plugin 140, 141
  Jetpack 151
  Social Share Starter 148-150
  W3 Total Cache 142, 143
  Wordfence Security 145-147
  WordPress Backup to Dropbox 137-139
  WordPress SEO plugin 143-145

N

net2ftp
  URL 25
non-blog type websites
  corporate or business websites 305
  e-commerce stores 305
  membership websites 306
  must-do tasks 307
  niche business websites 306
  one-page websites 305
  photo blogs 306
  product websites 306
  social networks 306
  static websites 305
  video blogs 306

O

one-page websites
  about 321, 323
  elements, branding 324
  high quality images 324, 325
  one-page theme, features 323
  one-page theme, picking 323

P

pages
  about 99, 100
  About Karol 102
  adding 100, 101
  Custom Menus 102, 103
  managing 102
  order 102
  Page Attributes 101
  parent 102
  selecting 118
  structuring 102
page template
  about 214
  creating 214, 215
permalinks
  enabling 358
  URL 358
PhotoArtist
  URL 336

photo blog
about 334
features 335
plugins, obtaining 336, 337
themes, exploring 336
pingbacks
about 72
URL 74
Plugin API
URL 276
Plugin Directory
URL 14
Plugin Resources page
URL 276
plugins
about 5, 127, 256
admin page, adding 265
auto-installation 134-136
building, from scratch 256
code requirements 257
features 128
installing 131, 255
manual installation 131-133
must-have pack 137
obtaining 128, 129
podcasting 246
reference links 276
searching 130
testing 270, 271
URL 255
using 269, 270
plugin, with DB access
management page functions,
adding 273, 274
running, when activated 272
searched words, capturing 271
using 274, 275
PodBean
URL 248
podcast
about 242
adding 242
audio files, hosting with service 247, 248
creating 243
dedicated podcast, setting up 245, 246
post, creating 244, 245
URL, for tutorial 243

voice, recording 243
podcasting
URL 246, 247
Podcasting Plugin by TSG
URL 246
Podlove Podcast Publisher
URL 246
Portfolio Press
URL 336
post
about 4, 52
selecting 118
post_class() function 217
post slug 78
PowerPress
URL 246
premium plugin directories
URL 130
Press This 81
ProTools 243

Q

Qumana
URL 83

R

RDF/RSS 1.0 feed
URL 238
Really Simple Syndication (RSS) 236
Recent Posts widget 316
Recipes 4
responsive design/structure 169
Revive Old Post plugin
about 251
settings 252
URL 251
right-to-left (RTL) support 10
RSS 2.0 feed
URL 238

S

salt keys
URL 32
search engine optimization (SEO) 143

secret keys
  URL 32
Secure FTP (sFTP) 26
shortcodes
  about 286
  double-tag shortcodes 286
  enabling, in widgets 290
  shortcodes with attributes 287
  simple shortcode, creating 287-289
  single-tag shortcodes 286
  types 286
  working 286
simple plugin
  core functions, writing 260, 261
  creating 257
  hooks, adding 261-264
  link icons, adding 257, 258
  plugin files, naming 258-260
  plugin files, organizing 258-260
  using 264
simple post
  adding 52-54
single template 212-214
site
  customizing 112, 113
  security 145
slug 96
SmartFTP
  URL 25
social media integration
  about 148, 248
  automatic content distribution,
      setting up 250
  blog, making social media friendly 248
  social media APIs integration,
      setting up 249, 250
  social media metrics tracking,
      setting up 253, 254
  social media share buttons, setting up 249
Social Metrics Tracker
  URL 253
social network
  about 338
  designing 341
  features 338
  functionality, extending 341

installing 339, 340
Social Share Starter
  about 148
  setting up 149, 150
  URL 148
Sonar X2 243
standard themes 161
starter themes 162
static websites
  about 307
  easy-to-grasp menus, creating 311
  home page, building 309, 310
  process 308
Studio One 243
StudioPress
  URL 163
subscriber 298

T

tags 4
template files, WordPress theme
  archive template 211, 212
  classes, generating for body
      and post 216, 217
  creating 207, 208
  custom page template, creating 218
  custom page template, using 218-224
  index.php file 210, 211
  index.php file, breaking up 208
  page template 214, 215
  single template 212-214
template hierarchy
  URL 217
template tags
  about 369
  conditional tags 371
  header and informational tags 369
  using, for including PHP files 371
  using, inside loop 370
Thematic
  URL 181
theme. *See* **WordPress theme**
theme development
  class styles 372
  template tags 369-371
  tips 369

Theme Directory
  URL 14
ThemeForest
  URL 164
theme frameworks
  about 162
  URL 181
ThemeFuse
  URL 164
ThemeIsle
  URL 164
theme selection, factors
  about 164
  customizable factor 169
  documentation 170
  purpose 165, 166
  responsive design/structure 169, 170
  reviews 170
  structure 164, 165
  support 170
  theme licensing 168
  up-to-date themes 168
theme stores
  StudioPress 163
  ThemeForest 164
  ThemeFuse 164
  ThemeIsle 164
  WooThemes 164
Thesis
  URL 181
trackbacks
  about 72
  URL 74
troubleshooting
  about 366
  WordPress 368, 369
  WordPress installation FAQs 367, 368
Twenty Fifteen theme 152
Twenty Fourteen theme 44

U

Underscores
  URL 173
upgrade, WordPress
  .htaccess, updating 362
  database, backing up 361

permalinks, updating 362
running 361
steps 360
themes, installing 362
updated plugins, installing 362
WordPress files, backing up 361
user management plugins 303
user roles
  about 294
  administrator 294
  authors 296, 297
  contributor 298
  editor 295
  subscriber 298
users
  about 7
  enabling, to self-register 301, 302
  managing 299, 300

V

video blog
  about 334
  features 334, 335
  plugins, obtaining 336, 337
  themes, exploring 336
Visual editor
  versus Text editor 67, 68

W

W3 Total Cache
  about 142, 265
  installing 142
  URL 142
web feed 235
weblog 3
widget area 152
widget-friendly theme
  creating 225
widgetizing
  about 225
  functions.php file, working with 226
  options 227
  sidebars, setting 225
  URL 227
  widgets, adding to theme 226, 227
  working 225

widgets
  about 6, 152, 276
  bundling, with existing plugin 286
  controlling 152-154
  custom tag cloud widget 276
  URL 285
Windows Live Writer 83
WishList Member
  about 330
  URL 330
WooThemes
  URL 164
Wordfence Security
  about 145
  setting up 146, 147
  URL 145
WordPress
  about 1, 2
  admin conventions 49
  advantage 18
  blog 3, 4
  built-in feeds 238
  common reasons, for site crashing 364, 365
  downloading 24
  features 7-10
  installation FAQs, troubleshooting 367, 368
  installing 27-30
  installing, through auto-installer
     script 33-36
  installing, through hand-built
     configuration file 30-32
  lists of items 50, 51
  manual installation 24
  online resources 12
  plugin directories 14
  reference, for requisites 24
  resources 373
  staying updated, through news 12
  step-by-step guide for
     manual installation 33
  templates 217
  theme directories 14
  upgrading 25, 360
  URL 5
  URL, for forum 14
  using, for blog or website 3
  wp-admin panel 37

WordPress, administrating
  about 357
  backups 358
  permalinks, enabling 358
  system requirements 357
WordPress app
  URL 83
WordPress Backup to Dropbox plugin
  about 137, 138, 359
  installing 138
  setting up 139
  URL 137
WordPress Codex
  about 13, 33
  URL 13
WordPress family 8, 9
WordPress plugins
  URL 128
WordPress SEO plugin
  about 143, 144, 265
  settings 145
  URL 143
WordPress theme
  about 5, 208
  adding, within wp-admin 170-172
  building, from ground up 180
  building, with framework 180
  building, with starter theme 181
  changing 170
  child themes 161
  CSS, examining 184-189
  design, converting into code 182
  design, setting up 178
  developer license 168
  developing 179
  downloading 173-176
  extracting 173-176
  finding 158-164
  HTML structure, examining 182-184
  installing 170
  main types 161
  menu, enabling 228
  selecting, factors 165
  sharing 231, 232
  standard, one-site license 168
  standard layouts 178, 179
  standard themes 161

starter themes 162
stores 163
structure 164, 165
template files, creating 207
theme frameworks 162
uploading 173-176
URL, for hierarchy 217
URL, for stores 166
WordPress Theme Directory
about 158-160
URL 158
WordPress version 3.7
features 10, 11
references 11
WordPress website
building 18
content, publishing 22, 23
migrating 363
restoring 363, 364
URL 20
using 20-22
versus WordPress.org 19
WordPress Widgets API
URL 285
World Wide Web Consortium (W3C)
standards 9

wp-admin panel
about 37-41
admin bar 38
comment, creating 44-46
general blog information, changing 41-43
lost password, retrieving 47
post, creating 43, 44
top bar 38
wp-admin (WordPress Administration panel) 52
wp-config.php file
URL 33
WP-Member
about 330
URL 330
WP Migrate DB
URL 363
wp_nav_menu() function 228
WP Smush.it
about 337
URL 337

Z

Zerif Lite
URL 159

Thank you for buying
WordPress 4.x Complete

About Packt Publishing

Packt, pronounced 'packed', published its first book, *Mastering phpMyAdmin for Effective MySQL Management*, in April 2004, and subsequently continued to specialize in publishing highly focused books on specific technologies and solutions.

Our books and publications share the experiences of your fellow IT professionals in adapting and customizing today's systems, applications, and frameworks. Our solution-based books give you the knowledge and power to customize the software and technologies you're using to get the job done. Packt books are more specific and less general than the IT books you have seen in the past. Our unique business model allows us to bring you more focused information, giving you more of what you need to know, and less of what you don't.

Packt is a modern yet unique publishing company that focuses on producing quality, cutting-edge books for communities of developers, administrators, and newbies alike. For more information, please visit our website at www.packtpub.com.

About Packt Open Source

In 2010, Packt launched two new brands, Packt Open Source and Packt Enterprise, in order to continue its focus on specialization. This book is part of the Packt Open Source brand, home to books published on software built around open source licenses, and offering information to anybody from advanced developers to budding web designers. The Open Source brand also runs Packt's Open Source Royalty Scheme, by which Packt gives a royalty to each open source project about whose software a book is sold.

Writing for Packt

We welcome all inquiries from people who are interested in authoring. Book proposals should be sent to author@packtpub.com. If your book idea is still at an early stage and you would like to discuss it first before writing a formal book proposal, then please contact us; one of our commissioning editors will get in touch with you.

We're not just looking for published authors; if you have strong technical skills but no writing experience, our experienced editors can help you develop a writing career, or simply get some additional reward for your expertise.

WordPress 3.7 Complete

Third Edition

ISBN: 978-1-78216-240-7   Paperback: 404 pages

Make your first end-to-end website from scratch
with WordPress

1. Learn how to build a WordPress site quickly
   and effectively.

2. Find out how to create content that's optimized
   to be published on the Web.

3. Learn the basics of working with WordPress
   themes and playing with widgets.

WordPress 3 Cookbook

ISBN: 978-1-84951-460-6   Paperback: 328 pages

Over 100 recipes to help you enhance your
WordPress site!

1. Take your WordPress site to the next level
   with solutions to common WordPress problems
   that make your site better, smarter, faster, and
   more secure.

2. Enhance your SEO and make more money
   online by applying simple hacks.

3. Rich with screenshots and practical tasks that
   you will find quite useful .

Please check **www.PacktPub.com** for information on our titles

[PACKT] open source ✳
PUBLISHING
community experience distilled

WordPress 3 Complete

ISBN: 978-1-84951-410-1   Paperback: 344 pages

Create your own complete website or blog from scratch with WordPress

1. Learn everything you need for creating your own feature-rich website or blog from scratch.

2. Clear and practical explanations of all aspects of WordPress.

3. In-depth coverage of installation, themes, plugins, and syndication.

WordPress 3 Site Blueprints

ISBN: 978-1-84719-936-2   Paperback: 300 pages

Ready-made plans for 9 different professional WordPress sites

1. Everything you need to build a varied collection of feature-rich customized WordPress websites for yourself.

2. Transform a static website into a dynamic WordPress blog.

3. In-depth coverage of several WordPress themes and plugins.

Please check **www.PacktPub.com** for information on our titles

CPSIA information can be obtained at www.ICGtesting.com
Printed in the USA
LVOW09s1515120716

496015LV00009B/342/P